ILYUSHIN IL-2 AND IL-10 SHTURMOVIK

Other titles in the Crowood Aviation Series

ILYUSHIN IL-2 AND IL-10 SHTURMOVIK

Yefim Gordon and Sergey Komissarov

The Crowood Press

First published in 2004 by
The Crowood Press Ltd
Ramsbury, Marlborough
Wiltshire SN8 2HR

www.crowood.com

British Library Cataloguing-in-Publication Data
A catalogue record for this book is available from the British Library.

ISBN 1 86126 625 1

Typeset by Florence Production Ltd, Stoodleigh, Devon

Printed and bound in Great Britain by CPI Bath

Contents

Introduction

This book is devoted to a family of aircraft which occupies a prominent place in the history of Russian (Soviet) aviation and of world aviation too. These aircraft, originating in the work of Sergey V. Ilyushin, one of the best known and most prolific Soviet aircraft designers, had their inception at the time when events in Europe erupted into the Second World War. Subsequently, when Russia was invaded by Germany, they were destined to play an important role in the war, making a sizeable contribution to the victory of the Red Army in its struggle against the invaders and thereby to the victory of Russia and its Western allies over German Fascism. The aircraft in question are the famous Il-2 and its derivatives, notably the Il-10.

The Il-2 occupies a special place among the progeny of Sergey V. Ilyushin as a designer. He began his career as the leader of a design team by producing a bomber which had preceded the Il-2, and, under the name of the DB-3 and later the Il-4, also formed an important part of the Soviet arsenal in the war. Bombers were to become the predominant work of his bureau in the first post-war years. Gradually the emphasis shifted to commercial aircraft, and Ilyushin earned a prominent place as a creator of Soviet passenger aircraft, among which the famous Il-18 turboprop airliner deserves a special mention. However, all this could not overshadow the role played by the Il-2 during the war. This aircraft continues to fascinate aviation researchers and the general air-minded public.

The Il-2 was built in greater numbers than any other attack aircraft in the history of aviation, an estimated 36,154 rolling off the production lines. Like the T-34 tank, Shpagin PPSh sub-machine-gun and BM-13 Katyusha multiple rocket launcher, it was the epitome of Soviet weaponry. For the Russian people in the war it was probably just as significant morally and emotionally as the Spitfire was for the British and the Zero fighter for the Japanese. The Il-2 was boosted by Soviet propaganda as an invulnerable 'wonder airplane' striking terror into the enemy. Understandably, every nation in time of war strives to extol the virtues of its soldiers and its weapons, indulging sometimes in pardonable exaggerations.

For many years after, the image of the Il-2 created during the war years was upheld in the Soviet Union unflinchingly by all those who wrote on the subject. Patriotism came first. However, as the events of the war grew more distant in time, a more sober and objective approach set in among those who study the history of the Soviet aviation. Democratic changes that had taken place in Russia since the beginning of 1990s also played their part in stimulating a desire to arrive at a balanced picture of both the achievements and setbacks that had fallen to the lot of the Soviet aircraft industry. Access to previously secret archives enabled researchers to undertake fresh studies, bringing to the fore many unknown facts. It is hardly surprising that, against this background, a certain reappraisal of some well-established notions has taken place. As is usual in such cases, some researchers are prone to go to the opposite extreme. The authors of several articles and books published in Russia in recent years assert that the Il-2 was generally an unsuccessful combat aircraft, responsible for the loss of a great many pilots – a 'widow maker'. Such assertions are not readily accepted by everyone. One might say that they have called forth a kind of overt or covert polemics on the subject in Russian aeronautical publications and even in the general press, opinions ranging from an adamant refutation of any 'revisionism' to attempts at a serious consideration of new facts without succumbing to cheap sensationalism. It is precisely this balanced approach that the authors of this book have tried to adopt. An example of this can be found in the thorough research by the aviation historians V. Perov and O. Rastrenin; their writings contain a wealth of facts and a sober, detailed analysis of combat efficiency of Ilyushin's machines which cannot be ignored. A valuable source of information on hitherto unknown aspects of the history of Ilyushin's attack aircraft was provided by a documentary chronicle of the development of Soviet aviation in the period 1938 to 1946, painstakingly compiled by I. Rodionov and made available on the Internet (*see* Bibliography).

A few words are called for concerning the choice of the subject matter of the book. Naturally, the description of the Il-2 – its origins, its development, the numerous versions and modifications and its operational use – forms its core. The Il-10, as the worthy successor and companion-in-arms of the Il-2 during the war, is entitled to the same treatment and due attention is given to the careers of both aircraft in foreign service. In addition, a few development projects closely associated with the same line of development are described in the book. These are the two Il-8 prototype versions that lost out to the Il-10, and the post-war Il-16, which was a logical termination of the design philosophy embodied in the Il-2–Il-8–Il-10 lineage. The description of this family of designs is preceded by a chapter outlining the background against which Ilyushin's activities should be considered. It will be seen that Ilyushin was not alone in perceiving the importance of attack aircraft for the warfare of his time, and the work conducted in the Soviet Union in this direction was truly impressive. Some idea will be given of the rival designs that failed to find their way into the arsenals of the Red Army.

Sergey Vladimirovich Ilyushin, head of OKB-240 which created the Il-2 attack aircraft and its successors. Sergey and Dmitriy Komissarov archive

CHAPTER ONE

Predecessors and Competitors

To understand better the circumstances which accompanied the emergence of Ilyushin's attack aircraft it is useful to look at the preceding development of the whole concept of attack aircraft, or battlefield aircraft. The following account will be concerned primarily with the efforts of Soviet aircraft designers.

The Concept

The idea of creating a dedicated aircraft for direct battlefield support appeared in 1911 during the fighting between Italy and its opponents, Turkey and Tripolitania. Combat sorties flown by Italian aircraft soon brought home the need for an aircraft possessing a powerful weapon fit and providing good protection for the crew. Yet, when the First World War began, the armies of the belligerents had no specialized close-support aircraft and this mission, to begin with, was fulfilled by fighters, reconnaissance aircraft and light bombers. However, the use of aircraft for strafing missions was soon adopted in the Russian army and in the armies of her allies Great Britain and France. The aircraft employed for the purpose were subjected to a minimum of modifications, which included primarily the provision of armour protection for the pilot against rifle fire from the ground. In Germany, specifications for a dedicated close-support aircraft of the J class provided with armour protection were evolved in late 1916, and in January 1917 the Junkers J.1 heavy, two-seater attack aircraft made its maiden flight. The front of the fuselage was manufactured as an armour shell protecting the engine, the fuel tank and the crew stations. The aircraft was put into series production and was later joined by two more types of armoured attack aircraft – the AEG J.1 and Albatros J.1 and J.2. Concurrently, the need was recognized for unarmoured light attack aircraft; accordingly, several types in the CL class were produced by Germany during the war.

Similar developments took place in Great Britain and France where several types of armoured attack aircraft and light attack aircraft made their appearance. The Sopwith TF2 Salamander was an example of the first, whose armour shell formed an integral part of the fuselage and sustained stresses generated by the wings. This novel feature helped to lessen the structural weight and thereby enhanced the aircraft's performance.

Thus the Germans, the British and the French came to the same conclusion: effective close support of ground troops required two types of attack aircraft, the one being a light, highly manoeuvrable aircraft and the other a heavy, armoured aircraft. The two types complement each other in performing combat missions. Subsequent experience in local and regional conflicts in the period between the two World Wars, as well as during the Second War, corroborated the correctness of the concept.

Soviet Beginnings

In the USSR the Air Force was undergoing a process of build-up in the early 1920s. The Soviet military leaders were acutely conscious of the discrepancy between the performance of the aircraft available at the time and contemporary military doctrines. This was not least applicable to the attack element of the Air Force. Work on specifications for new attack aircraft started as early as 1924, and in January 1926 a decision was taken to embark on the design of attack aircraft in conformity with the new specifications. These envisaged the use of armour to ensure the protection for the crew, the engine and the fuel tanks against anti-aircraft shell splinters and rifle-calibre fire from beneath, on the sides and from the rear. In addition, the armour was supposed to form part of the aircraft's structure.

Practical design work aimed at creating the new aircraft was conducted in several

Soviet design bureaux under the supervision most notably of Polikarpov and Tupolev – designers who were to gain world renown later. This work was hampered by numerous ailments afflicting the young Soviet aircraft industry, not least the shortage of sufficiently powerful engines. This was one of the reasons that prevented Polikarpov from bringing to fruition his project of a twin-engined attack aircraft called *Boyevik* (Attacker). It was a biplane powered by two M-5 (licence-built Liberty-12) engines, featuring armour protection of the front fuselage and engines. The project was under consideration in 1926, but it failed to receive approval. Nor did Polikarpov have a chance to implement his intention to adapt his first fighter – the IL-400 (I-1) monoplane – to the attack role. In the absence of a dedicated attack aircraft the Red Army Air Force had to make do with the R-1 reconnaissance aircraft in the close-support role; this was actually the Airco DH-9A built in Russia in a modified form; it lacked armour. Attempts were also made to modify other types of reconnaissance aircraft for use as attack aircraft. Thus the Tupolev R-3 (ANT-3) in its M-5-powered version was evaluated for this role, but was not proceeded with; in its Lorraine-Dietrich-powered version it formed the basis for the ShR attack aircraft project which also remained on the drawing board. The 400kg (882lb) extra weight of the armour proved too much for the available engine power. The attempt was also made to develop an attack version of the successful twin-engined TB-1 bomber designed by Tupolev. Designated TSh-1 (*Tiazholyi Shturmovik*, heavy attack aircraft) in its new role and bearing the OKB designation ANT-17, it was envisaged as featuring several versions of armament, one of which included recoilless cannon designed by L.V. Kurchevskiy. Yet designers ran into insurmountable difficulties and had to give up the project which, in Tupolev's words, could not be implemented due to the excessive weight of the strap-on armour and to the absence of engines delivering 1,300hp.

Curiously, according to some sources, the designation ANT-17 is applicable also to another attack aircraft project from the Tupolev stable bearing a parallel designation TSh-B (*tiazholyi shturmovik bronirovannyi* – heavy attack aircraft, armoured). Unlike the ANT-17, this was a four-seater biplane with two M-34 engines placed atop the lower wing; its armament was expected to include 75mm (3in) recoilless guns, eight 7.62mm machine-guns and a bomb load of 1,000 to 1,500kg. The armour plating is quoted as having a total weight of 1,000kg (2,205lb), of which 380kg (838lb) were part of the structure. Yet another project was under development in the Tupolev bureau – this was the ANT-18, based on the R-6 (ANT-7) reconnaissance aircraft. This project was also abandoned through the lack of sufficiently powerful engines.

Tupolev's bombers were the objects of highly unorthodox modifications with a view to producing battlefield support aircraft. Thus a TB-1 twin-engined bomber was fitted with a recoilless cannon vertically mounted in the fuselage, the ends protruding from the upper and the lower side of the fuselage. This 76mm cannon was intended to hit ground targets. Ground trials showed the weapon to be dangerous for the aircraft and the experiment was abandoned. Even the four-engined TB-3 (a heavy bomber by the standard of the day) was adapted for the attack role. On the initiative of P.I. Grokhovskii, a prolific military inventor, an example of the aircraft renamed G-52 was fitted with three fixed 76mm cannon – one in the nose and one in the leading edge of each wing. It remained as a single example. No test results are available, but the accuracy of fire, especially at the promised large distances, was likely to be low due to inadequate sighting devices.

A series of designs emerged as a result of the work undertaken under the auspices of the so-called Central Design Bureau, known under its Russian abbreviation of TsKB (*Tsentral'noye Konstruktorskoye Biuro*). In 1930 N.N. Polikarpov, a leader of one of the TsKB design teams, was tasked with producing an attack aircraft. In this he was assisted by S.A. Kocherigin. The first result of this work was the LSh-1 (TsKB-5) (LSh stands for *lyogkiy shturmovik* – light attack aircraft). It was a two-seater biplane featuring relatively weak armour protection. Its armament comprised two forward-firing 7.62mm PV-1 machine-guns and four PV-1s mounted under the gunner's cabin with their barrels set at an angle (variable on the ground) of 30 or 60 degrees relative to the longitudinal axis of the aircraft, to fire forward and downward. This battery, although lacking in its accuracy of fire, could be used for strafing infantry columns on the march. Rear protection was ensured by two PV-1 machine-guns on a flexible mounting. No bomb armament was provided. Several difficulties encountered during the work led to its cancellation. The TsKB took a decision to rework the LSh-1 into a heavy attack aircraft to meet another Air Force specification. The new machine, featuring heavier armour plating and more effective armament, was designated TSh-2 (TSh: *tiazholyi shturmovik* – heavy attack aircraft). Its first version bore the number 6 in the TsKB programme (TsKB-6; some sources give it the name of TSh-1 which would be a second use of the designation). The aircraft, powered by a BMW-VI engine, featured an armour shell forming the front of the fuselage and providing protection for the engine, oil and coolant radiators, fuel tanks and the pilot and gunner cabins. The armour shell was assembled from plates that were flat or had single curvature. This resulted in an angular shape to the fuselage and poor aerodynamics. The new machine had two synchronized PV-1 machine-guns and two batteries comprising four PV-1s each under the lower wings. During flight tests begun in 1931, the aircraft developed a speed of 180km/h (112mph) which was insufficient for a battlefield support aircraft. Teething troubles included malfunctions of the armament. The aircraft was returned to the factory for development work. Meanwhile, a second version of the TSh-2, also designated TsKB-21, was produced; it passed its flight test in the period between 2 November and 20 December 1931. It featured improved armour-plating and better engine cooling, which enabled the aircraft to reach a higher speed of 213km/h (132mph). Armament changes included the placing of the underwing machine-guns inside the thickened section of the lower wing to improve aerodynamics. An initial batch of as many as seventy machines was originally ordered for full-scale service evaluation. The pro-duction model was to be powered by the M-17 – a Soviet copy of the BMW-VI produced under licence. However, problems with the cooling of the M-17 engine resulted in a decision to halt the production at the end of 1932 after the completion of only ten examples.

Another attack aircraft created on the basis of the LSh-1 in parallel with the work on the TSh-2 was the ShON (*Shturmovik osobogo naznacheniya* – attack aircraft for special missions), also known as TsKB-23. This biplane was intended, among other things, for the Soviet aircraft carriers which were on the drawing boards at that time. It featured limited armour-plating protecting the engine and the pilot's cabin on the underside only. The armament of the ShON comprised a quartette of PV-1 machine-guns mounted under the floor of the gunner's cabin in a swivelling installation which permitted the guns to fire at a downward angle forwards and backwards. The aircraft was completed by 1 April 1931 and underwent flight testing until the summer of 1932. Its performance was on the whole satisfactory, yet no series production was undertaken – plans for the construction of the carriers were shelved and the aircraft was no longer needed.

An interesting design evolved at that time was the TSh-3 (TsKB-4) heavy attack aircraft designed by the team of S.A. Kocherigin in 1933. It was a two-seater, low-wing, braced monoplane with non-retractable undercarriage powered by a single M-34F engine delivering 830hp at take-off. Its armament comprised ten wing-mounted 7.62mm ShKAS machine-guns arranged in two batteries of five in the leading edges of the wings, supplemented by a flexible machine-gun for rear protection and a 250kg (551lb) bomb load. Like its predecessors, the TSh-3 had an armour shell assembled from flat panels of thickness varying from 5 to 8mm. The armour-plating weighed 576kg (1,270lb). In the course of factory tests successfully completed by the spring of 1934 the TSh-3 achieved a maximum speed of 247km/h (154mph) at ground level at the flight weight of 3,557kg (7,843lb). However, the new machine's performance fell short of the updated requirements of 1934 and it was not placed in production.

The machines that have been reviewed here had some common features in their design and shared some fundamental failings. Paramount among the latter was the fact that they were underpowered; this was further aggravated by persistent problems with the cooling of engines in an armour shell. All ground-attack prototypes of this period had extremely restricted visibility forward and downward, which limited the ability to spot targets during a sortie and precluded any accurate sighting. All this explains why all these efforts bore no fruit by the middle of the 1930s. In consequence, the Red Army had to rely upon light ground-attack aircraft that were straightforward adaptations of reconnaissance aircraft already in production. Moreover, the design philosophy and tactical thinking of the period had a strong tendency to concentrate upon combining in one aircraft type the properties of a reconnaissance aircraft and a ground-attack machine. This had a profound influence on the work of the design bureaux engaged in evolving and developing battlefield support aircraft.

Before the War

We now review some of the designs that dominated the scene in this sector of Soviet aviation in the years preceding the outbreak of the Second World War and the German invasion. Foremost among these was the R-5 reconnaissance biplane designed by N.N. Polikarpov which was built in large numbers and gained a reputation as a thoroughly reliable and effective machine. In 1932 the Red Army Air Force took on strength a light, unarmoured, ground-attack version of this aircraft – the R-5Sh, which differed from the baseline aircraft in having four PV-1 machine-guns mounted on the upper surface of the lower wings and being provided with bomb racks under the fuselage to carry a 240 to 500kg (530 to 1,100lb) bomb load. In 1934 a small batch was produced of the R-5LSh (LSh: *lyogkiy shturmovik* – light attack aircraft) – essentially the same R-5Sh but armed with eight forward-firing ShKAS machine-guns. In 1935 the R-5Sh attack aircraft began to be supplanted by a new version – the R-5SSS (*skorostnoy, skoropodyomnyi, skorostrel'nyi* – high-speed, high-rate-of-climb, high-rate-of-fire). It featured improved aerodynamics, a more powerful M-17F engine and more effective armament, comprising two synchronized ShKAS machine-guns above the engine and four ShKAS on the lower wings. A total of 620 examples of this aircraft were built between 1935 and 1937.

In 1933 a design team led by S.A. Kocherigin created the LR (*lyogkiy razvedchik*) light reconnaissance aircraft; powered by an M-34 engine delivering 750hp at take off (as against the 680hp of the M-17), it had a better performance than the R-5 while retaining the same layout and armament. The performance of the LR was further improved on the second prototype through the installation of a more powerful M-34N engine fitted with a supercharger. The aircraft successfully passed its acceptance trials and could be considered as suitable for the role of reconnaissance and light attack aircraft. But in the latter, its offensive armament had to be increased. However, it was not chosen for series production, having lost to a rival – the R-Z light attack aircraft. The latter was a thoroughly reworked R-5 biplane of smaller dimensions, powered by the M-34RN engine with a rating of 825hp at take-off. The armament of the R-Z comprised one synchronized, forward-firing PV-1 machine-gun, one flexible ShKAS machine-gun for rear defence and a bomb load of 300kg (661lb) The number of the R-Zs manufactured between 1935 and 1937 reached 1,031.

The R-5Sh, R-5SSS and R-Z aircraft were on the strength of the attack air regiments of the Red Army Air Force and took part in combat in China, Spain and in the Soviet-Finnish war of 1939–40. Combat experience showed all ground-attack versions of the R-5 to have the following weak points: slow speed, weak offensive armament and absence of armour protection for the crew, the engine and other vital elements of the airframe; this made the aircraft extremely vulnerable to battle damage. They could be reasonably effective only when there were no significant anti-aircraft defences and adequate protection against enemy fighters was ensured.

Not only reconnaissance aircraft, but fighters as well were adapted to the ground-attack role during the 1930s. These included the I-15bis, I-153 and I-16 single-seaters and the DI-6 two-seater fighters.

The Polikarpov R-5Sh (*shturmovik*), an attack version of the R-5 reconnaissance biplane. Note the twin machine-guns installed on the lower wings.
Yefim Gordon archive

The R-5SSS (*skorosnoy, skoropod"yomnyy, skorostrel'nyy* – fast, with a high rate of climb and a high rate of fire) was another attempt to enhance the potential of the R-5 as a combat aircraft. Yefim Gordon archive

Yet another attack derivative of the R-5 was the R-Z. This view shows the quadruple bomb shackles under the lower wings carrying 50kg (110lb) FAB-50 HE bombs. Note the wires securing the propeller-like vanes of the fuses when on the ground. Yefim Gordon archive

Chronologically, it was the last that preceded the single-seaters into service. A small batch (sixty-one) of the DI-6Sh armed with six forward-firing PV-1 machine-guns was manufactured after 1936. In 1939 the I-15bis fighters, armed with four PV-1 machine-guns, bombs and/or rocket projectiles, were turned over to attack air units. In 1940 the I-153 fighters began to be transferred to attack air units. They featured a similar armament fit: four ShKAS machine-guns, a 150kg (330lb) bomb load or four to eight RS-82 rocket projectiles. It must be noted that these fighter ground-attack aircraft enjoyed only a limited success in their new role, being incapable of destroying well-protected targets. The I-16 fighter was not built in an especially modified attack version (one such variant was produced in prototype form in 1937), but some examples of the late-series I-16s (type 24) were fitted with rocket projectiles for use against ground targets.

The period of the mid 1930s was marked by far-reaching changes in Soviet military doctrines involving, among other things, a reappraisal of the role of air power in warfare and the appropriate structural changes in the build-up of the Air Force. All this resulted in aerial warfare acquiring a considerably more significant place in the military operations, not least in their tactical aspect. Thereby ground-attack aircraft were also acquiring a more significant role. Deliberations on the subject yielded the idea of the so-called 'general purpose army co-operation aircraft' (which, in essence, is equivalent to the notion of a battlefield aircraft). In June 1935 Chief of the Red Army Air Force Yakov Alksnis endorsed the specifications for the 'general purpose army co-operation aircraft' in two versions: a reconnaissance and artillery-spotting air-

craft and a ground-attack aircraft. The two versions were supposed to be based on a single design, differing only in the mission equipment and the armament fit.

At the beginning of 1936 the Chief Directorate of Aviation Industry in the People's Commissariat of Heavy Industry commissioned three Chief Designers – I.G. Neman, S.A. Kocherigin and P.O. Sukhoi – with preparing designs for a long-range, high speed, reconnaissance aircraft powered by a 1,200hp AM-34FRNT engine, which, in addition to the reconnaissance role, also had the capabilities of a ground-attack aircraft and light bomber. This meant, in effect, that, instead of the concept of two different aircraft sharing a common airframe and supplementing each other, the Directorate of Aviation Industry opted for a single design of a multipurpose machine for which reconnaissance would be the primary role, while ground attack and bombing would be secondary roles. Presumably, this decision was influenced to a certain extent by the impression produced on Soviet aviation experts by the Vultee V-11GB high-speed, multipurpose aircraft which combined the roles of a reconnaissance machine and a light bomber/attack aircraft. In September 1936 the Soviet Union acquired a licence to build this American aircraft for the Soviet Air Force as the BSh-1 (*bombardirovshchik-shturmovik* – bomber /ground-attack aircraft; note that the same acronym later came to stand for *bronirovannyi shturmovik* – armoured attack aircraft). The decision in favour of a multipurpose aircraft was fraught with consequences: it delayed the emergence of a dedicated battlefield-support aircraft by at least two years and thus left the country without effective means of ensuring air cover for ground troops during the first period of the war.

Alongside Neman, Kocherigin and Sukhoi several other designers were also involved in the design work on the multipurpose aircraft. These included Polikarpov, Grigorovich and, interestingly, Ilyushin, although in fact his participation did not progress further than preliminary studies. Original specifications were revised with greater emphasis being placed on the ground-attack role of the aircraft. Several projects were submitted in course of time. Of these, only the Polikarpov and the Sukhoi machine reached the hardware stage. Both were evolved under the auspices of the so-called 'Ivanov' programme ('Ivanov' was Stalin's alias for telegrams) and, accordingly, both machines were known as 'Ivanov' for some time. They were similar in layout and general appearance, being single-engined, low-wing, cantilever monoplanes with retractable undercarriage, powered by radial air-cooled engines. Both had a crew of two – a pilot and a gunner manning a turret for rear defence. Their performance was closely similar, the maximum speeds being of the order of 400km/h (250mph) at ground level. The armament was also similar, comprising in the case of Polikarpov's machine seven forward-firing, 7.62mm machine-guns and a bomb load of up to 900kg, while the Sukhoi machine had a forward-firing armament comprising six SHKAS machine-guns and a bomb load of up to 600kg. However, Polikarpov was hampered for some time by a lack of production facilities and his aircraft

A prototype of the Kocherigin DI-6, two-seater fighter in DI-6Sh assault configuration. This photograph shows the twin machine-gun packs under the lower wings and the UKhAP chemical weapons dispensers suitable for pouring liquid phosphorus or other toxic agents. Yefim Gordon archive

Close-up of the starboard gun pack on the DI-6Sh prototype with the fairing removed, giving a detailed view of the PV-1 machine-guns. Yefim Gordon archive

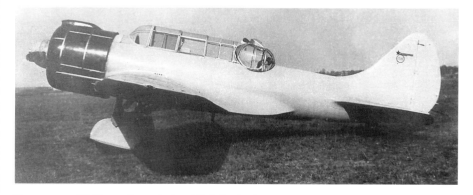

The prototype of Polikarpov's attack aircraft/light bomber known as the 'Ivanov'. The number 156 in the circle on the tail refers to the plant that built it. Yefim Gordon archive

The Vultee V-11GB (alias BSh-1), the twin machine-guns well visible. Yefim Gordon archive

began its flight tests with a considerable delay, while Sukhoi's machine had made considerable progress in its testing and in overcoming teething troubles. As a result, a decision was taken to discontinue all work on Polikarpov's 'Ivanov', and Sukhoi's machine (designated BB-1 – *blizhniy bombardirovshchik*, or short-range bomber, later renamed Su-2) successfully completed flight testing and was eventually put into production in 1939. Like all the projects mentioned above, it lacked armour protection, which reduced its value as an attack aircraft (its use in this role was also envisaged). A dedicated attack version of the BB-1 – the BB-2, also designated ShB (*Shturmovik-bombardirovshchik* – attack aircraft/ bomber) and Su-4, was developed by Sukhoi, the prototype entering flight test stage in April 1940. Its armament comprised four forward-firing ShKAS machine-guns, two machine-guns of the same type for rear defence, and a bomb load of 600kg (1,323lb), but, again, the machine was not provided with any substantial protection. Despite its generally satisfactory performance, it was not accepted for production because, by that time, the Il-2 was already entering series manufacture. Yet another offspring of the BB-1 (Su-2) was envisaged in 1940 – the BB-3, differing in being powered by the AM-37 inline, liquid-cooled engine. Like its predecessors, it was a short-range bomber with ground attack and reconnaissance as secondary duties. It did not progress to the hardware stage, nor did a BB-1 version intended to be powered by the M-90 radial engine.

The Polikarpov I-15 fighter could be equipped with launch rails for 82mm RS-82 rockets for ground attack. This aircraft with the tail number 4 Red is pictured during trials at the Red Army Air Force Research Institute (NII VVS). Yefim Gordon archive

The Polikarpov I-16 *tip* 24 could be outfitted with six RO-82 launchers for RS-82 rockets as standard. Yefim Gordon archive

The Sukhoi SZ-2 (*Stalinskoye zadaniye* – Stalin's task), the second prototype of the Sukhoi Su-2 light bomber. The aircraft was powered by a Shvetsov M-62 radial. Yefim Gordon archive

A prototype of the BB-1 short-range bomber – an example of the most common version of the Su-2 powered by a Nazarov/Tumanskiy M-88B radial (note the difference in cowling shape). Yefim Gordon archive

The Su-2M-82 (alias Su-4) was powered by a Shvetsov M-82 radial (note the dorsal carburettor intake). This one has been equipped with skis. Yefim Gordon archive

The ShB was an improved version of the Su-2. Note the different landing gear design (the main gear units retracted aft, the wheels turning through 90 degrees to lie flat in the wings *à la* Curtiss P-40). Yefim Gordon archive

Other Candidate Aircraft

As will be seen from the following chapter, the work on the aircraft that eventually came to be known as the Il-2 was initiated at the beginning of 1938 and its introduction into service started on the eve of the German invasion in June 1941. This was, however, by no means the only contender for the role of a dedicated ground-attack or battlefield-support aircraft. Concurrently, several other design bureaux were developing aircraft to similar specifications; they included both single-seater, single-engined machines and heavy, twin-engined aircraft, the latter often being multipurpose aircraft capable of performing the missions of escort fighters, light bombers or dive bombers. An account of these types will give a general idea of the scope of the efforts devoted in the last pre-war years to create an acceptable ground-attack machine.

To begin with, there were some single-engined types that were developed or modified for the ground-attack role. The work of the team headed by Kocherigin merits attention here. In 1938–39 his OKB, taking its R-9 reconnaissance aircraft as a starting point, developed two lightweight, two-seater attack aircraft – the Sh-1 with the M-88 engine and the Sh-2 powered by the M-87A (in some documents they are designated Sh M-88 and Sh M-87A, respectively). Both were cantilever, mid-wing monoplanes with non-retractable, spatted undercarriage.

Apart from the engines, they differed in their armaments. The Sh-1 M-88 was fitted with two 20mm ShVAK cannon and two ShKAS machine-guns (this was the first aircraft ever to carry wing-mounted 20mm cannon); the Sh-2 M-87A was armed with four wing-mounted ShKAS machine-guns. Both machines had a single ShKAS for defence from the rear. The normal bomb load was 200kg (441lb), but could reach 400 or even 600kg (882 or 1,323lb) in overload versions. State acceptance trials of the first machine were completed in the middle of 1939, those of the second in November 1939 (according to some sources, in July–August 1939). Their performances were closely similar: speeds at sea level were 360 and 350km/h (224 and 218mph), respectively, speeds at altitude were 437 and 439km/h (271.6 and 272.8mph), respectively. Due to several shortcomings, neither machine was put into production. The two designs were subsequently reworked by Kocherigin, who introduced retractable undercarriage and separate cockpits for the pilot and the gunner, not connected by the 'greenhouse' glazing, as distinct from the previous machines. This work resulted in two projects: the BMSh (*Bol'shaya Modifikatsiya Shturmovika* – Major Attack Aircraft Modification) and the MMSh (*Malaya Modifikatsiya Shturmovika* – Minor Attack Aircraft Modification) which were based on the Sh-1 and the Sh-2, respectively and were to be powered by the M-90 and the M-81 engine, respectively. However,

they did not proceed further than the drawing board.

In 1940 Kocherigin came up with a project for a single-seater, armoured, ground-attack aircraft (a flying tank, as he put it); the project was rejected, as was his tank-busting aircraft powered by two AM-37 engines. Another project developed in the Kocherigin OKB was the OBSh (*Odnomestnyi Bronirovannyi Shturmovik* – Single-Seat Armoured Attack Aircraft), powered by the M-81 radial engine. In its dimensions and contours it was strongly reminiscent of the German Fw 190. The aircraft featured armour plating as an integral part of the load-carrying structure. The armament in the attack version comprised two 12.7mm BS machine-guns and two 7.62mm ShKAS machine-guns, supplemented by a 100kg (220lb) bomb load carried internally. The project was included in the plan for prototype construction for 1940, but was later abandoned due to the unavailability of a sufficiently trouble-free M-81 engine. In the same year 1940 Kocherigin presented yet another project – the OPB (*Odnomestnyi Pikiruyushchiy Bombardirovshchik* – Single-Seat Dive Bomber) powered by the M-90 radial engine. This was actually a multipurpose aircraft, which could also be used as a ground-attack machine; in this version it was to be fitted with enhanced armour plating. The aircraft had a promising design performance, including a top speed at altitude in excess of 600km/h (373mph) and a bomb load of 500 to

Another contender for the attack/light bomber role was Kocherigin's Sh-1M-88, pictured here at NII VVS (note the hexagonal pavement slabs).
This view shows the fixed spatted landing gear and the bulged dorsal turret enclosure. Yefim Gordon archive

700kg (1,102 to 1,543lb). The project attracted much interest and construction of the prototype was started, but, for various reasons, not least because of the delays in M-90 engine development, the work proceeded slowly. To remedy the situation, Kocherigin reworked the design to accept the M-89 radial and then the AM-37 in-line, water-cooled engine. The M-90-powered prototype was completed, but its first testing had to be started with the M-89 engine, which also proved to be problematic. In the meantime, the AM-37 engine was withdrawn from series manufacture. This sealed the fate of this interesting machine, which, according to some assessments, could have proved useful in the approaching war.

Several contenders for the role of a dedicated ground-attack aircraft were produced by the OKB headed by P.O. Sukhoi, in addition to the already mentioned BB-1 (Su-2) light bomber and its derivatives. An aircraft from Sukhoi's progeny that deserves special attention is the Su-6 attack aircraft. It started life under the designation OBSh (the same as one of Kocherigin's projects) which stands for single-seat armoured attack aircraft. Two versions of this aircraft powered, respectively, by the M-88 and the M-71 engine were submitted by Sukhoi in September 1939. It was the OBSh M-71 that was proceeded with; in 1941 it was renamed Su-6 M-71. The first Su-6 was completed in February 1941 and made its first flight on 13 March. Its performance was superior to that of the Il-2 powered by the AM-38 engine (*see* next chapter).

The first prototype of the Su-6M-71, a single-seater attack derivative of the Su-2.
Yefim Gordon archive

Head-on view of the Su-6M-71 carrying ten RS-82 rockets during State acceptance trials at NII VVS. Note also the bomb-bay doors just aft of the wings.
Yefim Gordon archive

The Su-6M-71F reverted to two-seater configuration with a gunner's station for self-defence. This view shows clearly the 37mm 11P37 cannons and the addition of wheel-well doors.
Yefim Gordon archive

The Su-6AM-42 differed from the previous model mainly in having a Mikulin AM-42 V-12 liquid-cooled engine instead of the Shvetsov M-71 radial. Neither aircraft reached production.
Yefim Gordon archive

In brief, the Su-6 M-71 was for the most part developed further after the outbreak of the war; this lessened its chances of winning a production order. The Il-2 was in mass production by that time, and to introduce a new aircraft was a luxury the country could ill afford. Besides, the armament of this initial version – six ShKAS machine-guns and a 200kg (441lb) bomb load – was considered too weak by the standard of the day. In the course of the war, Sukhoi created two-seater versions of this aircraft: the Su-6 M-71F and the Su-6 AM-42. The former possessed excellent performance and firepower, being superior to the Il-2, and, at one time, serious consideration was given to launching it into series production. However, the M-71F engine was still unsuitable for large-scale manufacture. The AM-42-powered version was closely comparable to the Ilyushin Il-10 and lost to this aircraft.

Other types of Soviet single-engined attack aircraft developed in the immediate pre-war years include P.D. Grushin's unorthodox, tandem-wing Sh-MAI (Tandem-MAI). This two-seater, ground-attack aircraft and light bomber powered by the M-87A engine was tested in prototype form in 1940 and attracted considerable interest, but failed to find acceptance due to a number of serious shortcomings, such as insufficient performance, poor directional stability, faulty undercarriage and low production standards. The same year saw the testing of Borovkov and Florov's I-207 cantilever biplane fighter, which was also considered promising in the ground-attack role by the Air Force Command, yet failed to reach production status. It was expected to be particularly suitable for dive bombing, with two 250kg (550lb) bombs suspended under the wings. Very similar to the I-207 in concept was the OKO-4 cantilever sesquiplane designed by V.K. Tairov. This was a fighter with a secondary attack capability, powered by one M-88 engine. Its armament comprised two 12.7mm BS machine-guns and a bomb load of 100kg (220lb). The construction of a prototype was started in 1938, but in 1939 all work was discontinued – presumably because the project was not deemed to be promising. The newly established design bureau of A. Mikoyan and M. Gurevich produced the PBSh-1 and the PBSh-2 attack aircraft projects (PBSh: *Pikiruyushchiy Bronirovannyi Shturmovik* – Armoured Dive Bomber), which, however, remained on the drawing

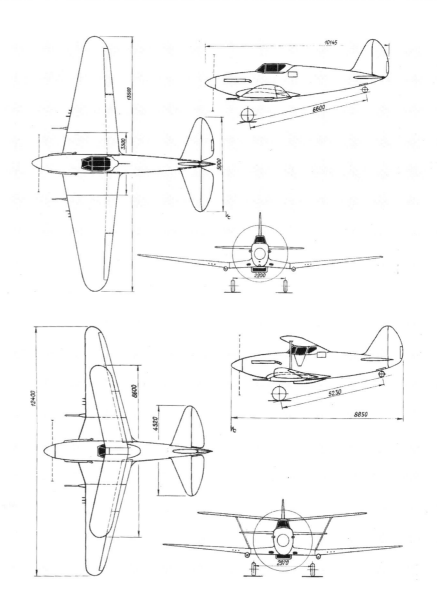

board. The same fate befell the OSh-AM-35 single-seater, armoured attack aircraft project presented by A.F. Dubrovin in September 1939. The armour was an integral part of the aircraft's primary structure. Its design performance was somewhat superior to that of the future Il-2, the maximum speed ranging from 435km/h (270mph) at sea level to 480km/h (298mph) at rated altitude, and the Air Force took some interest in the project, but it failed to receive the go-ahead. Polikarpov's last fighter biplane projects – the I-190 and the I-195 – were envisaged as having a secondary attack role. A similar application was foreseen for his cannon-armed, heavy fighters built in prototype form during the war – the ITP(M-1) and the ITP(M-2). M.I. Gudkov, one of the three designers behind the LaGG-3

Top: A three-view drawing of the projected Mikoyan PBSh-1 attack aircraft. Ivnamin Sultanov

Bottom: The PBSh-2 was a sesquiplane derivative of the PBSh-1. Note that the upper wings intended to increase lift and hence payload have forward sweep. Ivnamin Sultanov

fighter, strove to adapt this fighter for ground attack, albeit with limited success. Some of his proposed projects, based on the LaGG-3, such as the PIT M-105, remained on the drawing board. The same was true of the Gu-2 – a derivative of his ill-fated Gu-1 fighter, copying the P-39 Aircobra layout.

Another line of development was concerned with heavier, twin-engined machines – either dedicated attack aircraft or multipurpose machines suitable for the role. The SB bomber, well known as a participant in the aerial war in Spain, was experimentally adapted for ground strafing as the SB-Sh. Notable steps were made on this path by N.N. Polikarpov with his VIT-1 and VIT-2 machines (VIT: *Vozdushnyi Istrebitel Tankov*, Aerial Destroyer of Tanks) and their further development, the SPB (*Skorostnoi Pikiruyushchiy Bombardirovshchik*: High-Speed Dive Bomber), the latter having a secondary ground-attack role. They were tested in 1939–40, initially with encouraging results, and were considered for series production. However, several fatal crashes compromised them and prevented them from reaching service status. Equally promising in the ground-attack role was Polikarpov's wartime twin-engined TIS (*Tiazholyi Istrebitel Soprovozhdeniya*: Heavy Escort Fighter).

Despite its quite commendable performance, this machine also failed to go into production. The same can be said about the heavy, twin-engined fighters designed by Tairov (OKO-6, Ta-1 and Ta-3), which were tested in prototype form in 1940–41. In the course of the war, Sukhoi's bureau designed and built a prototype of the Su-8 (DDBSh: *Dalniy Dvukhmestrnyi Bronirovannyi Shturmovik*, Long-Distance Twin-Engined, Armoured Attack Aircraft) – an aircraft capable of considerable punch due to its potent armament fit. The aircraft's weak spot was its dependence on the unreliable M-71 engines. Before the war and during it attempts were made to adapt twin-engined tactical bombers and dive bombers for ground-attack duties. The aircraft in question were the Pe-2 dive bomber, the Tu-2 and the Yak-2 tactical bombers, which were experimentally fitted with potent multibarrel batteries of movable cannon or machine-guns intended for strafing; however, they failed to gain acceptance. Ilyushin embarked on a project for the TsKB-60 (Il-6) twin-engined, heavy attack aircraft intended to provide a valuable supplement to the single-engined Il-2.

At the opposite end of the scale, some designers proposed light-weight, slow-speed machines that were supposed to be cheap in production – such as Pegas, developed by Tomashevich or SAM-23 designed by A. Moskalyov. The first of them was built in prototype during the war, but not ordered into production. Alexander Yakovlev's light aircraft – the

The Polikarpov VIT-1 'tank killer' featuring a conventional tail unit. Note the long barrels of the Shpital'nyi ShFK-37 cannons. Yefim Gordon archive

The VIT-1 showed poor directional stability and was developed into the VIT-2, featuring twin tails. Note the main-gear fairings creating the false impression that the aircraft had a fixed, trousered landing gear. Yefim Gordon archive

The Polikarpov SPB fast dive bomber, which was the immediate precursor of the famous Pe-2. Yefim Gordon archive

The Polikarpov TIS heavy escort fighter, seen here in incomplete condition. Yefim Gordon archive

The Taïrov OKO-6 (Ta-3) escort fighter would have been a potent fighting machine had it gone into production. These photographs show the installation of four ShVAK cannon and two ShKAS machine-guns, as well as the marked contrast between the fighter's narrow fuselage and the Shvetsov M-89 radials. Yefim Gordon archive

Top: **Close-up of the Ta-3's nose with the cowling removed, showing the four-cannon installation.** Yefim Gordon archive

Middle: **The Su-8, aka DDBSh (long-range, twin-engined, armoured attack aircraft). This view illustrates the type's potent armament of four N-37 cannon in a ventral pack and four ShKAS machine-guns in each wing.** Yefim Gordon archive

Bottom: **The Petlyakov Pe-2Sh attack derivative featuring two ShVAK cannon and two Berezin UBK machine-guns installed in the bomb-bay for strafing ground targets.** Yefim Gordon archive

Above: Close-up of the AKAB ('automatic combined artillery battery') installation on the Pe-2Sh. Yefim Gordon archive

Left: A heavily modified Yakovlev Yak-2 light bomber featuring the Mozharovskiy/Venevidov KABB installation which comprised two ShVAK and two ShKAS. The extensively glazed nose offering good visibility for ground attack gave the aircraft a Messerschmitt Me 210-like appearance. Yefim Gordon archive

Close-up of the KABB installation on the modified Yak-2. Yefim Gordon archive

UT-1 and the UT-2 (respectively a single-seater sports plane and a two-seater, dual-control trainer) were modified during the war for ground strafing duties. The UT-1b, UT-2V and UT-2MV versions were used in this role in limited numbers.

Mention must also be made of exotic projects such as the BSh-MV attack aircraft featuring a twin-boom layout with a pusher engine and a flexible cannon battery in which the barrels could be deflected to fire forward and downward. The aircraft was proposed by Mozharovskiy and Venevidov – aircraft armament specialists; design work was conducted by them with assistance from A.A. Arkhangelskiy, a prominent associate of Tupolev. This was a direct rival to the Il-2; it possessed excellent visibility from the pilot's cockpit and was fitted with a potent battery of movable machine-guns for ground attack. Prototype construction was started early in 1941 with the first and the second prototype scheduled to be completed in September and October, but work was stopped with the outbreak of the war. There were some other equally unorthodox projects proposed and developed by other designers. Among these, one may mention the 'T' project by Arkhangelskiy, which was a light bomber and attack aircraft with a layout similar to that of the P-39 Aircobra. Most of them failed to materialize – the exigencies of war severely restricted the scope for new prototype construction.

As we can see, the number of designs of attack aircraft under development between 1938 and 1941 was impressive. Some of them were promising and, given the right circumstances, could in due

Imagine a bomber carrying a regiment of soldiers firing at ground targets? The Tupolev Tu-2Sh came close to this, featuring an experimental installation of 88 Shpagin PPSh sub-machine-guns installed on a sloping mount in the bomb-bay. The installation was intended for strafing enemy personnel and soft-skinned vehicle convoys; these photographs show it in both hoisted and lowered positions. Yefim Gordon archive

The second prototype of the Tomashevich Pegas low-cost, light attack aircraft. These views accentuate the basic design and limited protection afforded to the pilot. Yefim Gordon archive

course prove to be competent and effective aircraft. In particular, the Su-6 M-71F and the Su-8 (DDBSh), in the opinion of some specialists, would have become a combination eminently suitable for the type of fighting occurring on the Eastern Front. However, for various reasons they all were doomed to fail and give way to the Il-2 – the sole aircraft that had emerged as a series-produced machine by the time the war started. Paramount among these factors were the exigencies of war, with its emphasis on mass production, dislocation caused by the hasty evacuation of aircraft plants and design bureaux to the East, and persistent troubles with new aircraft engines – the perennial weakness of the Soviet aircraft industry which prevented many a project from reaching fruition. The only new attack aircraft type to join the Il-2 in squadron service and see action during the war was its stablemate, the Il-10, which will be described in a separate chapter.

The second prototype of the Tomashevich Pegas low-cost, light attack aircraft. Yefim Gordon archive

The Yakovlev UT-1b, a light attack version of the UT-1 single-seater trainer, was armed with a pair of machine-guns atop the wings and four RS-82 rockets on underwing launchers. The wheel spats were deleted to save weight. Yefim Gordon archive

CHAPTER TWO

The Il-2: Genesis and Development

From Concept to Hardware

In December 1937 Soviet military specialists, proceeding from the battlefield experience of the Spanish Civil War, voiced a need for a dedicated ground-attack aircraft possessing potent offensive and defensive armament; they strongly recommended that the creation of such an aircraft be included into the plan for prototype development and construction for 1938. Somewhat later, in February 1938, a similar idea was proposed by Sergei Ilyushin, who, at that time, held an important post in the Chief Directorate of Defence Industry and also headed a design bureau as Chief Designer of Plant No.39. He made his proposal in a letter addressed to the Soviet leaders I.V. Stalin, V.M. Molotov and K.Ye. Voroshilov, as well as to M.M. Kaganovich and A.D. Loktionov (the latter two heading, respectively, the aircraft industry and the Air Force). Stressing the need to create an armoured attack aircraft – a 'flying tank', as he termed it – Ilyushin put forward a specific project proposal and asked that he be given an opportunity to design and build this aircraft which, he claimed, could be submitted for state acceptance trials as early as November 1938. The project was appropriately designated LT AM-34FRN (*Letayushchiy tank*: 'flying tank', with the AM-3FRN engine). Ilyushin's request was granted and he was tasked with designing the aircraft. On 5 May 1938 the government approved the plan for prototype construction in 1938–39, which stipulated that three prototypes of a single-engined, two-seater attack aircraft designed by Ilyushin and powered by the AM-34FRN engine be built by Plant No.39. The first was to be submitted for acceptance trials in December 1938; the second in March 1939; and the third in May 1939 (later prototypes were reduced to two). At the same time, the aircraft was redesignated BSh (*bronirovannyi shturmovik*: armoured attack aircraft) and was known for some

time as BSh AM-34FRN. This was a service designation, the in-house designation of the design bureau (factory designation) being TsKB-55 (TsKB: *Tsentral'noye Konstruktorskoye Biuro* – Central

Design Bureau). Accordingly, the code TsKB-55 AM-34FRN may be found in documents (at that time the engine type was often included in an aircraft's designation).

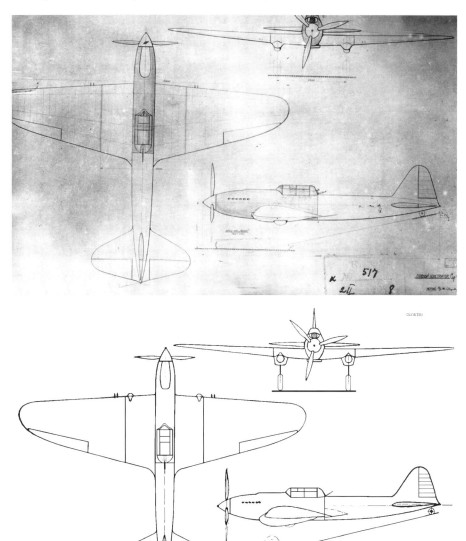

Top: The LT-AM-34FRN project was the immediate precursor of the BSh attack aircraft which evolved into the Il-2. This is an authentic factory drawing signed by S.V. Ilyushin. Via AVICO-Press

Bottom: A provisional, three-view drawing of the BSh-2 endorsed by Chief Designer S.V. Ilyushin on 15 January 1939. Via AVICO-Press

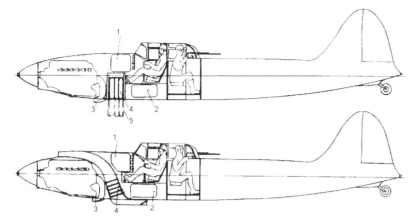

These two diagrams show how the BSh-2 evolved at the design stage. The upper diagram illustrates the original version featuring a semi-retractable water radiator; this was rejected in favour of a buried radiator in a sloping tunnel with a dorsal intake and a ventral outlet. The figures indicate: (1) and (2) upper and lower fuel tanks; (3) carburretor inlet; (4) water radiator; (5) radiator in fully extended position for take-off and landing. Via AVICO-Press

The first prototype BSh-2 (alias TsKB-55) during manufacturer's flight tests, showing the water radiator air intake atop the nose. Yefim Gordon archive

The origin of the TsKB prefix calls for some explanation. In 1931–36 the design bureau headed by S.V. Ilyushin at Plant No.39 comprised several design teams under their own leaders. One of these was led personally by Ilyushin; in 1933 it started the work on the prototype TsKB-26 and TsKB-30 bombers, later developed into the DB-3 and the Il-4 production versions. By mid 1936 most of the other teams had become independent and moved to other plants; in August 1936 Ilyushin's team was renamed OKB-39 (Design Bureau of Plant No.39), and the Central Design Bureau ceased to exist. However, for some time, up to the outbreak of war, prototypes built by the OKB-39 bore designations starting with the TsKB prefix.

The AM-34FRN engine rated at 960hp at sea level was ill-suited for the new machine and had been chosen by Ilyushin only for want of a better one; however, it was phased out of production in the meantime. This made it impossible to ful-

fil the stipulated schedule for prototype construction. Faced with this problem, Ilyushin opted for the new high-altitude AM-35 (A. Mikulin) for his TsKB-55. It had a take-off rating of 1,350hp, the nominal rating being 1,130 at sea level and 1,200 at the critical altitude of 4,500m (14,700ft). Revised specifications for the TsKB-55 AM-35 were endorsed by the Air Force (VVS: *Voyenno-vozdooshnyye seely*) chief A.D. Loktionov on 15 February 1939. The TsKB-55 was a two-seater, cantilever, low-wing monoplane with a semi-retractable main undercarriage housed in underwing fairings. The most distinctive feature was its streamlined fuselage of high-tensile, armour steel, developed by the All-Union Institute of Aviation Materials (VIAM: *Vsesoyuznyi institut aviatsionnykh materialov*) under the guidance of S. Kishkin and N. Skliarov. The armour steel had good impact strength and, most importantly, structural members made of it could be pressed into forms having double curvature. This allowed aircraft to be

designed with stressed armour skins, whereas the earlier TSh-1 and TSh-3 attack aircraft had been fitted with strap-on armour.

The TsKB-55's armoured body contained the vital parts: the engine, crew stations (the cockpits of the pilot and the navigator/gunner), fuel and oil systems. The coolant radiator and oil radiator were initially designed to retract into the armoured body in the event of intense anti-aircraft fire and extended to provide normal cooling when the danger was past, but such a system limited the aircraft's time over the battlefield. A different arrangement was adopted during the design stage. The radiator and oil cooler were fixed side-by-side behind the engine in a special duct in the armoured body; the air intakes of this obliquely placed duct were mounted over the engine cowling, and the exit for the air was arranged under the fuselage. This configuration was not as effective as the previous one but the aircraft's structure was greatly simplified.

Front view of the BSh-2 at the factory airfield, surrounded by Ilyushin DB-3F bombers. This view shows the lattice-like landing gear design with twin shock absorbers for each main wheel. Yefim Gordon archive

This side view illustrates the BSh-2's cockpit canopy design. Note that the aircraft is totally devoid of markings. Yefim Gordon archive

Three-quarters rear view of the BSh-2 prototype. Note that the gun turret is completely enclosed; a similar design would be used much later on the Il-10. Yefim Gordon archive

Close-up of the armoured cowling of the AM-35 engine on the BSh-2. Note the individual apertures for exhaust stubs. Yefim Gordon archive

Specification – TsKB-55 (BSh-No.2)			
Crew	2	Landing speed, km/h (mph)	140 (87)
Engine type	AM-35	Range at sea level, km (miles)	618 (384)
Engine power, hp		Take-off run, m (ft)	340 (1,115)
at take off	1,350	Landing run, m (ft)	260 (853)
at rated altitude	1,200	Offensive armament:	
Length, m (ft)	11,6 (38 ft 1in)	Bombs , kg (lb):	
Wing span, m (ft)	14,6 (47 ft, 10 ⁴⁄₅in)	normal bomb load	400 (882)
Wing area, m² (sq ft)	38.5 (414.45)	max bomb load	n.a.
Empty weight, kg (lb)	3,615 (7,971)	Cannon:	none
All-up weight, kg (lb)	4,725(10,419)	Machine-guns	ShKAS
Max speed, km/h (mph):		number × calibre, mm	4 × 7.62
at sea level	362 (225)	ammunition load, rounds	3,000
at rated altitude, m(ft)	422 (262) at 5,000 (16,400)	Defensive armament:	ShKAS
		number × calibre, mm	1 × 7.62

The armoured body was almost entirely included into the fuselage primary structure. It was assembled from stamped sheets of armour of 4 to 8mm (³⁄₁₆ – ⁵⁄₁₆ in) thickness, weight reduction being achieved by the optimum distribution of thickness of the armour panels, taking into account both the effective resistance to shell fragments and bullets and the structural loads applied to the armoured body members. Besides, the engineers were aware that at speeds of about 400km/h (248mph) the effectiveness of even thin armour panels increased. The cockpit windshield was made of K-4 bulletproof glass (or, in the Soviet terminology of the time, 'transparent armour'). This was the first time this material had been used on an attack aircraft produced in the USSR.

Ilyushin paid great attention to the survivability of unarmoured structural members. For instance, the mainwheels were semi-exposed when retracted, allowing the aircraft to force-land on unprepared surfaces with the gear up, thus suffering minimum damage to the airframe.

It was originally planned to arm the attack aircraft with five 7.62-mm (.30 calibre) ShKAS (*Shpital'nyi/Komarnitskiy*) machine guns – four in the wings and one on a flexible mount in the rear cockpit. The normal bomb load was 400kg (880lb), the bombs being housed in wing bomb-bays.

Approval

All of these proposals by Ilyushin were accepted. In January 1939 the preliminary design was submitted and the mock-up was approved. The mock-up review commission protocol was signed by Soviet Air Force chief A. Loktionov, who also endorsed the new specification, as we have seen. On the day after this endorsement, 16 February, the manufacture of two TsKB-55 prototypes started at Plant No.39 (for some time they were also referred to as BSh AM-35 in documents). The two TsKB-55 prototypes were of mixed construction, with wooden rear fuselages and fins, all-metal wings and horizontal tails, and fabric-covered control surfaces. The first of them (TsKB-55 No.1) was completed by the beginning of July, but it was not until 2 October 1939 that it made its maiden flight with V.K. Kokkinaki at the controls. On 30 December he took up the second prototype (TsKB-55 No.2). Factory testing of the two prototypes proved to be a protracted affair. Difficulties were encountered in achieving a proper functioning of the engine- and oil-cooling systems, and it took some experimenting before they acquired their final shape. As

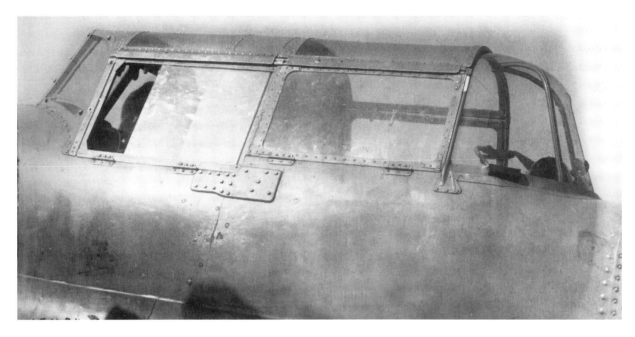

The BSh-2's cockpit canopy in closed and open configuration. Yefim Gordon archive

noted above, the coolant and oil radiators were placed in a duct passing from the top of the engine cowling to the underside of the fuselage. One more version was tested, with the coolant radiator and the oil radiator placed in an armoured bath under the fuselage; it was abandoned in favour of yet another arrangement, in which the coolant radiator remained in the obliquely placed duct within the fuselage, while the oil radiator was transferred to a separate armoured housing under the fuselage. At the same time, the original glycol cooling system was supplanted by water cooling.

The factory testing was completed on 26 March 1940. A few days later the second prototype was transferred to the Air Force Research Institute (NII VVS: *Nauchno-issledovatel'skiy institut Voyenno-vozdushnyye sily*) for its acceptance trials which lasted from 1 to 19 April and were conducted by leading engineer N. Kulikov and pilot Maj A. Dolgov, Maj I.D. Sokolov acting as test navigator. It was after the completion of the trials that the designation BSh-2 AM-35 (with the 2 digit) was

officially adopted and used in the test report. The test results were generally positive: the aircraft could be used as an attack aircraft/short-range bomber, provided its main faults were eliminated. The pilots noted that the BSh-2 was quite easy to fly and similar in handling to the Neman R-10 (KhAI-5) and the Sukhoi BB-1 tactical bombers. The general conclusion of the military specialists was favourable. In their opinion it was necessary to manufacture a batch of AM-35-powered BSh-2s and subject them to service trials in order to investigate tactical performance and to develop combat tactics.

Strictly speaking, these conclusions tended to understate the shortcomings of the machine revealed in the course of testing and were duly recorded in the test report. The BSh-2 fell short of many of the requirements. The maximum speed of 362km/h (225mph) at sea level and range of 618km (384 miles) were less than stipulated in the specification, which called for a speed of 385 to 400km/h (240 to 249mph) and a range of 700 to 1,000km (435 to 620 miles), while the landing speed and take-off run exceeded the design figures; manoeuvrability and stability were clearly insufficient and the rate of climb left much to be desired. The pilot visibility was considered inadequate, owing mainly to the single-engined configuration in which the engine cowling obscured the view ahead and downwards. It was also noted that the AM-35 engine suffered from teething troubles. These were caused in no small part by the powerful centrifugal, high-altitude supercharger which allowed the engine to attain a critical altitude of 4,500m (14,750ft) which was completely unnecessary for an attack aircraft flying at low altitude. In low-level flight the supercharger was a considerable drain on the engine's power. In response to a request made by Sergey Ilyushin at the manufacturer's test stage, the Mikulin design bureau (OKB: *opytno-konstruktorskoye biuro*) developed the AM-38 without waiting for a state order. The new engine had no supercharger and was more powerful than the AM-35 at low altitudes but had the same weight and dimensions. The AM-38 was installed in the first prototype TsKB-55 for flight tests. In addition, the aircraft's structure was modified to eliminate the shortcomings revealed by the official tests. Longitudinal stability was improved by increasing the tailplane area and moving the centre of gravity forward.

Front view of the same single-seater Il-2 at NII VVS. Yefim Gordon archive

From Two Seats to One

Now we come to one of the crucial points in the development history of the aircraft which later came to be known as the Il-2. It is the transformation of the two-seater BSh-2 into a single-seater. As mentioned above, the two-seater was deemed to be generally acceptable by the military, albeit with reservations. The Technical Council of the NII VVS (Research Institute of the Air Force) recommended the construction of a batch of sixty-five aircraft for service trials, but this was contested by People's Commissar for Defence Marshal S.K. Timoshenko who insisted that this be reduced to between ten and fifteen, bearing in mind the shortcomings of the aircraft. Accordingly, a resolution issued by the Defence Committee of the Council of People's Commissars (the government) on 26 June 1940 called for the construction of a batch of ten BSh-2 AM-35 for

Two more views of the same pre-production Il-2. Note the test equipment sensors on the rudder and elevators, the uniform green camouflage and the old-style star insignia on the fuselage.
Yefim Gordon archive

service tests. However, fulfilment of this order ran into difficulties.

In the meantime, the military increased their pressure on the design bureau, demanding that the two-seater attack aircraft be urgently modified to meet the requirements set out in the official specification. According to the version of events that until recently was generally accepted, it was the military who demanded that the BSh-2 be modified into a single-seater, and Ilyushin, although initially opposed, finally and reluctantly agreed. Some researchers, however, are now calling this version into question, citing the absence of corroborating documents. In their view, it was Ilyushin himself who came to the conclusion that a mere change of the engine (substituting the more powerful AM-38 for the AM-35) would not solve the problem; additional, radical modifications were necessary. He took the decision, simultaneously with the installation of the AM-38 engine, to turn the machine into a single-seater. This weight-saving measure was accompanied by the installation of a 12mm (1/2in) armoured wall and an additional fuel tank behind the pilot's seat instead of the gunner's cockpit. Thus, the decision to convert the BSh-2 into a single-seater, looks like being entirely the bureau's initiative – no official decision on that account had been issued by a government body at that moment. The exact reasons that prompted Ilyushin to take this decision can now be only guesswork; apparently, he came to the conclusion that this was the only way to ensure a speedy introduction of the new machine into production. He may have reckoned with the possibility of reinstating the gunner's cockpit later, when the new AM-38 engine no longer presented any special problems. However, the concept of a single-seater attack aircraft did, in fact, establish itself in the thinking of Air Force leaders. In the light of experience gained during the initial testing of the BSh-2, new specifications were drawn up for armoured ground-attack aircraft; they called for the development of single-seater machines. In the spring of 1940 they were sent out to the design bureaux headed by Ilyushin, Sukhoi, Kocherigin, Mikoyan and Arkhangelskiy. It was generally believed at that time that the protection of attack aircraft from aerial attack would be ensured by escort fighters. No one could foretell the events that happened later . . .

The TsKB-55 (BSh-2) No.1 converted into a single-seater was redesignated TsKB-57 – and, judging by the available documents – its existence was officially recognized and endorsed only on the eve of its first flight by an order issued by NKAP (People's Commissariat of the Aircraft Industry) on 11 October 1940. The order required Ilyushin to present the modified aircraft for manufacturer's trials on 15 October. Curiously, it required him to present the AM-38-powered BSh-2 No.1 for testing in a single- and a two-seater version, which was obviously impossible and may be regarded as face-saving by officialdom. Be that as it may, the single-seater BSh-2 AM-38 (TsKB-57) made its first flight on 12 October with Kokkinaki at the controls. The pilot's cockpit canopy had an elongated, non-transparent fairing aft of the seat; the engine was moved forward by 50mm (2in), the wings acquired an additional 5 degrees of sweepback on the leading edges and the stabilizer area was increased by 3.1 per cent. As a result, the centre of gravity was shifted from 31 to 29.5 per cent of the mean aerodynamic chord.

An AM-38 engine is lowered into position on an Il-2. Yefim Gordon archive

A view of the BSh-2's defensive ShKAS machine-gun installation, looking aft. Note the ammunition box and belt guide on the right; the air hose on the left was for the machine-gun cocking mechanism. Yefim Gordon archive

The BSh-2's port flap in fully open position, showing the ribs. Yefim Gordon archive

A pre-production Il-2 at NII VVS during State acceptance trials. Note the deeper intake for the water radiator and the anti-flutter booms near the wing-tips. Yefim Gordon archive

There were also other, less significant changes. The aircraft was to be armed with two 23mm MP-6 cannon, but these were not yet available, and the TsKB-57 retained the four ShKAS machine-guns that had been installed on the preceding version. During factory tests the aircraft attained a maximum speed of 423km/h (262mph) at sea level and 437km/h (272mph) at 2,800m (9,190ft); its range with a normal bomb load reached 850km (528 miles). Its handling qualities and airfield performance displayed an improvement on the previous model. Yet, the TsKB-57 was not presented for state acceptance trials because of troubles with the AM-38 engine which proved to be the IL-2's weak point later on. Difficulties encountered with this engine prompted NKAP to issue an order dated 11 December 1940 requiring Plant No.18 in Voronezh to start series production of a single-seater version of the Il-2 (the name of the BSh-2 allocated in accordance with the new system of designations that was introduced in mid December 1940) with the AM-35A engine instead of the AM-38; it was to be based on the second prototype of the BSh-2 with some changes which, in addition to the AM-35A instead of the AM-35 and to the single-seater configuration, included replacing two of the four wing-mounted ShKAS machine-guns with two 23mm MP-6 cannon.

In the meantime, the BSh-2 (TsKB-55) No.2 was, likewise, converted to a single-seater configuration. It incorporated a number of improvements intended to remedy the shortcomings revealed in previous testing of this machine and of the TsKB-57. The modified machine received the factory designation TsKB-55P (P presumably stands for *pushechnyi* – cannon-armed) and was first flown on 29 December 1940. It differed in some

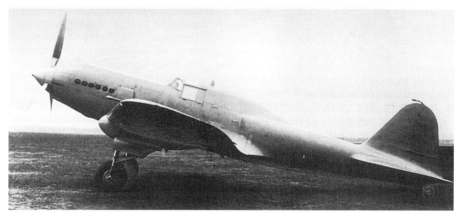

The first prototype was built in single-seater configuration as the TsKB-57. These views show the long fairing aft of the cockpit. Again the aircraft lacks markings. Yefim Gordon archive

The cannon-armed TsKB-55P was effectively the prototype of the initial production, single-seater Il-2. Yefim Gordon archive

Side and three-quarter rear views of the TsKB-55P, showing the lower-slung engine with five exhaust stubs on each side and the redesigned cockpit with a shorter rear fairing. Note the aerial mast and the black/green camouflage. Yefim Gordon archive

Specification – TsKB-57 (BSh-2 AM-38)	
Crew	1
Engine type	AM-38
Engine power, hp	
at take off	1,626
at rated altitude	1,500
Length, m (ft)	11,6 (38 ft 1in)
Wing span, m (ft)	14,6 (47 ft, 10 $^4/_5$in)
Wing area, m^2 (sq ft)	38.5 (414.45)
Empty weight, kg (lb)	3,792 (8,361)
All-up weight, kg (lb)	4,988 (11,021)
Max speed, km/h (mph):	
at sea level	423 (263)
at rated altitude, m(ft)	437 (272)
	at 2,800 (9,187)
Landing speed, km/h (mph)	140 (87)
Range at sea level, km (miles)	850 (528)
Take-off run, m (ft)	250 (820)
Landing run, m (ft)	260 (853)
Offensive armament:	
Bombs , kg (lb):	
normal bomb load	400 (882)
max bomb load	600 (1,323)
Cannon:	none
Machine-guns	ShKAS
number (calibre, mm	4 × 7.62
ammunition load, rounds	3,000
Defensive armament:	none

respects from the TsKB-57. Thus, in an effort to improve the pilot's forward view, the engine was lowered 175mm (6³/₄in) and the pilot's seat and canopy were raised 50mm (2in). An armoured glass panel and a short, transparent cowl were mounted behind the pilot's head to improve rearward visibility. Thus the TsKB-55P acquired the characteristic outward appearance of the future production single-seater Il-2. Later, production aircraft of this type earned a nickname 'the hump-back', reflecting the peculiar profile of the cockpit canopy.

Originally the TsKB-55P was intended to retain the AM-35A engine with which it was actually regarded as a production standard-setter at a certain moment, owing to difficulties with the AM-38 development. However, thanks to some progress in rectifying the faults of the AM-38 engine, it was soon found expedient to install it in the TsKB-55P as well. There were further changes as compared with the original configuration of the BSh-2 No.2. To improve longitudinal stability and controllability, the engine was moved forward by 50mm, the wing outer panels received an additional 5 degrees of sweep

on the leading edges and the stabilizer area was increased by 3.1 per cent (the same had been done on the TsKB-57). A new armour shell providing better protection was installed; it featured an increased thickness of armour plating, ranging from 6 to 12mm. The place previously occupied by the gunner was now used to install an additional fuel tank, bringing the total fuel load of the aircraft to 470kg (1,036lb). The engine was fitted with individual exhaust stubs. Carburettor air intake was transferred to the starboard wing root. The PBP-1b gunsight was installed; it was suitable also for low-altitude bombing, and the aircraft was fitted with a gun camera.

The factory testing of the TsKB-55P was proceeding at a slower pace than originally planned and was still in progress when NKAP, without waiting for the completion of the tests, issued orders placing the single-seater Il-2 with the AM-38 engine into series production at four plants simultaneously. These were plants No.18 (Voronezh), No.35 (Smolensk), Nos 380 and 381 (Leningrad). Plant No.18 was designated the 'chief' plant responsible for keeping up the uniform

standard of production at all four. Appropriate orders were issued by NKAP on 7 January and 14 February 1941. It may be added that of these only Plants No.18 and No.381 succeeded in starting the manufacture of the Il-2 before the outbreak of the war. Later they were joined by Plant No.1, evacuated to Kuibyshev, and by No.30. The latter had actually started preparations for the manufacture of the Il-2 before the war, but had to be evacuated before getting under way. In January 1942 it returned to the capital and got new premises at the Khodynka Central airfield in Moscow, at the site of the evacuated Plant No.1; it started the manufacture of the Il-2 in February 1942. Plant No.35 had produced only a few examples and was taken off the list, being lost to the Germans after the capture of Smolensk. Plants No.380 and 381 were evacuated to Nizhny Tagil in the Urals and merged into one Plant No.381 which turned out the Il-2s until October 1942; then it switched over to the manufacture of the La-5 fighter. In January 1942 Plant No.135 in Kharkov was tooling up for Il-2 manufacture, but later that month was closed down due to the German

Single-seater Il-2s on the final assembly line.
Yefim Gordon archive

Above: Assembling the Il-2's armoured nose sections. Yefim Gordon archive

Left: This view of Il-2s at the final assembly stage shows details of the engine mount and the water radiator duct. Yefim Gordon archive

offensive and the subsequent capture of Kharkov. Thus Plants No.1, 18 and 30 remained the three that produced the Il-2 throughout the war. All these relied on co-operation with subcontractors for the deliveries of armour shells and engines; to some extent the manufacture of wings was also subcontracted (for example, in January 1942 Plant No.156 in Moscow was tasked with making wings for the Il-2 and ensuring daily deliveries of six wing sets from March onwards).

The production version of the Il-2 was to be armed with two Taubin MP-6 cannon and two ShKAS machine-guns, supplemented by eight guide rails for RS-132 rocket projectiles. However, fitting the MP-6 cannon to the Il-2 was beset with problems and delays. Ilyushin showed a marked unwillingness to install this weapon in his aircraft. He raised objections, citing the MP-6's excessive recoil force, which, he pointed out, was more than double the level promised by the designer (Taubin) and far in excess of the design stress limit of the wing structure. In fact, it is more likely that he was guided by other considerations, namely, by his mistrust to the ability of the bureau headed by Taubin to produce a reliable and trouble-free weapon. Nevertheless, after some pressure from the top brass of NKAP, Taubin's cannon with eighty-one-round ammunition boxes were installed in the prototype Il-2 AM-38 (TsKB-55P). This proved faulty in many respects and required much development work; in particular, it was found necessary to provide the cannon

with a belt feed instead of ammunition boxes. In the meantime, the prototype Il-2 was equipped with less powerful 20mm ShVAK cannon, and in this configuration it successfully completed its factory tests.

On 27 February 1941 the Il-2 AM-38, after having some minor modifications, was officially turned over to the NII VVS for State Acceptance trials. They lasted from 28 February to 20 March. The tests revealed a general improvement in the aircraft's performance as compared with the original AM-35-powered, two-seater version. Thus, top speed at sea level with bombs carried internally was 419km/h (260mph) – 57km/h (35mph) more than that of the BSh-2; the rate of climb was increased, controllability and manoeuvrability were considerably improved. There was some decrease in range because of the greater all-up weight and fuel consumption of the AM-38 engine as compared with the AM-35. However, the Il-2 AM-38 was assessed as 'fully meeting the requirements posed to a battlefield aircraft, as regards performance and armament'. True, the State Commission also noted a number of defects and shortcomings which had to be eliminated. They included, among other things, faults in the functioning of the AM-38 engine and of the oil and fuel systems, insufficient armour protection for the pilot's head, short range and the poor quality of the radio communication.

Series manufacture of the Il-2s started concurrently with the acceptance trials and initially encountered great difficul-

ties. Many problems arose in connection with the manufacture of the armoured shells which were in short supply for some time. In mid January 1941 NKAP, citing a delay in deliveries of the shells, requested the Air Force command's consent to a suggestion that the first twenty production machines at Plant No.18 be manufactured with front fuselages made from boiler plate instead of armour steel 'in order to speed up mastering the series manufacture'. These machines, NKAP said, could be used for training. At least one such machine (actually, a mock-up) had, indeed, been built at the plant. Extraordinary efforts had to be undertaken to get the production of the Il-2 under way at the plants designated for this purpose. Plant No.18 (the chief plant) achieved the most satisfactory results among them. The first production machines started rolling off at the beginning of March 1941.

Into Production

On 10 March 1941 Maj K. Rykov, head of the factory's flight test facility, flew the first production aircraft. Despite fears that the AM-38, which had entered production recently, might not pass its 50hr tests, the engine operated reliably under all conditions. The second Voronezh-built Il-2 was completed by the end of March and in April the rate of production started growing. Plant No.18 built seventy-four aircraft in May 1941 and 159 in June. Interestingly, the first four production

An early-production Il-2 AM-38 armed with Volkov/Yartsev VYa cannons and eight RS-82 rockets, pictured during trials. Yefim Gordon archive

machines of Plant No.18 had each its own type of cannon. The first was armed with modified, belt-fed, MP-6 23mm cannon; the second had two VYa-23 cannon of the same calibre; the third production machine was fitted with two 20mm ShVAK cannon; and the fourth had two SG-23 cannon, designed by Salishchev and Galkin. In addition, all production Il-2s had retained two ShKAS machine-guns. Beginning with the fifth production machine, all subsequent Il-2s were initially armed with ShVAK cannon. A special order issued by NKAP on 17 January 1941 tasked the directors of all the production plants with manufacturing the single-seater Il-2 in a version armed with two ShVAK cannon and two ShKAS machine-guns. It was followed by a government resolution dated 12 February which sanctioned this armament version, citing the unavailability of the intended Taubin MP-6 cannon with belt feed. The MP-6 was given a second chance in the event of successful development. Concur-

rently, Ilyushin was tasked within developing and testing the production version of the ShVAK installation within twenty days. Interestingly, according to some documents, delays with the delivery of the MP-6 cannon resulted in a few production examples of the Il-2 being fitted with a quartet of the ShKAS machine-guns (the original BSh-2 armament version).

The belt-fed version of the MP-6 eventually made its appearance. Comparative testing of the VYa-23 and the MP-6 cannon was first conducted, according to one source, on the two TsKB-55 prototypes between 7 January and 22 February 1941. It was followed by comparative tests of early production examples of the Il-2 equipped with belt-fed VYa-23 and MP-6 cannon which took place between 21 March and the beginning of May. Both types of cannon showed satisfactory results and displayed no marked advantages over each other. However, the State Commission gave its preference to the VYa-23 cannon in view of its more mod-

ern and advanced design. A contributing factor was the low production standard and reliability of the series-manufactured MP-6 cannon. As a result, the MP-6 was withdrawn from series production, while the VYa-23 was recommended for introduction into service.

Later, the more potent VYa-23 cannon replaced the ShVAK cannon on many production models of the Il-2 and acquitted itself well in combat. As for the SG-23 cannon, all work on it was discontinued after unsatisfactory tests were conducted on a LaGG-3 aircraft in April 1941. There were two basic arrangements of cannon and machine-guns on production Il-2s. In the ShVAK-equipped version, produced by Plant No.381, the cannon were placed inboard of the ShKAS machine-guns, while the VYa-armed version and some ShVAK-armed machines featured the reverse arrangement (the cannon outboard of the machine-guns). At a later stage, in the summer and autumn of 1941, studies were

This winter-camouflaged Il-2 AM-38 armed with ShVAK cannons and RS-82 rockets is equipped with non-retractable skis. It is seen here during State acceptance trials in January 1942. Yefim Gordon archive

made of yet another version of the armament fit for the Il-2, comprising two 20mm Berezin B-20 cannon in addition to the usual pair of ShKAS machine-guns. Appropriate directives and orders were issued by the State Defence Committee and NKAP in July 1941. Information on the results of this work is not available; there is no evidence of this version having been produced in series.

Into Battle

By the time Germany invaded on 22 June 1941 only eighteen Il-2s had been delivered to the units of the Soviet Union's western military districts; worse, they had arrived in crates, and none of them had

been flown on site and mastered by the pilots (266 Il-2s had been built in the first half of 1941, but they were mostly assigned to training units and research institutions). Thus not a single Il-2 engaged in combat with German aircraft on the first day of the Great Patriotic War. The Il-2s received their baptism of fire on 27 June at the western front when a group of five Il-2s made a strafing attack against tanks and infantry columns in the vicinity of Bobruisk.

Combat experience and the service record of the Il-2 are dealt with in greater detail in the next chapter; here it is important to note that the first air battles subjected the aircraft to a severe test in the course of which both its strong points and weaknesses came to the fore. Ilyushin's

OKB and the production plants were faced with the task of rectifying numerous shortcomings resulting both from the faulty design of some units and items of equipment, and from poor production standards. Thus the ShVAK cannon proved to be capricious, jamming after a few rounds; much effort had to be put into improving their reliability. Combat experience also showed deficiencies in the armour protection: early batches of the Il-2 lacked plating above the pilot's head, over the engine and the aft fuel tank. It had been assumed that fighter attacks from above would be rare, but reality turned out to be different. Complaints were made about the insufficient fuel load, which severely limited the aircraft's combat range. Struts of the retractable

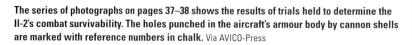

The series of photographs on pages 37–38 shows the results of trials held to determine the Il-2's combat survivability. The holes punched in the aircraft's armour body by cannon shells are marked with reference numbers in chalk. Via AVICO-Press

This winter-camouflaged and unspeakably dirty Il-2 with a short aerial mast carries only two RS-82 rockets under each wing. Yefim Gordon archive

undercarriage proved to lack the necessary strength, which resulted in numerous breakdowns and even crashes. The poor quality of the armour-glass windshield limited the forward visibility for the pilot; this was further compounded by the spraying of the windshield by oil spilled from the propeller hub and the front end of the crankshaft. The PBP-1b reflector gunsight caused discontent because it posed a danger for the pilot in case of a forced landing: many pilots received serious injuries by striking their heads against the gunsight. In response to wishes expressed by pilots, a new, simple, mechanical gunsight – the VV-1 – was introduced at the beginning of 1942; it comprised a bead placed in front of the cockpit and sighting lines marked on the armour-glass windshield. These simple devices could not ensure a high level of precision, and eventually the PBP-1b gunsight returned, albeit in a modified form – it was made easily detachable so as to enable the pilot to put it out of the way in case of an emergency landing.

In May and June 1942 aircraft in service were plagued by numerous failures of the AM-38 engines. The cause was traced to dust at unprepared airfields which penetrated the carburettors and then into the cylinders of the engines, causing excessive wear of engine parts. Urgent steps were

taken to remedy the situation. A special dust filter mounted on the carburettor air intake was quickly developed and introduced on all production machines (it can be seen on the starboard side of the wing leading edge near the engine).

But the Il-2 quickly proved its worth, and deliveries of this aircraft to frontline units in large numbers became a matter of high priority. In the weeks following the outbreak of the war the Il-2's daily production rate at the Voronezh plant was ten to twelve aircraft. This could have been higher, but Plant No.18 was still building the Yermolayev Yer-2 bomber at the same time. The main problem at the end of 1941 was the drop in production rates owing to the evacuation of the factories. In late October production at Plant No.18 temporarily ceased because the plant had to be evacuated. After moving to Kuibyshev (now Samara), the Voronezh plant did not deliver a single aircraft for thirty-five days. Meanwhile, Il-2 production had just begun at Plant No.1 in Kuibyshev and No.381 that had been evacuated to Nizhni Tagil in the Urals, but the few aircraft assembled there could not save the day.

Production of the Il-2 at the new location had to be organized in harsh conditions: the personnel worked in unheated

shops which still lacked roofs, the plants suffered an acute shortage of skilled labour and had to recruit a new labour force from the local population, including many women and youngsters with no experience of factory work. The difficulties were compounded by housing problems and food shortages bordering on hunger. It was then that Shenkman and Tretyakov, the directors of the plants, received a telegram:

> You have let down our country and our Red Army. You have the nerve not to manufacture Il-2s until now. Our Red Army now needs Il-2 aircraft like the air it breathes, like the bread it eats. Shenkman produces one Il-2 a day and Tretyakov builds one or two MiG-3s daily. It is a mockery of the country and the Red Army. . . . I ask you not to try the government's patience, and demand that you manufacture more Ils. This is my final warning. Stalin.

The words 'We need the Il-2s . . . like air, like bread' became the motto of the aircraft industry. Extra efforts were made to complete the assembly shops and organize the delivery of components and materials sourced elsewhere. As a result, by the end of January 1942 the leading Il-2 manufacturer, Plant No.18, had a daily output of seven aircraft. In February the newly-established Plant No.30 in Moscow launched Il-2 production, and in March Plant No.1 was turning out three aircraft per day.

Difficulties experienced by the relocated factories were compounded by the fact that initially they lacked the necessary airfield facilities for testing the manufactured aircraft before acceptance by the military. As a temporary measure, a decision was taken to dismantle the finished aircraft and send them by railroad to Moscow where they were to be reassembled and flown. An order to this effect was issued by NKAP on 2 January 1942; it stipulated that plants No.1, 18 and 381 send their production by rail to factories No.165 and 23 in Moscow for reassembly and acceptance by the Air Force representatives (factory No.165 was set up specially for this purpose at the site of the evacuated aircraft plant No.84). Arrangements were also made for the reassembly of the Il-2 in Voronezh, at the site of the evacuated Plant No.18. This cumbersome procedure entailed much extra work and was discontinued as soon as the evacuated plants had put into operation all the necessary facilities.

In late July–early August 1941 the Ilyushin OKB (Design Bureau) had been evacuated from Moscow to Plant No.381 at Nizhnii Tagil (the order was issued by NKAP on 27 July 1941). One of the chief designer's last tasks before leaving the city was to devise measures enabling the Il-2 to operate from snow-covered airfields. As a stopgap measure, non-retractable skis were fitted to the Il-2s both by front-line units and at production plants. This version was subjected to State acceptance trials in January 1942. Non-retractable skis caused a marked drop in speed, which was considered unacceptable by the frontline pilots. In response to their demands, a retractable ski landing gear was promptly designed; in flight, the skis lay flat against the main gear fairings, minimizing drag. The speed was reduced by a mere 10 to 12km/h (6.2 to 7.4mph). The retractable skis were then put into production. The ski undercarriage led to a marked increase in the length of the landing run and the skis of the parked aircraft had a tendency to freeze to the snow surface. Later, it was decided that packing the snow to achieve a reasonably solid surface was more practical, and the use of skis on the Il-2 was discontinued (no doubt to the relief for the production factories which had complained that the fitting of the skis was a painstaking job, placing in jeopardy the delivery schedule).

Interestingly, there were some highly unorthodox projects with regard to the Il-2's undercarriage. In 1942 an Il-2 version with caterpillar undercarriage designed by Chechubalin was under development; it was intended to tackle operations from dirt strips soaked with water during springtime. There is no information as to whether this version was actually built and tested. Still more unusual was a project proposed in July 1941 by the engineers Nadiradze and Yefremov. Having successfully tested an air-cushion undercarriage on a specially modified example of the UT-2 trainer, they proposed that a similar one be fitted to the Pe-2 dive bomber and the Il-2 attack aircraft. This, they claimed, would enable the Il-2 to operate from any unprepared surface – a ploughed field, a swamp – at the expense of some loss in speed. Some preparatory work had been done on the Il-2 version by the engineers, but, apparently, the idea was not proceeded with, while the same project was actually put into effect on a single Pe-2 – with disappointing results.

Experiments with the landing gear included also the use of wheel tyres made of solid foam rubber instead of the usual tyres with inflatable inner tubes. These, on the Il-2, were notoriously short-lived; still more important was the fact that, in the case of one wheel inner tube being pierced by an enemy bullet during a sortie, the landing usually ended in a heavy incident or a crash. One production Il-2 armed with ShVAK cannon was fitted with such modified wheels in August 1941.

The Il-2 Comes of Age

Combat experience revealed the Il-2's vulnerability to attack by fighters from behind. From the first days of the war, frontline pilots realized the necessity for an aft-mounted, remotely-controlled machine-gun, rear-firing rockets or a rear gunner's cockpit, as on the TsKB prototype. In a letter to Stalin, Capt Ye. Koval', a navigator in the 243rd ShAP (Attack Air Regiment), wrote:

I consider it my duty to demand that the designer and the aircraft industry improve our formidable attack aircraft. Its main shortcoming is that the aircraft is absolutely unprotected against enemy fighters attacking from behind. In most cases the fighter approaches from behind and opens fire at 10 to 15m [32 to 50ft], trying to damage the engine or kill the pilot. Compensating for this shortcoming by providing fighter escort does not seem to be effective.

Koval' further wrote that attack aircraft operated at low and extremely low altitudes, while the escorting friendly fighters had to fly at 1,000 to 1,500m (3,300 to 5,000ft) over the target and often lost visual contact with their charges. He concluded that a rear gunner was essential.

In an effort to remedy the situation, Ilyushin's OKB developed two types of

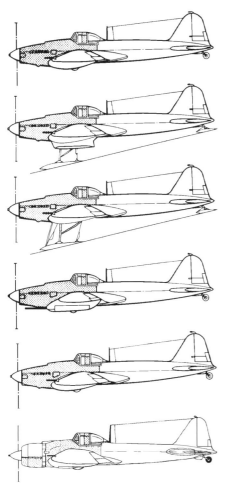

Top to bottom: a standard single-seater Il-2 on wheels, a single-seater with retractable skis, a single-seater with fixed skis, the experimental single-seater Il-2 with ShFK-37 cannons, a late-production single-seater and a proposed single-seater Il-2 powered by an M-71 radial. The shading indicates the areas featuring armour protection.

fixed machine-gun installations intended to protect the Il-2 from the rear. The first of them comprised two fixed rearward-firing ShKAS machine-guns, the other consisted of one 12.7mm UBT machine-gun. Small changes in the direction of the machine-guns were possible in both cases; sighting was effected with the help of mirror devices. On 28 July 1941 Ilyushin suggested to Shakhurin that fifty machines be equipped with the fixed installation of two machine-guns for defence. Prototypes of the two versions were to be manufactured and tested in the middle of August 1941. After testing, the installation with two guns was found to be more acceptable, yet both of them afforded a low degree of protection and were not put into production. There were also some field conversions involving the installation of fixed aft-firing machine-guns, but this was not a widespread practice. It was obvious that a rear gunner was needed.

Without waiting for the OKB and production plants to produce factory-built two-seaters, from the spring of 1942 onwards some frontline units started converting the Il-2s to a two-seater configuration in the field. Local craftsmen made use of whatever weapon was available: a DA, UBT or ShKAS machine-gun, which was placed on an improvised flexible mount (sometimes it was a turret ring taken from the R-5 reconnaissance aircraft or the Pe-2 dive bomber). The 243rd Attack Air Division developed its own variant of such a conversion which was demonstrated to the Air Force command in September 1942. It could easily be effected at the division level and was recommended for widespread introduction. According to some reports, nearly 1,200 machines were modified in the field in this fashion.

Interestingly, some frontline pilots also suggested that the Il-2 be provided with a machine-gun in the extreme tail under the tail surfaces, or with one firing downwards and backwards through a ventral hatch. These suggestions were not followed up.

Ilyushin's first two-seater version of the Il-2, specially designed as a response to frontline demands, appeared in the process of modifying this aircraft to accept the air-cooled, radial M-82 engine. The primary purpose of this modification was to enable the aircraft to make use of a wider range of engines and to provide a back-up in case production of the AM-38 should run into trouble; at the same time, the radial engine, capable of taking much punishment, would serve to enhance the aircraft's survivability. It was proposed that, concurrently with the installation of the M-82 with a take-off rating of 1,675hp, the aircraft be made a two-seater, 'taking into account the war experience'. The second crew member would ensure protection from attacks from the rear. Ilyushin made the proposal to create this version of the Il-2 in his letter to Shakhurin, dated 21 July 1941.

A production Il-2 armed with ShVAK cannon and ShKAS machine-guns was modified to take the new engine. The section of the armoured body up to the front spar, which formed the engine cowling, was removed and a double armoured wall, absorbing the loads from the welded engine bearer of the M-82, was installed along the front spar of the wing centre section. The engine was not armour-protected. By making a few changes to the equipment, the designer increased the Il-2's fuel capacity to 535kg (1,179lb). A gunner's cockpit with a flexible UBT machine-gun, designed by M. Berezin, was provided. The gunner was well protected with armour plating on the sides and the rear wall of the cabin, as well as above his head. Besides, the blister mounting of the UBT machine-gun was provided with armour-glass. The aircraft was designated Il-2 M-82 (in some documents it is called

This photograph, taken on 16 September 1941, shows the Shvetsov M-82 radial of the first prototype Il-2M-82 uncowled for maintenance. Yefim Gordon archive

The second radial-engined prototype differed in having a geared M-82IR. Note the RS-82 rockets under the wing. Yefim Gordon archive

When combat experience proved the Il-2's protection against fighters attacking from the rear to be inadequate, service units started incorporating makeshift machine-gun installations to protect the tail. These two Il-2s have been modified in the field, featuring primitive rear cockpits for tail gunners, equipped with flexible ShKAS machine-guns. Yefim Gordon archive

This twin-ShKAS installation was tested by NII VVS in February 1942 (hence the ink stamp on the photograph reading *Sekretno*, 'Classified'). The machine-guns were aimed by the pilot, using a periscopic sight.
Via AVICO-Press

Il-2 M-82A); it was sometimes referred to as the Il-4 (not to be confused with the bomber of the same name).

On 8 September 1941 the new attack aircraft made its first flight at the hands of Vladimir K. Kokkinaki. The manufacturer's tests were quickly completed, showing that, at a normal weight of 12,466lb (5,655kg), the Il-2 M-82 had a top speed of 382km/h (237mph) at S/L and 421km/h (261mph) at 2,600m (8,500ft). The rate of climb and field performance had deteriorated, but handling qualities were virtually unchanged. In Ilyushin's opinion, the new two-seater version should lead formations of single-seater Il-2s and protect them from attack by enemy fighters. The new machine passed State acceptance tests between 4 February and 27 March 1942 and was recommended for series production. A second prototype of the radial-engine-powered Il-2, tested in February and March 1942, was powered by the M-82IR engine, with a boost in power rating at low altitudes. It had some armour plating fitted to the underside of the engine cowling. Plans were drawn up for the manufacture of the Il-2 M-82 at Plant No.381 and Plant No.135, starting

in the second quarter of 1942. A total of 678 machines of this version were to be manufactured by the end of the year. However, as early as April 1942 these plans were abandoned because by that time the AM-38 engines were well-established in production and AM-38-powered Il-2s were already being mass-produced; the M-82 engine was deemed more urgently required for re-engining the LaGG-3 fighter. It is known that at least one production Il-2 M-82IR was built by Plant No.381; for some reason, it reverted to a single-seat configuration. Interestingly, in August 1942 Ilyushin made an attempt to reverse the fate of the Il-2 M-82, urging on Shakhurin the expediency of launching this version into series production; he suggested that it should be renamed Il-6 (this designation had previously been used for the TsKB-60 attack aircraft project; later it came to denote a twin-engined bomber). At the same time he ventured to provide full armour plating for the cowling of the M-82. On 3 September 1942 NKAP issued order No.674s tasking Ilyushin with installing armour protection on the M-82 engine on the Il-2; a prototype of the modified aircraft

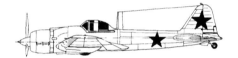

A drawing of the projected Il-2M-71. Via AVICO-Press

was to be flight-tested on 10 October. Technical drawings for series manufacture were to be prepared by the same date. Yet the series manufacture failed to materialize.

The Il-2 M-82 was not the only version of the Il-2 to be powered by a radial, air-cooled engine. There was a project of a derivative powered by the more powerful M-71 engine and bearing the designation BSh M-71. It will be described in the chapter dealing with the Il-8.

Failure of the two-seater Il-2 M-82 to obtain production status made it imperative for the OKB to produce an AM-38-powered, two-seater version. By the beginning of September 1942 projects for two such versions were developed. Both required a minimum of changes to be introduced into the structure and featured a rear cockpit equipped in one case with a ShKAS and in the other with an UBT machine-gun. By the end of September two suitably modified machines were

The first prototype of the experimental Il-2M-82 (c/n . . . 4714). Apart from the radial engine (a feature meant to increase combat survivability), it reintroduced an aft-facing gunner's station. Note the shape of the cockpit canopy.
Yefim Gordon archive

submitted to the NII VVS for comparative State acceptance trials. They featured a gunner's cockpit placed behind the pilot's seat outside the armour shell. The gunner, facing aft, was accommodated on a belt seat; he was protected by a 6mm armour plate from the rear, but otherwise lacked any protection. The cockpit canopy was swung to starboard for entry.

The ShKAS and the UBT machine-guns were mounted on a semi-turret mount and were belt-fed. The UBT machine-gun could be fired at angles of up to 35 degrees upwards, 35 to starboard and 25 to port. The ShKAS installation had slightly wider angles of fire.

The provision of the second cockpit and extra armament increased the aircraft's AUW. Therefore, to avoid increasing the take-off run unacceptably, the flaps were provided with locks allowing them to be set at 17 degrees for take-off. Increased loads on the tailwheel meant that the wheel had to be enlarged and its attachment point reinforced.

Both aircraft passed acceptance tests, the results of which were officially

Above: The open cockpit canopy of the second prototype Il-2M-82 gives details of the defensive machine-gun installation. Yefim Gordon archive

The prototype of the two-seater Il-2 pictured during State acceptance trials in 1942. Unlike later production aircraft, this one had a ShKAS machine-gun in the rear cockpit. Note the short aerial mast and the vertically cut-off rear end of the gunner's glazing. Yefim Gordon archive

A two-seater Il-2 undergoing static tests at TsAGI. Yefim Gordon archive

The starboard wing of an Il-2 fails as the ultimate load is reached during static tests. Yefim Gordon archive

endorsed on 3 October. Despite its lower performance, it was the UBT-armed version that was recommended for series production. What mattered was the greater firepower of the UBT, which afforded a greater degree of protection against enemy fighters. The two-seater Il-2 with the UBT defensive machine-gun was officially ordered into production at Plants Nos 1, 18 and 30. It replaced the single-seater Il-2 as the standard production version and was subsequently manufactured in large quantities. Powered initially by the AM-38 and later by the AM-38F engine, the two-seater Il-2, like its single-seater predecessor, could be armed with either ShVAK or VYa cannon. The introduction of the gunner on the Il-2s was enthusiastically welcomed by the pilots of attack air units at the front; the UBT proved to be a sufficiently effective defensive weapon on the Il-2. However, the two-seater machine did possess certain weak points, the most important being the lack of adequate armour protection for the gunner.

As for the ShKAS-based version of the rear-mounted machine-gun installation,

A production-standard, two-seater Il-2 with a UBT machine-gun in the rear cockpit. Note the engine inlet air filter at the starboard wing root.
Yefim Gordon archive

it was not wasted. In October 1942 NKAP sent instructions to the same three production plants requiring them to manufacture parts that were necessary for installing a turret ring on the Il-2 intended for the ShKAS. These were to be delivered to the Air Force, which would use them for converting the single-seater Il-2s to a two-seater standard. In all,

750 sets of parts were to be delivered in the course of three months (November 1942–January 1943).

In the course of manufacture, the two-seater version was subjected to constant improvements and modifications. Most of the resulting variants had no special designation and can be identified only by the number of production batches. In the

post-war literature one often encounters designations such as Il-2M, Il-2M3 or Il-2 type 2, denoting different variations of the basic two-seater Il-2. However, there is no documentary confirmation of these designations. Externally, notice-able differences between two-seater Il-2s belonging to different production batches included, in particular, variations in the

Above: Two-seater Il-2s nearing completion. Note the lozenge-shaped lines on the bulletproof windshield which probably functioned as reference lines during diving attacks. Yefim Gordon archive

Left: Workers outfitting an almost complete two-seater Il-2 (c/n 6103). This photograph shows how the rear cockpit canopy swung open to starboard. Yefim Gordon archive

Il-2 production proceeded on a huge scale to meet the needs of the Air Force. The banner stretched across the assembly shop reads *Vsyo dlya fronta, vsyo dlya pobedy* ('Everything for the frontlines, everything for victory'). Note how aircraft are moved around the final assembly shop by an overhead crane. Yefim Gordon archive

A further view of the same assembly shop. Yefim Gordon archive

A mid-production Il-2 with a tall aerial mast (its length was increased from 350 to 800mm, 18–31in). Note the altered shape of the rear cockpit canopy and the different shape of the cannon fairings; no wing cannon are fitted. Yefim Gordon archive

This early two-seater features an abbreviated rear cockpit canopy. Note the angle to which the machine-gun could elevate. Yefim Gordon archive

A retouched photograph of a late Il-2 (often incorrectly referred to as the Il-2m3). Note the cannon fairings at the wing leading edge. Yefim Gordon archive

This two-seater Il-2 has the late-model outer wings with sweep-back increased to 15 degrees. Note the late-style insignia outlined in white. Yefim Gordon archive

shape of the aft glazing of the gunner's cockpit. It was found to be limiting the movement of the machine-gun; to remedy this, cut-outs were made in the aft part of the rear cockpit canopy. For the same reason the gunner's canopy was sometimes deleted altogether, as may be seen on many wartime photographs of the Il-2. The rear cockpit canopy was dismantled in frontline units to improve visibility for the gunner.

Several other two-seater models of the Il-2 deserve to be mentioned here. The first was the Il-2bis which was developed at Plant No.1 in parallel with the above-mentioned ShKAS and UBT-armed versions. The Il-2bis (c/n 4434) had a gunner's cockpit with full armour protection and a blister machine-gun mount (called BLUB – *blisternaya ustanovka Berezina*, Berezin's blister mount) for its UBT; the cockpit was similar to those of the BSh-2 AM-35 and the Il-2 M-82. The gunner was protected by armour plating from all sides and by bulletproof glass in the rear glazing (blister) where the machine-gun was mounted. To make the gunner's cockpit sufficiently spacious, the rear fuselage fuel tank was deleted; instead, two tanks of the same total capacity were accommodated in the inboard bomb-bays. The aircraft was armed with two ShVAK cannon, two ShKAS machine-guns and eight launching rails for 82mm unguided rockets. In October 1942 the Il-2bis successfully passed its factory tests and State acceptance trials. These were followed by service trials at the front where the prototype machine made nine sorties before being shot down by ground fire. It won praise from the flying personnel; the gunners were especially

The Il-2bis, a refined version of the two-seater featuring a fully enclosed gunner's cockpit, seen at NII VVS during trials. The aircraft wears early-style insignia.
Yefim Gordon archive

Close-up of the Il-2bis's streamlined canopy. Note that the gunner also enjoyed the protection of a bulletproof glass panel. Yefim Gordon archive

impressed by the roomy rear cockpit, affording good protection and ease of operation of the weapon. However, this modification required significant structural changes connected with the relocation of the fuel tanks and its internal bomb load was reduced to 200kg (440lb) because two inboard bomb-bays were occupied by fuel tanks. For these reasons this version was not adopted for full-scale production.

Neither did the version fitted with the Mozharovskiy/Venevidov MV-3 turret go into wide use. A prototype of this version was built in May 1943. The turret was fitted with a UBT machine-gun and had an aerodynamic balance. It had appreciably greater angles of fire compared with other

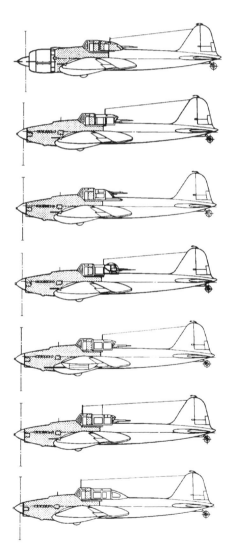

Top to bottom: the Il-2M-82, an early-production two-seater, the Il-2bis, the experimental Il-2 with a Mozharovskiy/Venevidov MV-3 'ball turret', the Il-2KR and the Il-2U.

versions of defensive armament, and the aerodynamic balance enabled the gunner to use his weapon at speeds in excess of 400km/h (249mph). However, the turret was too bulky and caused a considerable deterioration in the aircraft's performance. Therefore it was not introduced on production Il-2s.

In response to frontline pilots' wishes, the semi-turret ring for the UBT machine-gun on the Il-2 was replaced by a Toropov-designed VUB-3 turret with the same weapon; its angles of fire were increased to 45 degrees upwards, 35 to the sides and 12 downwards.

In 1944 two more versions of defensive armament were tested on the Il-2. One of them was the UBSh with a UBT machine-gun having a greater ammunition load (200 rounds) and wider angles of fire. It was found to have no advantages over the VUB-3 installation already in service, and it was felt that an increase in the firepower of the defensive weapon was called for. Accordingly, an installation with a 20mm UB-20 cannon on a standard VUB-3 mount was developed and tested on a production Il-2. The results were satisfactory, yet the installation was not adopted for series production due to the poor reliability record of the cannon itself.

Meanwhile, the Ilyushin design bureau kept working on improving the Il-2. In the summer of 1942 the OKB resorted to a change of power plant to enhance the aircraft's performance. A prototype AM-38F (forsirovannyi – boosted) engine giving improved performance for take-off and at low altitude was installed in a single-seater Il-2. The new engine produced 1,700hp (1,268kW) at take-off and its critical altitude was 750m (2,500ft), compared with 1,650m (5,400ft) for the AM-38. The engine speed was increased from 2,150 to 2,360rpm and the compression ratio reduced from 6.8 to 6.0, allowing the use of low-octane fuel. The design bureau sought to increase engine reliability by changing the inlet configuration, and the installation of an air filter proved helpful. However, it took some time before the teething troubles of the new engine were eliminated. Deliveries of two-seater attack aircraft powered by the uprated AM-38F engines giving improved performance for take-off and at low altitude began in January 1943; the new engines were installed on the single-seater machines as well. The uprated engine

enabled the Il-2 to attain greater speed and rate of climb at ground level; airfield performance was improved and a greater warload could be carried.

Concurrently with the work on the AM-38-powered, two-seater versions of the Il-2, Ilyushin's bureau started, at the Chief Designer's initiative, project work on a two-seater Il-2 powered by the M-250 engine. This engine, developed under Dobrynin's direction by the KB-2 MAI design bureau, had a take-off rating of 2,270hp and a nominal rating of 1,900hp at an altitude of 1,000m (3,280ft). Ilyushin was so impressed by the promised performance of the M-250 that he called it 'the engine of the future' and ventured to install it in an Il-2 with a view to speeding up the engine's flight testing and development. The M-250-powered Il-2 was to be armed with two VYa-23 wing-mounted cannon and two 12.7mm wing-mounted UBK machine-guns, a single UBT machine-gun being provided for rear defence. Its normal bomb load was to reach 600kg, or 800kg in overload version (1,320 and 1,760lb, respectively); the maximum speeds at sea level and at altitude were to be 450 and 490km/h (280 and 305mph), respectively. There is no evidence that this version was actually built. One may surmise the opposite, judging by the comments in Ilyushin's report to NKAP on Plant No.240's activities in 1942 (in letter No.14/180s, dated 16 February 1943). He stated that design work on installing the M-250 engine on the Il-2 had been started in the second quarter of 1942; however, 'due to unavailability of the M-250, the design work on this installation was suspended and was not resumed in 1942'. Interestingly, the People's Commissar of the Aircraft Industry A. Shakhurin made the following comment in his letter to Stalin on the prospects of the M-250 engine:

Installing the M-250 engine in the two-seater Il-2 attack aircraft will entail an increase of its gross weight to 7,000 to 7,300kg [15,430 to 16,100lb] and cause some centre-of-gravity problems. The mentioned modification of the Il-2 will require an increase in the wing area and bigger tail surfaces, as well as a rearrangement of the coolant and oil radiators . . .

Indeed, it is difficult to visualize the Il-2 retaining its dimensions when fitted with this monster of an engine with twenty-four cylinders in six radially arranged banks; the engine's dry weight was as high as 1,200kg (2,646lb) – a good deal more than the 880kg (1,940lb) of the AM-38F.

An attempt to use water injection for boosting the power of the AM-38F engine on the Il-2s proved abortive. In 1944 a suitably modified Il-2 was tested in the NII VVS. The results were satisfactory, but the scheme had one drawback. The water tank, for want of a better accommodation, occupied the place of the gunner, thus depriving the Il-2 of its rear protection. This was characterized as unacceptable both by Ilyushin and by the military, and the project was abandoned.

Another question linked to the power plant was the automation of its control by the pilot. A hydraulic device was developed which automatically adjusted the propeller's pitch to the engine's rpm, relieving the pilot of the manual adjustment of the pitch. This was the so-called combined throttle-and-pitch control lever developed at TsIAM (Central Aero Engine Institute). An example of the Il-2 equipped with this device successfully passed State tests, which had demonstrated a significant improvement in the ease of handling and automated maintenance of the most economic flight mode. On 25 March 1944 the People's Commissariat of the Aircraft Industry (NKAP) issued order No.529s tasking the industry with starting the manufacture of the device. In a letter dated 25 July 1944 and addressed to a deputy People's Commissar of the Aircraft Industry, Ilyushin advocated introducing this feature on all the production Il-2s without prior service trials. However, it is not clear to what extent this recommendation was followed.

A series of further measures were taken to enhance the performance and combat efficiency of the Il-2. Counterbalance weights were installed in the elevator-control system, making it easier to lift the two-seater's tail at take-off and improving longitudinal stability. The aircraft's static longitudinal stability, which had worsened due to the rearward CG shift by approximately 3.5 per cent mean aerodynamic chord (MAC), improved when the CG was moved forward again by increasing the sweep-back of the outer wing panels to 15 degrees (that is, an increase of 6). As a result, the CG position moved from 31.5–32 per cent of MAC to 28 per cent. Better longitudinal stability brought an improvement in

combat qualities – it ensured more precise aiming when firing the guns or performing a bombing attack. Ilyushin proposed this modification to NKAP in May 1943. An AM-38F-powered Il-2 c/n 6767 produced by Plant No.18 and featuring the new wings, together with some other aerodynamic refinements, passed tests in the NII VVS between 20 September and 9 October 1943. Production of the Il-2 with increased-sweep outer wings began in late 1943.

Initially, the new outer wing panels were produced in both a wooden (or mixed) and a metal version. An example of the former was Il-2 c/n 303316 with wooden wing with increased sweep-back, produced by Plant No.30; it was tested in May 1944. However, Ilyushin insisted from the outset that preference should be given to the metal construction, which increased the aircraft's ability to absorb combat damage and made it more suitable for repairs. It also afforded a weight saving of 100kg (220lb) as compared with the mixed construction and required fewer man-hours in manufacture. Production of metal wings was started at Plant No.18; in January 1944 Ilyushin, together with the top leaders of the aircraft industry and Air Force representatives, wrote to Stalin and suggested that the other two production plants, Nos 1 and 30, also be switched to manufacturing Il-2s with metal wings, while the wooden wings were to be relinquished altogether. Accordingly, on 18 January the State Defence Committee issued a resolution No.4976ss which stipulated that the three aircraft plants should completely switch over to the manufacture of metal wings with increased sweep-back by the summer of 1944 (Plant No.18 – by 15 April, Nos 1 and 30 – by 15 May). This was to be achieved without reducing the total output of the Il-2s. Additionally, on 21 February 1944 NKAP tasked Plant No.64 in Voronezh with manufacturing metal wings of the new type for the Il-2.

In July 1943, at the initiative of TsAGI (the Central Aerodynamics and Hydrodynamics Institute), experiments were conducted at LII (the Flight Research Institute) to study the influence of horn balances on the elevators on longitudinal stability and controllability of the Il-2. It was established that the introduction of this feature did not affect the stability and controllability of the aircraft.

Improving Performance

In 1943, when the Red Army mounted successful offensive operations and was rapidly advancing, the inadequate range of the Il-2 became a more acute problem. Its solution was sought through the use of external drop tanks. Several types of such tank were developed and tested. They included, in particular, the PTB metal drop tanks housing 175ltr (38.5gal), and the PLBG-150 tanks made of compressed cardboard treated with a bonding agent, with a capacity of 150ltr (33gal). As a result of the trials, the choice fell on the PLBG-150 tanks which were adopted for production and service use. A two-seater Il-2 AM-38F fitted with two such tanks passed State acceptance trials between 19 September and 10 October. Their introduction, however, was not trouble-free; it took some time to overcome problems with the incomplete use of fuel from these tanks. The use of drop tanks carried on underwing bomb shackles entailed a reduction of the ordnance load and the armament had to be restricted to the gunnery and rocket projectiles.

In his quest to improve the performance of the Il-2, as regards speed, range, load-carrying capacity and airfield performance, Ilyushin attached considerable importance to choosing the propeller type that would make the most efficient use of the available engine power. Several propeller types were used or tested on the Il-2 in the course of its production life. First production models were equipped with the VISh-22T three-blade, variable-pitch propeller. It had a propensity to splash oil through the hub which caused Ilyushin to seek alternatives. These were found in the AV-5 series. On later aircraft the VISh-22Ts were successively replaced by new propellers, first by the AV-5L-124 and then the AV-5L-158 type, both being also three-bladed. The introduction of the new propellers was, in particular, associated with the switch-over to the boosted AM-38F engine. The AV-5L-124 propeller was tested on an Il-2 at Plant No.30 between 20 and 24 May 1942 (according to a NKAP order issued on 24 May) and later was fitted to some production machines. It was, however, regarded as an interim solution pending the availability of the AV-5L-158, transition to which was strongly urged by Ilyushin. This propeller had a diameter of 3.6m (11ft 9½in) and a blade width of 292mm (11½in), the figures for the AV-5L-124 being 3.4m (11ft 2in) and 260mm (10¼in). On 31 July 1942 a prototype propeller of this type was tested on a production Il-2 c/n 182412 powered by a prototype AM-38F engine; the testing was conducted in the NII VVS. According to 'preliminary conclusions', the AV-5L-158 propeller did not demonstrate any substantial advantages over the AV-5L-124. However, at the end of August Ilyushin in a letter to Shakhurin wrote of the successful testing of an Il-2 with the boosted AM-38 engine and the AV-5L-158 propeller, stressing the fact that the boosted engine and the new propeller in combination ensured a reduction of the take-off run from 550 to 370m (1,800 to 1,214ft), 32 per cent. He urged immediate steps to introduce both the new engine version and the new propeller on the production lines. A little later a fly-off was arranged between an Il-2 equipped with the AV-5L-158 propeller and landing flaps and an Il-2 with the AV-5L-124 propeller and no flaps. Both were two-seater machines with the UBT machine-gun in the defensive position. The results were convincingly in favour of the former, and on 5 October 1942 the State Committee for Defence issued a resolution ordering the two-seater Il-2 with the AV-5L-158 propeller, AM-38 engine, landing flaps and the UBT defensive machine-gun into series production instead of the single-seater Il-2.

In May 1942 Plant No.30 was, among other things, tasked with testing the new VISh-105 propeller on the Il-2. It was not adopted for production Il-2s. In 1943 one production Il-2 was experimentally fitted with a four-bladed AV-9L-158 metal, variable-pitch propeller. It was tested in the LII NKAP (Flight Research Institute); the new propeller afforded a modest reduction of the take-off run and virtually no increase in horizontal speed as compared with the standard version with the AV-5L-158 three-bladed propeller. On the negative side, the four-bladed propeller had a tendency to over-speed when the throttle was pushed forward at take-off or in level flight. In consequence, the AV-9L-158 was deemed unsuitable for series manufacture, and four-bladed propellers were never seen on production Il-2s.

Much attention was paid to constantly improving the efficiency of the aircraft's armament, including the bombing armament and rocket projectiles. The bombing accuracy of the Il-2 was severely hampered by the inadequate view forwards and downwards for the pilot, making accurate sighting impossible. As a means of enhancing bombing accuracy, a special timing device known as VMSh-2 was developed; it was an automatic device which released the bombs at a preset interval after the moment when the aircraft's nose obscured the target. An order issued by NKAP on 8 April 1943 stipulated that Plants No.1, 18 and 30 start equipping the Il-2s with these devices; the proportion of the Il-2s so equipped should be gradually increased and reach 100 per cent from July onwards. Another improvement of the bombing armament consisted in dispensing with the special KMB boxes for small-calibre bombs that initially had to be fitted into the wing bomb-bays. Modifications to the bomb-bay doors made it possible to load the bombs direct simply by placing them on the closed doors through hatches on the upper wing surface. Modifications were made to bomb-release mechanisms and underwing shackles for the externally carried bombs. The modernized bombing devices passed tests in August 1942 and were incorporated in production aircraft. Thus, from 15 October 1942, the Il-2s were manufactured with the modernized bomb-bays obviating the need for small bomb boxes.

At first, the Il-2 was equipped with RO-82 launching rails for eight RS-82 rockets. Experimentally, early in 1942, the number of launching rails on some single-seater Il-2s was increased, enabling them to carry fourteen projectiles of 132mm calibre (RS-132) or a combination of eight 82mm and eight 132mm projectiles. Presumably this was done at the expense of the bomb load. Pilots did not consider the RS-82 projectiles to be a very effective weapon and expressed their preference for the heavier 132mm rockets; they were particularly impressed by the armour-piercing RBS-132 and high-explosive/fragmentation ROFS-132 projectiles introduced in the course of the war (from the spring of 1942 the armour-piercing RBS-82 and RBS-132 came into use, supplemented by the V-8 and M-13 projectiles later in the year; the last-mentioned two types were improved versions of the RS-82 and the RS-132, respectively). It was suggested that rocket projectiles could be used for protection

against fighters attacking from the rear; in August 1941 some Il-2s were fitted with a pair of launching rails for rearward-firing rockets which proved useful in scaring away the attacking fighters. In mid 1943 a two-seater Il-2 AM-38F was fitted with no fewer than eight launching rails for rearward-firing rockets.

Experiments were made with different kinds of weaponry on the Il-2. Notably, in 1941–42 attempts were made to equip the attack aircraft with a flame-thrower. A series-produced, flame-throwing device of the UKhAP-250 type was used; it was filled with 100ltr (22gal) of gasoline mixed with 4.2kg (9¼lb) of aluminium naphthenate. Aerial tests showed that at speeds of 320 to 340km/h (200 to 210mph) that were usual for the Il-2 the density of the burning mixture at ground level was too low to produce a worthwhile effect, even if the aircraft were flying at a height of no more than 10m (30ft). The device was found to be unsuitable for combat use.

In August 1942 one example of the Il-2 was experimentally fitted with an aircraft mortar designed by Potanin. The testing was conducted in the NIP AV (Scientific Research Test Range of Aircraft Armament). The mortar tube, with an 82mm bore, was provided with a loading mechanism containing six rounds of ammunition. The mortar was mounted with its axis set at an angle of 43 degrees upwards and rearwards. To minimize recoil, an elastic mounting was used. The mortar shell was fitted with a special inertial fuse. Thirty aerial firings were performed in the course of six test flights. The automatic loading mechanism proved troublesome and there were three cases of the shell's jamming. When fired at a speed of 320km/h (199mph) at the altitude of 1,000m (3,300ft), the shell exploded at a distance of 280m (920ft) behind the aircraft and 70m (230ft) above it. The results were deemed generally satisfactory, but the load of six rounds was considered insufficient and it was decided that it should be increased to fifteen. The final results of the tests are not known.

At Sea

The Il-2 was widely used by the Soviet Navy's air arm (AVMF – *Aviatsiya Voyenno-morskogo flota*). Skip bombing was an especially effective method against surface ships: the aircraft approached the target at 100ft (30m) and at about 400km/h (250mph), dropping the bombs so that they bounced off the water into the ship's side. The Russian term for this method is *topmahchtovoye bombometahniye* (mast-top bombing) because the bomber approaches at mast-top level. More will be said about these operations in the next chapter. Here it should be noted that, according to some sources, the naval career of the Il-2 included its use as a torpedo aircraft. Descriptions have appeared of a torpedo-carrying version of the Il-2, allegedly designated Il-2T. One source claims that in the summer of 1944 a flight of Il-2Ts was operated on a permanent basis in the 23rd Independent Attack Air Regiment (OShAP) of the Black Sea Fleet. The aircraft in question were of the version with new outer panels featuring increased sweep-back on the leading edges. The VYa cannon were dismantled. The torpedo of the 45-36 AN type weighing 940kg (2,073lb) measured 5.45m (17ft 10 1/2in) in length and 450mm (17.7in) in diameter; it was attached to the underside of the fuselage at an angle of some 10 degrees by two curved, tubular struts with cartridges inside the attachment fittings of the torpedo. Another source claims that the 12th ShAP of the Black Sea Fleet Air Force equipped Il-2s with torpedoes of an American type measuring 533mm (21in) in diameter. This information has been contested by some Russian aviation historians who are extremely sceptical about the existence of the Il-2T. They point out that no documentary evidence to corroborate the use of torpedoes by the Il-2s has been found. Significantly, the book *Naval Aviation in the Great Patriotic War*, dealing in detail with Il-2 operations, makes no mention of the Il-2T.

Surviving Damage

The question of vulnerability to combat damage, understandably, was of utmost importance to service units. The Il-2's survivability was appraised in the 1st Attack Aircraft Corps, and Ilyushin's predictions were confirmed. As a rule, the lower armour could not be pierced by small-calibre projectiles, and the cockpit also turned out to be well protected. Experience showed that the armour shell provided adequate protection against 7.62mm bullets, while 20mm high-explosive

ammunition of German flak and large-calibre machine-gun bullets could pierce the armour and inflict serious damage. The Il-2s suffered heavy losses both from fighter attacks and ground fire. Nevertheless, there were many examples showing the aircraft's ability to absorb considerable damage and return to base with what might well be termed as 'fatal injuries' to the airframe. One pilot managed to land his Il-2 with the rudder and the port tailplane shot away by AA fire; another landed with the wing centre-section skin and flaps completely gone.

The rear fuselage, outer wing panels and oil cooler suffered most from AA fire. The use of non-strategic materials when metal became scarce created problems in this respect. A matter of concern was the wooden rear fuselage which had been standardized on the majority of production Il-2s (in May 1941 Plant No.18 was authorized to manufacture 200 Il-2s with metal rear fuselages due to temporary problems with wood supplies). The strength of the wooden tail was clearly insufficient to sustain heavy damage. Sometimes the rear fuselage failed in flight. Equally vulnerable were the wooden wings. There were cases when the plywood skin of the wings broke away. Experience showed that Il-2s with metal outer wing panels had a better chance of survival. When deliveries of metal to the aircraft factories became regular, all-metal wings were introduced (as noted above) and the rear fuselage structure was reinforced with angle extrusions (these had already been used on single-seater Il-2s earlier). These features were incorporated in Il-2s manufactured in the second half of 1944. In April 1994 the Air Force approached the NKAP with a request to switch over to all-metal Il-2 airframes, but this was not complied with. On 14 May 1944 People's Commissar of the Aircraft Industry A. Shakhurin wrote to N. Seleznyov, a senior Air Force official:

As a reply to your letter on series manufacture of the Il-2s with metal rear fuselages at Plants No.1, 18 and 30 I inform you of the following: the NKAP intends to switch the Plant No.18 to the manufacture of the all-metal Il-8 AM-42 aircraft in 1944, and Plants No.1 and 30 in 1945. Bearing this in mind, the NKAP considers it inexpedient to switch Plants No.1 and 30 to the manufacture of the Il-2s with metal rear fuselages, because this will require much rigging and tooling, while the workshops

must be tooling up for the production of the all-metal Il-8.

(This last aircraft, which lost to the Il-10 in production, is described in a separate chapter.) In fact, one may surmise that the top echelon of NKAP simply was reluctant to introduce major changes into the well-established production processes. After the war, complete metal rear fuselages were manufactured to replace the wooden ones.

In the spring of 1944, Ilyushin's OKB resorted to modifying the armour shell of the aircraft, extending it to aft to include the gunner's cockpit. This was done with a view to enhancing the Il-2's survivability and ensuring better protection for the gunner. An Il-2, c/n 305395, manufactured by Plant No.30 and provided with the extended armour, successfully passed State acceptance tests on 25 August. The all-up-weight was increased by 30kg (66lb); the bomb load of 400kg (880lb) remained unchanged. Concurrently, the OKB developed a 'repair' set of additional armour plating to be retrofitted to Il-2s in the field. These measures were received with enthusiasm by flying personnel of the attack air units, but their implementation was not as speedy as one might have wished. The repair sets reached service units with unpardonable delays. As for the extended-armour version, no immediate decision about its series manufacture was taken, despite insistence on the part of the Air Force. In November 1944 Shakhurin proposed in a letter to G. Malenkov that Il-2s with the extended armour shell be placed in production at Plant No.30, while Plants No.1 and 18 were to stick to the previous standard. It was not before the spring of 1945 that Plants No.1 and 30 started series manufacture of the new version, which, in consequence, reached the Air Force units mainly after the end of the war (593 machines of this type were produced by the two plants by the end of 1945).

In the spring of 1943 the combat survivability of the Il-2 was further enhanced through the introduction of self-sealing fuel tanks made of fibre. In contrast to metal tanks, the holes produced by bullets in the fibre tanks did not have lacerated edges; this speeded up the process of the protective layer sealing the hole. A batch of 100 Il-2s with such fuel tanks produced by Plant No.18 was sent to frontline units for service trials starting in

August. Among other measures intended to enhance the combat survivability of the Il-2 one must mention the introduction of duplicate elevator control linkages – something that was requested by front-line pilots who cited many cases of their mounts crashing after the control rods had been severed by enemy bullets. As early as August 1941 the director of Plant 18, Shenkman, and the chief of the plant's design section, Nazarenko, raised the question of introducing duplicate cable linkages instead of elevator control rods. Having obtained approval from Ilyushin, they tested the new control linkages on the Il-2 No.0-0. The tests were successful and the new feature was recommended for introduction on production machines; yet this recommendation was not put into effect then. Surprisingly, Ilyushin had come to the conclusion that the danger of control linkage failure due to combat damage was exaggerated. However, the short supply of tubes required for control rods prompted Shenkman to raise this question again in January 1942 and this time Ilyushin gave his consent to incorporating the duplicate cable linkages on production machines. This, however, was not the end of the story. Obviously, in actual fact the majority, if not all of the Il-2s, went on to be manufactured without the duplicate control linkages. Sometimes these were installed in the field by personnel of frontline units. Such was the case in the 18th Attack Air Regiment of the Black Sea Fleet Air Force, where several Il-2s were modified in this manner in December 1941. Only from mid 1943 did the factory-produced version of duplicate control linkages begin to be incorporated into the Il-2s. In the period 20 September to 12 October 1943 an Il-2 c/n 186767, fitted with duplicate control linkages was undergoing State check trials. There is evidence that Ilyushin's OKB was still developing the duplicate elevator controls as late as mid 1944 when a two-seater, AM-38F-powered Il-2 was fitted with such controls.

The Fighter, Reconnaissance and Training Role

The varied tasks fulfilled by Ilyushin's attack aircraft during the war included a rather unusual one: the use of the Il-2 as a fighter. Of course, the Soviet attack aircraft were inferior to the Bf 109 and the Fw 190 in the counter-air role; but they could conduct air attacks with a fair degree of success against the slower and less advanced aircraft of the *Luftwaffe*. The operational experience of many attack air regiments included a number of cases when Il-2s attacked formations of Ju 87 dive bombers whose 7.92mm defensive machine-guns were of little effect against the armoured attack aircraft.

During the winter of 1941–42 Il-2s were active fighting German transport aircraft. When the three-engined Junkers Ju 52/3m transports began intensive operations to relieve the troops encircled near Demiansk, they found the Il-2s to be one of their most deadly adversaries. The pilots of the 33rd GvShAP were the first to try their hand in these operations. Equally successful were Il-2 operations against transport aircraft near Stalingrad. There, in addition to the 'Auntie Ju', the Ilyushins attacked Heinkel He 111 bombers and Fw 200 Condor transports delivering supplies to the encircled troops.

The accumulated combat experience prompted the Soviet government to order in May 1943 the development of a fighter version of the Il-2. As early as July Ilyushin produced a version of the Il-2 optimized for use as a 'bomber killer'. It was designated Il-2I (*istrebitel*, fighter). It was a single-seater Il-2 converted from a standard production two-seater attack aircraft with an AM-38F engine (it was a machine manufactured by Plant No.1, c/n 7581). The wings were reinforced. The Il-2I was stripped of ShKAS machine-guns, internal bomb-bays and rocket launch rails. The armament was reduced to two VYa cannon with 150rpg. Thus the Il-2I's weight of fire was 4.0kg/sec, which was considerably more than contemporary Soviet fighters possessed.

In July–August 1943 the Il-2I underwent State trials in the NII VVS. The test report stated that the modified single-seater's performance improved only slightly as compared with the two-seater. The report added: 'The Il-2I can only be used to fight against certain types of aircraft possessing relatively low speeds at altitudes up to 4,000 m [13,123 ft].' The Il-2I could easily attack Ju 87 and He 111 bombers, as well as transport aircraft. However, it was no good against the latest German fast bombers and fighters. Hence the C-in-C of the Red Army Air Force concluded that there was no point in the further manufacture of the Il-2I as a fighter.

In response to insistent demands from the Air Force, Ilyushin developed one more version of his attack aircraft, the Il-2KR (*korrektirovschchik*) artillery spotter/reconnaissance aircraft. It was built in the prototype form in March 1943 and introduced into service in the summer. Actually, attempts to adapt the Il-2 to this role had started much earlier, when the combat two-seater versions were not yet available. Therefore a two-seater UIl-2 trainer (described below) was evaluated in the role. In July 1942 special comparative tests were conducted with two aircraft – an UIl-2 and a Yak-7 fighter – in order to determine which of them was the more suitable for adaptation to spotting/reconnaissance missions. As a result, it was stated that the UIl-2 was more suitable for the purpose, but required a number of modifications. When asked to develop the properly equipped prototype, Ilyushin at first claimed that the AM-38-powered, two-seater Il-2 was unsuitable for this modification and insisted that the two-seater Il-2 M-82 was the more easily adaptable. However, the demise of the latter left Ilyushin with no choice. The Il-2KR was developed from the two-seater Il-2 powered by the AM-38F. It retained the basic airframe and armament of the standard Il-2 AM-38F, changes being confined to equipment, fuel system and armour plating. The RSI-4 radio was replaced by a more powerful unit (RSI-3bis), and an AFA-1 or AFA-1M camera was installed in the rear fuselage. Outwardly the Il-2KR differed from the standard Il-2 in having the aerial mast mounted on the windscreen (instead of a more aft position). This version acquitted itself well in service and was well liked by pilots, but there were complaints about the lack of armour protection for the gunner/observer. An attempt to rectify this by extending armour plating to the sides of the rear cockpit was made only in April 1945, when a single example was so modified. It was not launched into series production because the end of the war was near. In the summer of 1944 the number of Il-2KR aircraft in the artillery spotting role in the Air Force amounted to 80 per cent of the required strength and requests were sent to the industry to step up production of this version. Some Il-2s were converted to

Left and above: This single-seater was the prototype of the Il-2I – an attempt to adapt the *shturmovik* for the fighter role. Yefim Gordon archive

Below: The prototype of the Il-2KR artillery spotter/reconnaissance aircraft at NII VVS. This version was identifiable by the forward location of the aerial mast. Yefim Gordon archive

the Il-2KR standard in the field, being fitted with various types of camera for oblique photography at low altitudes. Experience showed that one camera was insufficient to register the reconnaissance information and additional cameras were installed under field conditions in the front of the undercarriage fairings. In some cases these cameras were mounted externally on top of the fuselage, occupying the place of the rear machine-gun.

The training of attack aircraft pilots was no easy task. To cope with it the 1st Reserve Air Brigade was established in Kuibyshev (it was later awarded the Order of the Red Banner of Combat for its activities). By the beginning of August 1941 eight attack air regiments with 306 Il-2s and 292 trained pilots were transferred to the front. Later, more than a thousand pilots were undergoing training every month, and the need for a

dedicated trainer version of the Il-2 became increasingly acute. A dual-control version of the Il-2 was first requested in 1940 and was designed as early as April 1941 (some sources indicate that the first example of the TsKB-55, later modified and renamed as TsKB-57, was converted back to a two-seater configuration and fitted with dual controls by 9 April 1941 and was under testing from 17 July), but it took some time to get series manufacture under way. At the beginning of January 1942 the Air Force officially asked NKAP to make arrangements for the production of twenty dual-control machines at Plant No.1 in February and March, on the basis of drawings from Plant No.18. To simplify production, the Air Force found it acceptable to have them built without the armour steel and armour-glass that were in short supply. On 7 February the State Defence Committee issued a resolution providing for the manufacture of dual-control Il-2s, and, in pursuance of it, on 9 February NKAP ordered Plant No.18 to start producing the trainer version from 15 February onwards and to turn out twenty machines of this version every month. However, the plant failed to cope with the task, citing all sorts of difficulty. It was not before 1943 that the trainer version designated UIl-2 (also referred to as Il-2U, for *uchebnyi* [*samolyot*] – trainer) began to be produced in substantial numbers. On this aircraft the instructor's cockpit replaced the gunner's cockpit; this version differed externally in having an aft fairing of varying shape. Initial versions of the dual-control trainer had the front fuselage made of ordinary (not armour) steel, but from 1943 onwards the Il-2Us were manufactured with the normal armoured shell fuselage identical to that on combat types. Dual-control trainers were initially powered by the AM-38 engines, supplanted by the AM-38Fs at a later stage. A version of the Il-2U produced in January 1945 featured an extended armour shell, providing protection for the rear cockpit. The instructor pilot could correct the trainee's errors and demonstrate piloting techniques by means of dual controls. A special version of the UIl-2, armed with two ShKAS machine-guns, two RS-82 rockets and a 200kg (440lb) bomb load, was used to teach attack aircraft combat techniques.

A huge, manually-trained swivelling camera could be the installed in lieu of a machine-gun on the Il-2KR for oblique photography. Note the radio set installed for real-time voice-link transmission of intelligence data. Yefim Gordon archive

The Il-2U (alias UIl-2) dual-control conversion trainer lacked defensive armament and was easily identifiable by the longer and recontoured cockpit canopy. Yefim Gordon archive

In the course of production the Il-2U was repeatedly modified and improved. In July 1944 a production UIl-2, c/n 1881100109, manufactured by Plant No.1 was subjected to check-up testing which revealed a number of shortcomings, notably, in the equipment of the rear cockpit. Rectifying these defects continued even after the end of the war. Thus a modified UIl-2 AM-38F, c/n 18841133, manufactured by Plant No.18 in April 1945, passed State acceptance trials in the NII VVS between 31 May and 8 June. Some of the changes introduced into the new model were: to improve the second cockpit it was provided with a floor and control linkage fairings, the seat was provided with padded back-and armrests; the front cockpit received armour-glass in its windshield and special controls for fixing the flaps in the take-off position; equipment changes included installation of an RSI-3M1

transceiver. The new tests were completed with satisfactory results and the changes were recommended for production. The dual-control Il-2 was more docile in handling and possessed better longitudinal stability than the combat versions; it could actually sustain a prolonged horizontal flight with the pilot's hands off the control stick. Some UIl-2s were equipped for target-towing.

Large-Calibre Cannon on the Il-2

Attempts to enhance the firepower of the Il-2 by means of large-calibre cannon constitute a special chapter in the aircraft's history. Ilyushin was tasked with producing a version of the Il-2 armed with 37mm cannon as early as the spring of 1941. By mid 1941 an example of the Il-2 in its original single-seater production version was fitted with two 37mm (1.45 calibre) Sh-37 cannon designed by a team led by Boris Shpital'nyi (also known as ShFK-37). It passed its ground- and air-firing tests by 15 September and was subjected to State

acceptance trials between 23 September and 12 October 1941. Because of their large size, the cannon were installed in underwing fairings and lowered considerably to provide room for a high-capacity ammunition box (each box contained forty rounds). As a result, the gun attachment points became complex and large, draggy fairings had to be installed (identified by the front parts of the fairing protruding ahead of the wing's leading edge).

It was revealed during the trials that the performance of the ShFK-37-armed Il-2 was considerably inferior to that of the standard production version armed with VYa or SVAK cannon. During tests the aircraft attained 373km/h (231mph) at sea level and 409km/h (254mph) at 2,400m (7,900ft) at an AUW of 5,864kg (12,927lb). The rate of climb deteriorated and the take-off run increased; the landing speed was 146km/h (90mph). Moreover, the Sh-37 proved unreliable and the low position of the cannons relative to the aircraft's CG caused the Il-2 to pitch down when the cannon were fired, reducing the firing accuracy. The manoeuvrability of the aircraft

This single-seater Il-2 with anti-flutter booms has been fitted experimentally with two 37mm Shpital'nyi ShFK-37 cannons in huge pods. Additionally, the aircraft carries eight RS-82 rockets. Yefim Gordon archive

A close-up of the starboard ShFK-37 cannon with the fairing removed. Yefim Gordon archive

deteriorated markedly – it became more sluggish and difficult to handle.

At the end of December 1942 eight Sh-37-armed Il-2s arrived with the 688th Attack Air Regiment of the 228th Attack Air Division of the 16th Air Army for service trials (they were joined by one more in January). The aircraft took part in combat activities in the Stalingrad area in January. Combat experience revealed both the advantages of the new armament and its weak points. Armour-piercing incendiary shells fired from the Sh-37 pierced the armour of German light tanks and, under certain conditions, of medium-weight tanks and might be considered a generally effective weapon against armoured vehicles when used by skilled pilots. However, it was not easy to achieve the necessary precision of fire when using these weapons. This was due to the heavy recoil of the cannon and the poor synchronization of their firing. These combined led to the aircraft's veering off the sight line and to

a marked imprecision of fire. The pilot could not afford to use more than two or three rounds in a single burst if he were to retain any precision. Moreover, the new cannon proved rather unreliable, and not infrequently one jammed. Firing a single Sh-37 cannon was, for all practical purposes, impossible because the aircraft immediately turned in the direction of the firing cannon. All this lessened the usefulness of the new Il-2 version and hardly endeared it to frontline pilots who voiced their opinions of it. As a result, the Il-2 armed with the ShFK-37 (Sh-37) cannon was not placed in large-scale production.

Yet the need for an aircraft capable of effectively destroying German AFVs was felt acutely, and further efforts were made to provide one. In March–April 1943 two new, advanced 37mm NS-37 (11P-37) cannon designed by Noodelman and Sooranov were installed in a two-seater AM-38F-powered Il-2. The cannon were belt-fed, which allowed them to be

attached direct to the wing underside; they were enclosed by relatively small fairings, the front ends of which were sloping rearwards, as distinct from the forward-protruding fairings of the Sh-37 cannon. Each cannon had fifty rounds loaded direct into the wing, instead of traditional ammunition boxes. If necessary, the aircraft could carry up to 200kg (440lb) of bombs in overload configuration. Launch rails for rocket projectiles were dismantled.

A small batch of Il-2-37, as the type was designated, were manufactured at Plant No.30 and underwent service trials with the 208th ShAP during the Kursk battle. In the opinion of the pilots, the handling techniques for the new variant did not differ from those for a fully-loaded two-seater Il-2. The fairings and the distribution of large masses in the wings (one gun with ammunition weighed 237kg [552lb]) increased the aeroplane's inertia and made it more sluggish to manoeuvre. In addition, there were difficulties with

The port cannon mount on the same aircraft with the cannon removed; note also the rocket launch rails. Yefim Gordon archive

An early-production two-seater Il-2 armed with Nudelman/Suranov NS-37 cannons. The more compact and streamlined cannon pods are readily apparent. Yefim Gordon archive

aiming. It was practically impossible to fire more than one round at a time with any precision because the poor synchronization of the guns coupled with their powerful recoil and location far from the fuselage caused the aircraft to yaw violently. Thus the new weapon inherited the problems of the Sh-37 cannon. To ensure the most effective use of the NS-37 cannon, steps were taken to train frontline pilots in firing the weapon in short bursts against point targets. A recommendation was issued to designers and manufacturers of the weapon that the NS-37 cannon should be provided with a muzzle brake. Express instructions required that the Il-2 armed with the NS-37 cannon be provided with fifty rounds of ammunition per cannon and a normal bomb load of 100kg (220lb). That helped to enhance the efficiency of the aircraft to some extent. Again, in the hands of a skilled pilot the NS-37-armed Il-2 was a formidable weapon capable of destroying even Tiger tanks; it was considered to be especially effective against all kinds of motor vehicle, railway trains and ammunition and fuel depots. Yet it did not see widespread use. A contributing factor to this was the emergence of an effective 'alternative' method of destroying AFVs. It was the use of hollow-charge cluster bombs which had been developed

under the leadership of I. Larionov and put into production by the summer of 1943. The small bombs known as PTAB 2.5-1.5 were loaded direct into the bomb bay and dropped on enemy vehicles from altitudes up to 100m (328ft).

The NS-37-armed Il-2s could carry only a 100kg (220lb) bomb load as against the 400kg (882lb) carried by the standard-armament Il-2s. This reduction, in the opinion of pilots, was not compensated for by the greater firepower of the 37mm cannon lacking the necessary precision. Pilots who had flown the NS-37-armed machines were unanimous in their preference for the VYa-23-armed version capable of carrying a greater bomb load; they considered this armament fit more versatile and better suited for most types of mission. In brief, the results of service trials of the Il-2s armed with the NS-37 cannon were considered unsatisfactory, and in November 1943 a decision was taken to discontinue the series manufacture of this version. Plant No.30 received an order to switch over completely to the manufacture of the Il-2s armed with 23mm VYa cannon by 15 January 1944. Thus from January onwards, all aircraft factories engaged in the production of the Il-2s manufactured these aircraft only in the VYa-armed version. In all, 947 NS-37-armed Il-2s

had been produced by 7 December 1943; there were plans to bring this figure to 1,175 by 15 January.

In a further quest to enhance the firepower and combat effectiveness of the Il-2 against armoured and well-protected targets, a decision was taken to produce a version of this aircraft armed with 45mm cannon. On 22 August 1943 NKAP issued two orders (Nos 507s and 508s) requiring the Ilyushin OKB to build two prototype Il-2 aircraft armed with two 45mm cannon each; both were to be presented for State acceptance trials by 5 November. One of these was to be armed with the cannon designed by the OKB-16 (Nudelman and Suranov), later to be known as NS-45, the other one had a similar cannon designed by the OKB-15 (Shpital'nyi). A prototype Il-2 powered by the AM-38F engine and armed with two NS-45 cannon was submitted for acceptance trials on 10 September 1943 (in some sources the dates of 13 September and even 2 November are cited). The tests lasted until 8 February 1944.

A later two-seater armed with NS-45s seen during State acceptance trials (note the tall aerial mast). Yefim Gordon archive

Another mid-production aircraft with NS-45 cannons. Yefim Gordon archive

This Il-2 is armed with heavy cannons (possibly of 45mm calibre) whose type remains unknown. Note the shape of the cannon pods protruding beyond the wing leading edge. Yefim Gordon archive

Test air firing of the new cannon revealed its low effectiveness against point targets. This was due mainly to excessive recoil. In consequence, the machine with the NS-45 cannon was not put into series production. As for Shpital'nyi's weapon (the Sh-45), an official report dated 30 October 1943 stated that an Il-2 armed with Shpital'nyi cannon 'had been completed on 27 October and had not yet been flown to the NII VVS because of bad weather'. No further information on this aircraft is available, but some sources indicate that plans to install the Shpital'nyi 45mm cannon on the Il-2 were abandoned.

In response to criticism concerning his large-calibre cannon, Nudelman undertook successful attempts to reduce considerably the recoil force of both the NS-45 and the NS-37 by equipping them with muzzle brakes. He even claimed that the new version of the NS-37 could be fired singly on the Il-2 without compromising the precision of aiming. However, according to some researchers, these modified cannon (NS-45M and NS-37M, respectively) were not installed in the Il-2. There is, however, a photograph depicting an Il-2 with a large-calibre cannon (37 or 45mm), the barrel of which is apparently fitted with a muzzle brake.

Curiously, in seeking to enhance the Il-2's efficiency as a tank buster, Ilyushin did not rely solely on increasing the calibre of the cannon installed in the aircraft. In fact, he resorted to the opposite – at one time he seriously studied the possibility of reducing the calibre of the VYa cannon to 14.5mm. This would have enabled the VYa cannon to make use of the 14.5mm armour-piercing rounds of anti-tank rifles which had demonstrated their high penetrating power. On 14 November 1942 Ilyushin wrote to Shakhurin:

An armour-piercing shell has been developed for the Volkov-Yartsev cannon mounted on the Il-2 by reducing its calibre to 14.5mm while leaving the size of the shell case unaltered. Tests have shown that this armour-piercing shell penetrates the armour of 50mm

[2in] thickness at a distance of 150m [490ft]. It is necessary, as a matter of urgency, to design and manufacture a loading system for this kind of ammunition at the Il-2 aircraft and to conduct the appropriate testing.

Ilyushin sought Shakhurin's permission to design this new system and asked the People's Commissar to give instructions to Plant No.18 requiring it to install this new system on a production example of the Il-2. Accordingly, on 17 November NKAP issued order No.482s entrusting Ilyushin with the design of the new ammunition feed system for the VYa cannon adapted to the 14.5mm armour-piercing shell; the director of Plant No.18, Belianskii, was obliged to turn out two Il-2s equipped with the new ammunition feed for the VYa cannon by 15 December. No information is available on the results.

The End of the Story

Finally, a few words must be said about the final phase of the aircraft's production. It was manufactured in huge numbers, total production totalling 36,154. In 1944 the Il-2 was joined on the production lines by its more efficient stablemate, the Il-10. Production of the two types continued in parallel in 1945, the proportion between them gradually changing in favour of the Il-10. As the manufacture of the latter gradually increased, production figures for the Il-2 tapered off. This can be exemplified by figures referring to the activities of Plant No.18. In the second half of 1944 the plant was tasked with introducing the Il-10 into series manufacture without impairing the total output of attack aircraft. This was tackled successfully. In January 1945 the plant turned out fifty Il-10s and 225 Il-2s, in March the figures were ninety and 207, respectively, and in May 163 and 112. For 1945 as a whole, the figures for the Plant No.18 were 1,315 Il-10s and 943 Il-2s. After the end of the war the manufacture of the Il-2 continued for some time, but was quickly brought to a close. Plant No.1 stopped

producing the Il-2 in June 1945, Plant No.18 did the same in July, while at Plant No.30 it was not before October that the Il-2 was finally phased out.

The Il-2s that survived the war remained on the strength of attack air units of the Soviet Air Force for some time. The intention was to phase them out as soon as possible and rearm the attack element of the Air Force completely with more modern Il-10s and Il-16s (described below). However, this proved to be more time-consuming than was expected, and it was found expedient to prolong the period of service of the remaining Il-2s. In March 1946 a draft resolution of the government was prepared instructing the People's Commissariat of the Aircraft Industry to supply 1,500 metal rear fuselages for the Il-2s to the Air Force. The intention was to replace the wooden tails of the Il-2s and thus increase the service life of these aircraft. The appropriate order was issued to Plant No.30, but on 19 April 1946 the Air Force curtailed this order to 700 metal rear fuselages. This order was further halved to 350 on 1 May; moreover, now they were intended not for combat machines but for the UIl-2 trainer. The new rear fuselages were to be produced and mounted on the Il-2s before 1 January 1947. By 16 November this refurbishment was effected on 143 machines and the work went on. Events proved this curtailment of the order for the new tails to be a rash decision. On 21 December 1946 Commander-in-Chief of the Air Force Vershinin sent the following request to Minister of the Aircraft Industry Khrunichev:

Bearing in mind that the estimated manufacture of 1,900 Il-10 aircraft (including 200 combat trainer versions) in 1947 will fall short of our need for attack aircraft, the Il-2 aircraft must be retained in squadron service until the middle of 1948; their service life must be extended by replacing wooden parts of the fuselages by metal ones. To effect these measures, 1,298 metal rear fuselages of the Il-2s must be manufactured.

The sequel to the story is not known.

CHAPTER THREE

The Il-2 in Combat

Early Days

By the time the Great Patriotic War broke out, only eighteen Il-2s had been delivered to the western Military Districts of the USSR, yet none had been flown and mastered by aircrews. Not a single aircraft of this type succeeded in joining combat against the *Luftwaffe* on 22 June 1941. Among the first units to receive the new aircraft in Voronezh was the 4th ShAP (Attack Air Regiment) commanded by Maj S. Getman. It had been the intention that this unit should conduct the service evaluation of the Il-2. Before the outbreak of war the pilots had just enough time to make several circuit flights and flights into a designated zone. They had had no time to receive training in formation flying. None of the pilots had any skills in firing cannon and machine-guns, in precision bombing and in using rockets. Instead of the statutory complement of sixty-five Il-2s the unit had only seventeen on strength. Nevertheless, as early as 1 July the regiment had its baptism of fire in the vicinity of the Berezina river and the town of Bobruisk. Even inexperienced pilots were quick in appraising the simple handling of the Il-2, its potent armament and its invulnerability to small arms fire and, to some extent, even to the fire of small-calibre anti-aircraft guns. The Il-2s attacked enemy tanks when they gathered in large numbers in disembarkation or concentration areas or on the march. Less frequently the aircraft were used for destroying targets on the battlefield. The Air Force command and the senior officials of NKAP quickly became aware of the usefulness of the aircraft and did their best the ensure that as many as possible should reach the attack air regiments.

The multiplicity of the tasks to be tackled and the shortage of aircraft in the frontline units left their mark on the tactics employed in the initial stage of the war. As a rule, their sorties were performed by one or two flights consisting of three aircraft flying at low altitudes without the benefit of fighter protection. Should there be no opposition from German fighters, they made several passes at their target from different directions. That caused the flak to be less concentrated and helped to reduce their own losses. When undertaking a strike, two kinds of attack were mostly employed. The first consisted in bombing from altitudes that ranged from the minimally admissible (hedge-hopping flight) to 150m (490ft). The second was an attack pressed home after a zoom climb that was made after approaching the target area at low altitude; the Il-2s zoomed to an altitude of 300 to 400m (980 to 1,300ft) and then used their weapons in a shallow dive.

At that time official instructions stipulated that the Il-2s should undertake their attacks from different altitudes, the interval between the groups of aircraft being 10 to 15min. To make the aircraft less noticeable during the sorties, the use of cloud cover and the right direction relative to the sun were recommended; throttling back the engine during a diving attack was also considered expedient. To reduce the time between the issuing of a combat order and the actual strike, small groups of aircraft were stationed at airfields situated at a distance of 15 to 20km (9 to 12 miles) from the frontline. Air regiment commanders were tasked to ensure the preservation of a communication channel between the airfield where their unit was stationed and the headquarters of the army formations. Before performing a mission, especially when it was flown at extremely low altitudes, the pilots carefully studied the combat area, taking note of reference points and recognizable features near the target. When a respite in combat occurred, young pilots were sent on familiarization flights at low altitudes and only after that were they allowed to take part in combat missions, initially at altitudes of 400 to 500m (1,300 to 1,640ft) under fighter cover. However, it was no easy task even for experienced pilots to find and hit the target when flying at low altitude. Therefore attack air units enlisted the assistance of a pathfinder aircraft flying at medium altitude and seeking out the target. Usually the SB bombers served as lead aircraft. When the target was discovered the navigator of the SB released the bombs and thereby designated the target. A mixed battle formation was based on the following pattern: placed forward and flying under the protection of two or three I-16 or MiG-3 fighters, were the lead aircraft or a group of target-designation aircraft; they were followed by a strike force of attack aircraft accompanied by a flight divided into pairs; one of these was placed on a flank and the other one served as a rearguard.

Surprise blows delivered by aircraft flying at very low altitude formed the basis of their tactics which reflected the situation and the unequal balance of forces in the air during the first stage of the war. However, as the number of Soviet aircraft grew, the blows dealt by them became increasingly devastating and tactics were refined.

Having suffered substantial losses to Soviet aviation, the Germans gave up their practice of sending troops in compact columns along main roads. They began to use forest lanes and country roads; tanks and other vehicles using camouflage now advanced well spaced, making use of anti-aircraft defences. Under these changed conditions, attack aircraft concentrated their effort and chose as targets enemy troops at assembly and refuelling points and on the march. To put this into effect, precise intelligence was needed. At first, it was provided by reconnaissance aircraft not in the inventory of the attack air units. Thus these aircraft discovered in the vicinity of Mozhaisk a grouping of more than 300 tanks which were moving in column several abreast in the direction of Moscow. Acting in concert with bomber units, attack aircraft strafed the troop concentrations for two successive days. As a result, the advance of the enemy was

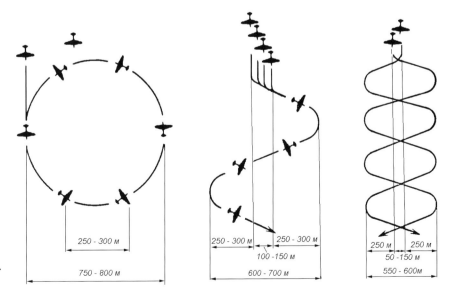

Soviet Army servicemen prepare a tactical airfield for Il-2 operations. The surface is sprinkled with water to reduce dust formation. Via AVICO-Press

This diagram illustrates three of the Il-2's battle tactics.
Left to right: 'wheel of death', S-turn and 'scissors' tactic.
Via AVICO-Press

В дни жестоких боёв не прерывалась традиционная связь
авиационных частей с трудящимися Ленинграда. На аэродромы
приезжали делегаты различных предприятий.
На снимке: группа рабочих Кировского завода в 174 ШАП.

halted and their opportunities for manoeuvre severely restricted with the ensuing destruction of these troops. A few days later, attack air units, acting in cooperation with fighters and making use of air reconnaissance information, performed several successful attacks against German tanks that were trying to penetrate to the Soviet rear. Groups of nine aircraft headed by a lead aircraft dealt successive blows to the enemy. Favourable conditions were thereby created for Soviet troops to counter-attack. When the area was liberated, eighty knocked-out German tanks were discovered. The next step in enhancing the effectiveness of missions to interdict the arrival of enemy reinforcements consisted in organizing air reconnaissance in attack air units. Reconnaissance missions were performed by the most experienced attack aircraft crews. At the same time, every pilot was obliged to be observant and to report everything worthy of note that he had seen on the battlefield and on the territory immediately behind the frontline.

New Roles

At the end of October the evacuation of the factories led to a temporary halt in the deliveries of the Il-2s to frontline units. Several machines that had been assembled at Plants No.1 and 381 which had begun the manufacture of the aircraft, could not remedy the situation. By that time the Germans started the 'decisive' offensive against Moscow known as Operation *Typhoon*. The number of Il-2s opposing the enemy at all fronts totalled 144, only half being in airworthy condition. Of this number, only thirty-six were assigned to the sector opposing the *Wehrmacht* in the direction of its main blow. In the Soviet air grouping note must be made of the 215th ShAP (Air Attack Regiment) commanded by Maj L. Reino, whose pilots fought courageously. In July the pilots returned their outdated I-15bis biplanes and began converting to the Il-2. But this training did not last long. Shortly after, the regiment was committed to action and performed strafing mis-

sions against vehicle and tank columns in the area Dukhovshchina–Yartsevo. Usually every group of the attack aircraft was led by a Pe-2 aircraft which performed target designation for Il-2 pilots. After the leader's signal, the attack aircraft made a zoom climb and, having gained altitude, dropped their bombs and fired unguided rockets at the target, then descended to a lower altitude and put their cannon and machine-guns into action. An heroic exploit was performed by Senior Lt A. Novikov on 3 October. When strafing a column, his aircraft was hit by flak and caught fire; Novikov directed his blazing machine at the column he was attacking. In recognition of this and other deeds the 215th ShAP was transformed into the 6th Guards Attack Air Regiment (GShAP) and became the first among attack air units to be awarded this coveted title.

Commander of the 65th ShAP Maj Vitrook was the first to use the Il-2 to attack enemy bombers. In one aerial combat the aircraft of the group headed by Vitrook, defending each other from

Above left: **Country roads were often used as runways by Il-2s and other combat aircraft. This shot was taken in the Moscow region in the autumn of 1941.** Yefim Gordon archive

Above: **Hidden among the trees, an early-production single-seater Il-2 with eight rocket launch rails is prepared for a mission.** Yefim Gordon archive

Left: **The pilots of a Soviet attack regiment mark the day's targets on their maps beside a single-seater Il-2 inscribed *Smert' fashistskim okkupantam!* ('Death to the Nazi invaders!').** Yefim Gordon archive

A briefing takes place in front of a filter-equipped Il-2 armed with ShVAK cannons and four RS-82 rockets. Two-seaters carried four rockets instead of eight due to the added weight of the second crew member. The aircraft's c/n (370640) is visible on the front fairing of the main-gear nacelle. *Yefim Gordon archive*

enemy fighters, succeeded in downing three Messerschmitts. That day, 11 November 1941, was also memorable for those Muscovites who remained in the city. On that day Lt G. Svetlichnyi from the 312th ShAP could not make it to his base at the Tushino airfield and landed his Il-2 on Gorky Street (the city's main thoroughfare), not far from Belorusski railway station, virtually in the centre of the Soviet capital.

In the winter of 1941–42 the Il-2s were active in combating the German transport aviation. When the three-engined Ju 52s started their flights into the 'Demyansk pocket' to rescue encircled troops, they found the Il-2s among their most dangerous opponents. This was done at the initiative of the pilots of the 33rd Guards ShAP. Just as successful were the actions of the Il-2s against the transport aviation near Stalingrad. There the Ilyushins fought not only the Ju 52s and the He 111s, but also the Fw 200s which were used for ferrying supplies to the encircled Germans.

The winter of 1941–42 raised the question of operating Il-2s from snow-covered airfields. As related previously, this was tackled by fitting the Il-2 with a ski undercarriage, first of a non-retractable and then of a retractable type. Conversion to the winter undercarriage did not take much time. Later, when airfields were rolled down to produce a hard-packed snow surface, there was no longer any need for skis and the Il-2s were switched to operation on wheels all year round. But the main problem at the end of 1941 was the drop in output caused by the evacuation of the aircraft plants.

In that winter the first summing up of the results of the use of the Il-2 in combat was made. Experience showed that a well-trained pilot could knock out on average two German tanks at a distance of 300 to 400m (980 to 1,300ft) using cannon and unguided rockets, provided that he had made a successful pass at the target; a pilot with a merely satisfactory level of training could knock out one. Cases were on record when German tank crews failed to withstand the nervous pressure caused by the assault and abandoned their machines during an attack. The success of the Il-2s was in no small part enhanced by the fact that some of aircraft were armed with the VYa cannon which were more potent than the ShVAK, albeit with a somewhat inferior rate of fire. Machine-gun fire was also effective against troops, transport vehicles and other unprotected targets. If the whole ammunition complement were spent, the result might be thirty to forty troops killed or wounded, should they fail to escape in time.

In the summer of 1942 German forces undertook a major offensive on the southern flank of the front. Attack air units, already with substantial numbers of aircraft on strength, tried to frustrate the enemy's advance near the Don river. The missions were usually flown by small groups of the Il-2s which attacked columns on their march across the steppes.

The main blow was made using cannon or unguided rockets. The average bomb load of the Il-2s at that time did not exceed 200kg (440lb); sometimes they carried no bombs at all. A special order issued by the People's Commissariat of Defence (NKO) contained an analysis of the shortcomings in the combat employment of the aircraft and recommendations as to their correct use:

We have at our disposal the Il-2 attack aircraft which are the most effective bombers for use against the enemy's tanks and personnel. No other army is in possession of such short-range bombers. We can and we must considerably increase our blows dealt to the enemy, but to achieve this, we must immediately give up the harmful practice of underestimating the Il-2 in the role of daytime bombers and see to it, that not a single Il-2 takes off for a combat sortie without a full bomb load.

In the wake of this order stringent control was set up so as to ensure that the bomb load should not be less than 400kg (880lb). Senior Lt I. Pstygo, a pilot of the 504th ShAP (subsequently a Hero of the Soviet Union and an Air Marshal) was among the first pilots to take on board a bomb load of 600kg (1,960lb).

New Version and Changing Tactics

On the 30 October 1942 the Il-2s of a new production version – the two-seater, AM-38-powered machine – were committed to action for the first time. On that day they successfully attacked an airfield in the vicinity of Smolensk. The machine-gun for rear defence became an effective means of ensuring protection against fighters. During the service evaluation period alone the Il-2 gunners shot down seven Bf 109s and repulsed many attacks by fighters.

Armourers prepare 100kg (220lb) FAB-100 bombs for loading on an Il-2 while technicians are at work on the aircraft itself which is 'unbuttoned' for maintenance.
Yefim Gordon archive

100kg bombs were hoisted into place under the Il-2's wings with the help of manually-operated winches. Yefim Gordon archive

Above: Small 25kg (55lb) bombs were loaded manually. Yefim Gordon archive

Left: This picture shows how FAB-50 bombs were loaded into the inner wing bomb-bays. Note the bomb-loading hoist. Yefim Gordon archive

Below: An early single-seater Il-2 (as evidenced by the wing-tip anti-flutter booms) taxies out for a sortie. Yefim Gordon archive

Commander-in Chief of the Red Army Air Force AM A. Novikov wrote that, during the battle of Stalingrad, much was staked on ground-attack aviation, and it fully justified the hopes pinned on it. 'Attack aircraft were simpler in design and cheaper in production; by virtue of their numbers multiplied by the excellent combat qualities they to a large extent compensated for a certain shortage of bombers that we experienced.' Novikov also noted that the Il-2s were to a lesser extent dependent on the vagaries of weather than bombers, which made it possible to use them in combat in adverse conditions. Gradually the number of the Il-2s in frontline air units grew. On the eve of the counter-offensive near Stalingrad there were 1,644 on strength, and on the eve of the Kursk battle 2,817. In both cases the Il-2 aircraft made up nearly a third of all Soviet combat aircraft. Thus the aircraft

became numerically the most important type on the Eastern Front.

In the course of the war the tactics of ground-attack aviation underwent a steady process of improvement based on the accumulated combat experience. Thus operational practice corroborated the expediency of employing formations incorporating pairs of aircraft. A group of three gave place to a group of four consisting of two pairs, a group of six aircraft was supplanted by a group of eight comprising two flights of four each. This immediately improved the effectiveness of strikes on a target from different directions. Provided a cleverly designed battle formation were chosen, the aircraft in the rear of the formation easily spotted the opposing anti-aircraft assets, immediately knocked them out and then proceeded to fulfil the main task of the mission. Mutual fire support within a group became more reliable.

The enemy, too, constantly studied Soviet ground-attack tactics and resorted to his own ways and means of counteracting them. Therefore it was risky to repeat the same tactics and make a routine of them. It was the search for novelty in the tactics of the ground-attack aircraft that ensured success in combat. However, certain principles and rules evolved through experience provided a starting point in devising the plan of a mission. For example, there existed definite rules for attacking the several types of target: moving, small-size, large-area, narrow, long, group or single targets. Certain 'standards' were also used when calculating the required number of aircraft, ammunition complement and the battle-formation type. Thus small-calibre bombs were used against light tanks, large-calibre bombs against heavy tanks; fragmentation bombs were suitable against troops, and incendiary bombs for destroying fuel tankers. In order

An Il-2 pilot receives a last-minute report from his crew chief. Despite the heavy snow cover, the aircraft lacks any form of winter camouflage; the action may have kept the airmen so busy that there was no time to repaint the aircraft. Yefim Gordon archive

Many Il-2s were captured by the *Wehrmacht* after either being shot up on the ground or force landing due to battle damage. Yefim Gordon archive

to achieve maximum efficiency, in every case the optimum version of the warload was determined. When establishing the number of aircraft for a given mission, due consideration was given to the size of the site to be attacked, to the killing radius of particular ammunition types (for example, eight Il-2s each carrying eight bombs 'worked' on a troop concentration area measuring 100m × 200m [330ft × 660ft]), to the possible opposition from enemy anti-aircraft defence, to the weather, terrain profile and the length of the route. The more numerous were the variants mastered by the aircrews, the quicker was the preparation for a mission and the more efficient its fulfillment.

A directive issued by the Commander-in Chief of the Red Army Air Force on 22 August 1942 pointed out that combat actions performed by ground-attack aircraft from extremely low altitude deprived the Il-2s of the chance to use their striking power to the fullest extent. Using bombs with instant-action fuses increased the risk of the aircraft's being hit by fragments of its own bombs, and the effectiveness of the strike was adversely affected by the bouncing of bombs. In addition, operations at extremely low altitude made it difficult to take one's bearings, to seek out the target and aim at it, as well as to counteract attacks by

enemy fighters. And it was also practically impossible to provide fighter cover for aircraft flying close to the ground because there was a high probability of losing them out of sight. The directive recommended that the bombing altitude be increased and the pilots master diving attacks and new battle formations. One should approach the target area at altitudes of 800 to 1,200m (2,625 to 3,940ft), in battle formations of such types as 'S-turn in pairs' or 'echelon formation' and perform

A single-seater Il-2 armed with ShVAK cannons and eight RS-82 rockets is refuelled on a snow-covered airfield. The fuel bowser is based on a GAZ-AA 1.5-ton lorry. Yefim Gordon archive

Another view of a single-seater *shturmovik* **on an unpaved airstrip, showing the canopy design details. Note the rockets under the wing.** Yefim Gordon archive

A shot of a group of Red Army Air Force pilots posing beside an early production Il-2 on a grass airfield. Yefim Gordon archive

an attack with due regard to the character of the target and its location; specially trained pairs or flights of aircraft should be designated in advance for the suppression of anti-aircraft defences; the bombing should be effected consecutively one by one in a dive or 'all at once', following a signal from the leader; the choice of target should be made independently by every pilot; after the first pass the aircraft should form a 'circle' and repeat their attacks using rockets, cannon and machine-gun fire.

The 'circle' battle formation used for group attacks against ground targets was an ellipse with its longer axis pointing in the direction of the target. After the attack the group leader took a position behind the rearmost aircraft in the group at a distance of 500 to 800m (1,640 to 2,625ft) and closed the 'circle'. Thereby mutual support and a prolonged fire action against the enemy were assured, as

A flight of four winter-camouflaged Il-2s equipped with retractable skis taking off. Yefim Gordon archive

well as the suppression of anti-aircraft fire. Strafing actions from extremely low altitudes or involving a zooming climb to about 300m (980ft) were recommended for those cases when it was necessary to achieve maximum surprise and when the targets were especially large. Thus ground-attack tactics were enriched by new elements, but older ones evolved through experience were also retained. To conduct defensive aerial combat, a group of the Il-2 aircraft made use of an ovoid formation elongated in the direction of their own territory. This presupposed that the group included at least six aircraft flying at distances of 300 to 600m (980 to 1,960ft) at an altitude of not less than 300m (980ft). Turns were made with a bank of 15 to 40 degrees.

Whereas in August 1941, due to attrition, the regiments often had no more than five or six serviceable machines on strength, in November and December this grew to thirty-two and then to forty. Their tactics imposed stringent demands and the growth in numbers had a direct tactical influence. However, the aircraft were as yet unable to operate within the whole scope of the enemy's defences. For example, during the counter-offensive near Stalingrad, air close support was effected by sequentially transferring the combat effort from one defensive position to another. In the 8th Air Army (VA – *Vozdushnaya Armiya*) commanded by Air Lt Gen T. Khriukin, when the VA was acting in support of the 57th and the 51st Army, the aircraft received target designations from forward air control posts and attacked targets situated in the immediate vicinity of the advancing Soviet troops. Experience showed that in penetrating fortified defence lines the blows must be concentrated and divided by minimal intervals between the groups. Bombers were employed in the first wave from medium and high altitudes to divert the enemy's attention from the subsequent air strike. As for small enemy groupings, they were attacked at long intervals, but systematically.

Ground-attack air regiments and smaller units acting in support of infantry and tanks received their missions direct from the land forces command. Thus, during the battle of Stalingrad, army scouts reported a concentration of enemy reserves within the city. Air Force units were tasked with suppressing the enemy's firepower and paralysing the resistance of

its infantry. At dawn bombers dropped their loads on previously located targets. Five minutes later ground-attack aircraft made a strike aimed at weapon emplacements. They were followed by fighters, which started to attack enemy infantry. After a 20min bombardment and strafing, infantry swiftly occupied the eastern outskirts of the city.

One more episode provides eloquent testimony in this respect. It was necessary to ensure that two large groupings of Soviet troops met each other, cutting through enemy's defences. To achieve this, Soviet aviation attacked incessantly. At the same time, the enemy was shelled. Target zones for the two kinds of fire were distributed from a combined air control post. The Il-2 aircraft made up to seven or eight passes against their targets. Every 15min a pair of attack aircraft protected by fighters appeared over the target. In the course of 12hr airmen and artillery units ensured an incessant bombardment and strafing of the area where the Soviet troops finally joined.

Battle formations of attack aircraft were remodelled to suit the special conditions associated with new tasks. Depending on the situation, they were supplemented by groups for the suppression of AA artillery, groups for spotting and target designation and a cover group (as a rule, this was a pair of aircraft which accompanied the main group at some distance and was intended

to build strength up in the eventual air combat). It was hoped that a surprise attack would become a turning point in the combat. Improvements were made also in the methods for controlling crews and groups in the air. Definite rules were evolved concerning the commander's place during a mission. Thus the commander of an air formation such as an Air Division personally took part in a mission when the task was of great importance and checked its results. A regiment's commander flew in those cases when the whole regiment or a predominant part of it was fulfilling the same combat task, and kept under control the activities of the squadrons. Squadron commanders always headed in person their sub-units, especially when the tasks were particularly difficult and important.

In the summer of 1943, after two years of war, the Soviet command took the decision to use hollow-charge ammunition from the air against heavy weaponry. The PTAB-2.5-1.5 hollow-charge bombs developed under the direction of I. Larionov were put into production especially for attack aircraft. These diminutive bombs were loaded direct into the bomb-bays of the Il-2s and dropped from heights of up to 100m (330ft) on tanks and similar vehicles. On impact, the bombs produced an explosion, the energy of which was concentrated in one direction; they literally burnt holes in the armour. Bearing in

These single-seaters have been retrofitted with carburettor inlet filters in the field. Via AVICO-Press

mind that every Il-2 could carry up to 192 of these bombs, it is easy to calculate that dropping these weapons created a blazing carpet 15m (50ft) wide and nearly 70m (230ft) long; enemy tanks covered by it would probably be destroyed. This was especially important because the low precision of the bombing sights on the Il-2 was a weak point of the aircraft. Among the first to use the PTAB-2.5-1.5 was the 291st ShAD (Attack Air Division). On 5 July 1943 during the Kursk offensive a group of six attack aircraft led by Lt Col A. Vitrook knocked out fifteen enemy tanks in one pass; in the course of five days the division claimed 422 knocked-out or damaged enemy tanks. During the massive Kursk battle Gen V. Riazanov became a genuine master in the use of attack aircraft en masse under conditions characterized by swift actions. He developed and perfected methods of using the Il-2s in cooperation with infantry, artillery and tanks. His command post was constantly within the battle order of the land forces. Many a time, in responding to the flow of the battle, he succeeded in reassigning targets to his air units, designating as the target now tanks, now infantry launching a counter-attack, now enemy bombers, which were to be deterred from fulfilling their mission. Subsequently Gen Riazanov was twice awarded the title of Hero of the Soviet Union, and the 1st ShAK (Attack Air Corps) commanded by him became the first to be awarded the Guards title.

Soviet Losses

However, successes were accompanied by a high rate of combat attrition. The German command asserted that in 1943 the Russians lost 6,900 attack aircraft, and in the following year 7,300. In fact, Soviet losses were exaggerated by a factor of 2.2 as compared with the real figures. Yet the losses in attack air units were indeed high. In 1943, on average, twenty-six sorties were made for one Il-2 lost in combat, and in some operations this figure was still

A single-seater Il-2 attacks German positions. Yefim Gordon archive

This two-seater taxiing out for a mission is a fairly late-production aircraft, as indicated by the tall aerial mast. The tactical number 35 is hand-painted.
Yefim Gordon archive

lower. Approximately half of the Ils were shot down by fighters and the other half was lost to ground fire.

Assessing the main reasons for the attrition, Commander-in-Chief of the Air Force A. Novikov came to the conclusion that it was due not so much to a poor standard of aircrew training nor inadequate preparedness of the air units as to a disastrous lack of originality in tactics. On almost all fronts attack aircraft made use of roughly the same pattern. Irrespective of the situation in the air and on the ground and the character of the target, the Ilyushins approached at the altitude of 1,000 to 1,500m (3,280 to 4,920ft), made their attack and then left in a shallow glide with a left banking turn. In these cases the enemy knew in advance what the Il-2s would do, and, before their arrival on the battlefield, took measures to prepare the AA guns to repulse the attack. The gunners trained their weapons to anticipated heights and the enemy made extensive use of local features to conceal the flak batteries.

One of the contributing factors to the battle losses of the Il-2s was the poor quality and insufficient availability of radio transceivers on the Il-2s. During the first period of the war only the aircraft of the group leaders were equipped with transmitters. If the leader's aircraft was shot down, the rest of the group was deprived of communication. Interaction between aircraft in the group and mutual fire support were adversely affected and attacking fighters had a better chance of success. Only from 1943 onwards were all Il-2s equipped with radios, ensuring stable communication both between the aircraft and with the forward air control posts.

The German Bf 109s and Fw 190s scored better results in their attacks on Il-2s when their gunners lost vigilance and when their battle formations were disrupted. Often it was the damaged aircraft and those lagging behind that became victims. It was far from always that attack aircraft pilots were capable of defensive tactics and gunners were proficient in the use of their weapons. The evaluation of the survivability of the Il-2s was conducted in 1st ShAK (Attack Air Corps). It turned out that the calculations made by the Ilyushin OKB when selecting the armour distribution layout were corroborated. The underside armour plating could, as a rule, withstand a direct hit of small-calibre flak ammunition. The pilot's cockpit proved to be comfortable and well-protected by armour. One Il-2 hit by flak lost an elevator, the left stabilizer surface and the rudder. On another the metal skinning of the wing centre section and the flaps were ripped off; a third aircraft had its fin riddled with bullets. Yet all returned safely to base.

Particularly vulnerable to ground fire were the rear fuselage, outer wing panels and oil radiators. As noted above, it was the wooden parts of the airframe that suffered the greatest damage. When the deliveries of metal to the aircraft industry improved and aircraft began to be manufactured with metal wings, this affected their survivability positively. Analysis of attack aircraft operations in the 3rd Air Army (VA) showed that total hull losses of Il-2s amounted to 2.8 per cent of the total number of sorties while battle damage amounted to half this number.

Pilots pointed out on many occasions that, during attacks performed by a group, it was the rearmost machine that was especially vulnerable. There are several cases on record when pilots in combat made a landing on the enemy territory to save a comrade whose damaged aircraft had made a crash landing. As a rule, it was the pilot of the rearmost aircraft in the group. For example, Junior Lt Beresnev made a landing near Dzhankoi in the Crimea and saved his squadron commander; L. Pavlov made a landing to save the aircrew of M. Stepanishchev. Such landings were made by pilots of both two- and single-seater machines. In this fashion a wingman saved his leader N.I. Nikolayev, who was later awarded the title of Hero of the Soviet Union for destroying a ship by ramming. On one occasion, in March 1944, an Il-2 from the 503rd ShAP made a landing to save the pilot of a damaged Yak-1 fighter. It turned out that a mainwheel tyre of the Il-2 was pierced by a bullet. Therefore one more Il-2 piloted by Lt A.V. Demekhin had to make a landing; Demekhin took on board and transported to safety the three airmen (for this he too was made Hero of the Soviet Union).

According to statistics, the number of the Il-2s lost in combat during the war years totalled 10,759, which amounts to nearly 29 per cent of all aircraft lost by the Red Army. An additional 807 were lost by the Naval Air Force. These losses were due to the following causes: shot down by enemy fighters 24 per cent (an average figure for the whole war; 60 per cent during the early period); attrition due to anti-aircraft guns 43 per cent; causes unknown (failed to return from combat) 32 per cent. About 1 per cent of the Il-2s lost were destroyed at their airfields by air attack.

Many attack aircraft pilots whose aircraft were shot down during a sortie survived and, getting back to their unit, continued to fly missions. A vivid example of this is presented in the recollections of V.S. Frolov, a pilot who started his wartime flying career in 1943 and later became a Hero of the Soviet Union. He was shot down five times. Frolov recalls his fourteenth sortie, when he was sent in a group of sixteen aircraft to suppress enemy artillery:

I hear the group leader's command: 'Attack, the bombs!' I pressed the button and then a heavy blow struck my head. I was unconscious for a moment, then I felt a jet of cold air burst into the cockpit. Opening my eyes, I pulled the control stick and levelled out from a dive just above the treetops. I shot a glance back and saw an enormous hole in the wing root and the fuselage. The instruments had gone out of action, the sliding window on the starboard side of the canopy was shattered, there was no response from the gunner, but the engine was running. My head, my shoulder, my arm and my leg were wounded by splinters of an ack-ack shell. Controlling the aircraft became difficult, my consciousness was dimmed; then I saw a church situated near our airfield, and blacked out. Later our flight controller who had been at the airfield on that day told me: 'An aircraft approached the airfield at an altitude of 200m. One undercarriage leg was extended, the other was dangling, a great hole was seen in the starboard wing panel and the fuselage. I wondered how an aircraft could fly in that condition without breaking up. The pilot made two passes and, finally, came in for landing at the side of the airstrip. He lowered the flaps, and the aircraft began to disintegrate in the air. The drag was already far too high, and now the flaps . . . The aircraft struck a shelter with one wheel and broke up into a multitude of parts. The gunner was killed, and the pilot, bleeding all over, was extracted from under the wreckage and taken to a hospital. A direct hit of a medium-calibre flak shell into the starboard wing root had not silenced the engine, nor severed the controls.'

Armourers load cannon ammunition belts into the outer wing ammunition boxes. Yefim Gordon archive

Il-2 pilot Pavlov, Hero of the Soviet Union, poses beside the two-seater Il-2 paid for by people from his home town of Kustanai. Yefim Gordon archive

Still sporting their summer camouflage, a pair of two-seater Il-2s armed with four RS-82s take off from a snow-covered tactical airfield. Note the late-style insignia. Yefim Gordon archive

This Il-2 pilot with the rank of captain has good reason to be pleased: he has won the Order of the Red Star and the Order of the Red Banner of Combat. The aircraft, which has an unusually high tactical number (100 or higher), belonged to a Guards unit, hence the badge painted on the canopy frame; the badge is also worn by the pilot. Note the artwork on the fuselage revealing that this was a unit known as 'The Singing Squadron' because all of its pilots could sing well and formed a folk ensemble. Yefim Gordon archive

A rare, air-to-air shot of a winter-camouflaged single-seater Il-2. Note that the rudder has been damaged and replaced, which is why half the star is gone; the tactical number is yellow. Yefim Gordon archive

Left: Caught by the camera just as it becomes airborne, two-seater Il-2 '44 Red' sports quick-identification markings – a white rudder and a white fuselage band just aft of the wings. The hinged portion of the gunner's cockpit canopy has been removed, apparently to improve his field of view. Yefim Gordon archive

Below: This Il-2 operated by the same squadron appears to lack rocket launch rails. Yefim Gordon archive

Ramming and Strafing

As mentioned above, Il-2 pilots resorted to ramming attacks both in aerial combat and against ground targets such as tank and vehicle columns, ships, trains and bridges. For example, on 3 November 1943 an Il-2 pilot rammed a Ju-88 in the air, and on 17 July 1944 Senior Lt S.V. Milashenkov directed his burning machine into a tank column (he was posthumously awarded the title of Hero of the Soviet Union). On 18 June 1944 N.I. Nikolayev, as mentioned above, rammed a ship and obtained the Hero title posthumously.

From 1943 onwards the Il-2 was also used against armoured trains (in 1943 at the Ukrainian Front and in the Baltic area). In efforts designed to frustrate enemy rail transportation, the primary object of attacks was rolling stock at stations and en route. As a rule, before starting for a mission the attack aircraft received target information from co-operating reconnaissance aircraft. They approached from the direction of the sun at 1,000 to 1,100m (3,280 to 3,610ft) with a subsequent steep dive. From 600 to 700m (1,970 to 2,300ft) pilots opened fire with guns and rockets and dropped their bombs from 300 to 400m (980 to 1,300ft). At the same time, fighters from the cover group that were not engaged in aerial combat also destroyed ground targets, first of all the locomotives. From 1943 onwards the Il-2s came to be used more extensively for strafing actions not only on the battlefield and in the immediate rear of enemy lines, but also deeper inside enemy territory, for example, against airfields, including those situated at up to 250km (155 miles) from base. An order issued on 4 May 1944 permitted attack air units to conduct a 'free chase' against enemy trains.

The methods of ensuring fighter cover for the attack aircraft were also constantly improved. Experience revealed that fighters did not attack Soviet aircraft immediately above the latter's target for fear of being hit by their own flak; they attacked mostly before or just after the Il-2 ground attack. Therefore the best protection of the Il-2s was afforded by covering patrols conducted on the approach to the target or on the return route. When the attack aircraft performed strike missions close to the Soviet frontline, the cover group took up a position at a distance of 10 to 15km (6 to 9 miles) from the front; when the attack aircraft began to leave the target area, the cover group moved forward, interdicting enemy attack.

Employment of the Il-2 en masse on all fronts was facilitated also by its simplicity and its mastering by air and ground crews alike. 'This was one of the easiest aircraft to master', recalled pilot, twice Hero of the Soviet Union, V. Yefimov,

In operations over the target and in an aerial combat the pilot's attention was not distracted by any complex manipulations with instruments and units. The aircraft forgave the pilot even gross mistakes in piloting. I don't know a single case when this aircraft became uncontrollable or entered a spin because of mistakes in piloting technique.

It must be admitted, though, that the Il-2 had its shortcomings as regards handling; for example, recovery from a dive was accompanied by excessive stick forces and required much physical effort on the part of the pilot. This, incidentally, imposed a limit on the practical feasible dive angle. The Il-2 also had a tendency to veer off a straight course during a take-off or a landing run, which sometimes led to accidents.

At Sea

The Il-2 was extensively used by the naval air force. The first attack aircraft squadrons were created in July and August 1941 in the Baltic Fleet and the Black Sea Fleet. Later, Attack Air Regiments and Divisions made their appearance in all fleets (that is, also in the Northern Fleet and the Pacific Fleet). They went into action against warships and transports at sea, attacked naval bases and havens, destroyed aircraft parked at coastal airfields, suppressed anti-aircraft artillery thus assisting naval bombers and torpedo aircraft, rendered support to ground troops and naval landing operations and took part in the destruction of coastal artillery batteries. The attack air units of the naval aviation performed their missions independently

This single-seater Il-2 bears the dedication *Za Otradnova* ('For Otradnov' – the last name of the pilot's friend killed in action). Interestingly, the aircraft has two prominent reinforcement ribs on the upper rear fuselage (obviously a field modification). The wire patterns on the bulletproof windshield and the windscreen side quadrants are reference lines for dive bombing and/or rocket attack (the pilot would unleash the rockets when the target filled the diamond in the centre of the windshield). Yefim Gordon archive

The Il-2 in the foreground – a single-seater example, judging by the heavy load of eight RS-82 rockets – wears a curious temporary winter camouflage pattern. Yefim Gordon archive

or in cooperation with other aviation elements.

In the course of the war naval attack air units made approximately 27,000 sorties, of which more than 50 per cent were flown against maritime targets, about 44 per cent were flown against ground troops and the rest were strikes against airfields, sorties to provide cover for their own ships at bases and reconnaissance missions. The number of sorties per fleet were: the Baltic Fleet, more than 17,000; the Black Sea Fleet, about 8,000; the Northern Fleet, about 1,500; and the Pacific Fleet (the war against Japan), over 300. The overall result of attacks undertaken by naval attack aircraft was the destruction of several hundred combat ships, transports and other naval craft, to mention the maritime targets alone. To tackle these, the

Il-2s made use of the all types of weapon available to them: gunnery, bombs, incendiary weapons and rockets.

Especially effective was the destruction of enemy ships by means of the so-called mast-top bombing performed by Il-2s: the attack aircraft descended to a height of 30m (100ft) and flew at a constant speed of about 400km/h (250mph) up to the moment when the bombs were released; the bombs rebounded from the sea surface and rammed the side of the target. People's Commissar for the Navy N. Kuznetsov assessed the effectiveness of this bombing as approximately five times as great as that of the usual level-flight bombing. But it was also fraught with great risk for the attack aircraft which had to break through a veritable wall of anti-aircraft fire from enemy ships. The events of 16 May 1944 illustrate this style of attack: aerial reconnaissance discovered in the Gulf of Finland a convoy which included landing barges, minesweepers, patrol ships and patrol boats (fifteen vessels in all). To destroy it, eighteen Pe-2 bombers and twenty Il-2s were sent under the cover of forty-nine escort fighters, in addition, a group of twelve La-5 fighters started patrolling a coastal area from which enemy fighters could appear. The Pe-2s, diving from 2,000m (6,600ft), were the first to hit the enemy using fragmentation and high-explosive bombs. In about 30sec they were followed by a group of eleven Il-2s which used their guns, rockets and small bombs to suppress the ships' AA weapons. Next came the turn of eight mast-top-bombing Il-2s (a ninth had been shot down by fighters). As a result of the strike three minesweepers and two patrol boats were sunk and one patrol ship was damaged. Eight Fw 190s were shot down. This was considered a satisfactory result. Soviet losses comprised three Il-2s shot down by fighters and three Yak-9s from the fighter cover group.

One of the best attack aircraft pilots in the Navy was Lt Col N. Stepanian. On 14 December 1944 he flew at the head of his 47th ShAP, comprising forty-two Il-2s, to strike the naval base of Libava. The attack aircraft together with the Pe-2 bombers sank seven transports and damaged six others in the harbour. Thirteen Il-2s were downed; one was the machine piloted by Regiment Cdr Stepanian who was killed in action. He was posthumously awarded a second title of Hero of the Soviet Union.

Soviet Air Force pilots show female guests from a nearby town around an airfield – obviously not near the frontline. All the unit's Il-2s wear all-over white camouflage and the legend *Yaroslavskiy komsomolets* ('Young Communist League member of Yaroslavl'); the nearest aircraft is a Moscow-built example (c/n 301257). Note the heat-insulating covers on the engines. Yefim Gordon archive

A picturesque local resident smoking a pipe watches mechanics servicing an Il-2. Note the empty air filter fairing (the filter itself is being cleaned) and the starboard landing gear nacelle dented by a hit. Yefim Gordon archive

The Il-2 was operated by the Naval Air Arm as well. Here, four naval officers pose beside a two-seater adorned with the Guards badge. Note the darker spot on the nearest propeller blade where a bullet hole appears to have been mended. Yefim Gordon archive

This air-to-air shot of an Il-2 by the gunner of a sister ship was taken on the way home. Note the open main gear doors as the landing gear begins to extend. Yefim Gordon archive

'8 Red', a summer-camouflaged, single-seater, takes off from a winter airfield. The star insignia has a thin white outline. Yefim Gordon archive

A shot of a field-modified, single-seater Il-2 equipped with a makeshift machine-gun installation to protect the tail; note the rear-view mirror on the windscreen frame. Equally interestingly, only one of the pilots in the group wears a fur-lined overall while the others are equipped with full-length leather topcoats – a famous article of apparel. Yefim Gordon archive

This single-seater Il-2 is armed with eight 132-mm RS-132 rockets. The fatter and shorter body of this weapon is obvious, the launch rail providing a reference point. Yefim Gordon archive

Attack aircraft of the naval air force were also used to attack ground targets. Thus in June 1944 it became necessary to blow the Svir-3 hydroelectric power station dam situated in the enemy rear. It was destroyed by a joint effort of A-20G and Il-4 bombers, the latter armed with naval mines, and of the Il-2 attack aircraft, whose task was to suppress the anti-aircraft batteries. At dawn on 15 October the Air Force of the Northern Fleet made a massed raid on a German convoy of twenty-six combat ships and transports under the protection of seven fighters. The first to attack were twelve Il-2s, followed by another dozen an hour later. In their wake came the third wave of ten A-20Gs accompanied by fifteen fighters. A similar combined strike mission involving Il-2s and Kittyhawk fighters in the dive-bombing role was undertaken on 10 May 1944; hits were scored on a transport with a displacement of 6,000t and a patrol-ship, the transport sinking as a result.

Learning from Experience

Up to 1943 the losses suffered by the Il-2s from fighter attacks were particularly heavy because fighter cover groups were small in numbers and lacked proficiency in combat. Obligatory training in aerial combat was introduced in the 11th Guards Attack Air Division (ShAD). The pilots Lysenko and Matveyev were the first to master the combat methods practised by fighter pilots; they shared their experience with young pilots. At the beginning of 1943 several mock aerial fights were organized for training and demonstration purposes over the Division's airfield; in these, Il-2s were pitted against different versions of Yakovlev and Lavochkin fighters. As it turned out, the Il-2 could hold its own in dogfighting against the fighters and even succeeded in being the first to open fire on several occasions.

On 5 February a group of Il-2s set off for its first mission, which consisted in providing cover for land forces. In the course of patrolling Lt Nalchik noticed a Bf 109 approaching him from behind. Maintaining self-control, the pilot allowed the enemy to come closer, almost to the distance for opening fire, and then made a sharp turn, putting his aircraft on an intersecting course, reducing his speed at the same time. The German pilot, who evidently had not expected such a manoeuvre, dashed forward past the Soviet aircraft. Nalchik went on confidently, as if he were training; he banked in the opposite direction and placed himself within the banking turn of his adversary. A precise burst followed and the German went down trailing smoke. Suddenly Nalchik became aware of a second Bf 109 sitting on his tail. Simulating unawareness, he let the fighter come closer and then

repeated the manoeuvre, which came as a surprise to the enemy. A salvo sealed the fate of this aircraft.

On 18 February a group of nine Il-2s led by Lt Col Lysenko, while over the target area, was attacked by six Bf 109s. The attack aircraft were performing their mission without fighter cover, and the leader radioed to the other aircraft in the group to halt their strafing and form a circle. As usual, the first attack of the fighters was directed at the leader of the group. However, Sgt Krapivko, a gunner,

had a say in the matter. A well-aimed burst hit the enemy. The German fighters redoubled the fierceness of their attacks against the ring of Soviet aircraft, but they were repulsed from all sides. Lysenko efficiently guided the actions of his subordinates by radio. The nine Il-2s returned to base safely.

The Fw 190 fighters that had arrived at the front resorted to diving attacks during which they passed through the defensive circle formed by the Il-2s and then made an ascending manoeuvre from

'6 Yellow', a two-seater Il-2 with hastily applied winter camouflage. Strangely, the forward fuselage rarely received any white paint.
Yefim Gordon archive

Below: A pair of mid-production two-seaters warms up the engines before a winter sortie.
Yefim Gordon archive

below. In response, the Soviet battle formations of attack aircraft and escorting fighters were rearranged and came to comprise several layers at differing altitude. The fighters engaged the enemy at the beginning of his attacks and the gunners of the Il-2s introduced changes into their pattern of fire. Soon the gunners Nikhanev, Shcherbinin and Vasnevskii had each a downed Fw 190 to his credit. They were joined by pilots Andreyev, Pchelintsev and Bartashevich, who further increased the number of shot-down Fw 190s.

In 1943 the training of the pilots of attack air regiments was conducted at thirteen field aerodromes. Every month a brigade commanded by A. Podolskiy trained up to twenty attack air regiments. This made it possible to increase the number of regiments at the front from seventy-nine in January 1943 to 104 in October. By the end of the war the number of regiments totalled 150; of these, at least 120 were at the front. To train the pilots, a dual-control trainer version of the Il-2 – the UIl-2 (also known as the Il-2U) was used, when available. Several Il-2s were converted into dual-control machines in the field, for example, in the Northern Fleet, in the 11th Field Aircraft Maintenance Workshop.

Attack aircraft played an important role in the closing stage of the war. During the battles before the liberation of Budapest the 715th ShAP was stationed at Tekel airfield, near the city. A pilot of this Air Regiment, Capt M. Niukhalov, directed his damaged aircraft into the midst of a tank column. The regiment's pilots made up to five sorties a day. When the unit was tasked with destroying a bridgehead and a concentration of troops near a bridge, but not the bridge itself, the airmen dismantled the UBT machine-guns in order to increase the bomb load and flew missions without gunners. More than twenty sorties were made on such aircraft. During combat in Germany the Il-2s encountered Me 262 jet fighters, which were on alert seeking out damaged machines returning to base. When one Me 262 was shot down by an escort fighter in April, such attacks ceased. On 2 May 1945 the Il-2s together with the A-20 bombers under the cover of Yak-9 fighters sank the training battleship *Schlesien*. In the assault on Berlin strafing attacks were conducted to

Not only fire and steel were used to defeat the enemy; the power of words was equally important. Here, the wing bays of an Il-2 with retractable skis (c/n . . .03) are loaded with propaganda leaflets to unload over German-held territory. Yefim Gordon archive

The Il-2 could take an incredible amount of punishment and still bring the crew home – or at least get it down safely. This badly shot-up single-seater converted with a makeshift gunner's cockpit and reinforcing ribs on the rear fuselage made a forced landing, whereupon the gunner removed the machine gun and took it away with him. Yefim Gordon archive

A classic air-to-air shot of a classic warplane. This brand-new Il-2 was probably photographed on a pre-delivery test flight. Note the dive-bombing reference lines on the upper part of the cowling. Yefim Gordon archive

support the troops that were advancing within the city; attacking aircraft refrained from the use of their guns to avoid the risk of hitting their own troops. On 25 April two groups of aircraft participated with a tank unit in taking control of Tempelhof airfield which was stubbornly defended and maintained in a functioning condition. Nine Il-2 aircraft landed on the airfield, took up position with their tails towards the airfield buildings and, using their aft-firing machineguns, opened fire on the buildings. At the same time Soviet tanks burst on to the airfield. Several other airfields, for example Schönefeld, were captured in a similar way. The last combat sortie was flown by Il-2s against German troops in Czechoslovakia. The Il-2s were the first to enter Prague when they landed on an airfield captured by insurgents.

No precise information is available concerning the participation of the Il-2s in the war against Japan (mention is made only of the Il-10).

Summing up the War

The Il-2 earned the reputation of being one of the most effective weapons of the Red Army and was held in high esteem by

A starter vehicle based on a GAZ-AAA (a three-axle derivative of the GAZ-AA) is about to be hooked up to a winter-camouflaged Il-2. Yefim Gordon archive

the soldiers. But despite its versatility and wide range of uses, in the course of the war some 80 per cent of combat sorties were made to a depth of 10 km (6 miles), very close to the battlefield.

As we noted in the Introduction, in recent years some Russian researchers have voiced the opinion that the traditional appraisal of the Il-2 and its role in the Great Patriotic War should be revised. As an example one may quote an article written by Vladimir Spasibo and pretentiously entitled 'The Il-2: the Truth versus the Legend'. In his opinion,

German soldiers inspect a damaged Il-2 which has belly-landed on a heath. Yefim Gordon archive

This early-production, two-seater Il-2 serialled '24 White' (note the short aerial mast) is inscribed *Za chest' Gvardii!* ('For the honour of the Guards!'). Note the three mission markers on the fin above the star. The gunner's section of the canopy has been removed to improve the view and increase the field of fire. Yefim Gordon archive

This still from a wartime documentary shows the muzzle flashes created when the Il-2's VYa cannons were fired. Yefim Gordon archive

'in 1941–1944 the Soviet Air Force did not have at its disposal a really effective close support aircraft', and only the advent of the Il-10 improved the situation to some extent. At the same time, according to his assertion, 'the German experience of creating and employing close support aircraft was more successful' (he refers to the experience with such aircraft as the Ju 87, the Hs 129 and the Fw 190). This article called forth a comment from Grigory Sivkov – a former pilot of attack aircraft who made 203 sorties on the Il-2 during the war and was twice awarded the title of Hero of the Soviet Union. He resolutely disagrees with Spasibo and states categorically that 'in 1941–1944 the Il-2 was unequalled as a close support aircraft'. It is worth quoting him more fully:

As for the close support of the troops, not a single operation of any significance was conducted without close cooperation with attack aviation. As an example one may cite the successful defensive operation near Vladikavkaz [in the north Caucasus] as far

back as November 1942, when we struck massed blows at concentrations of German tanks and made havoc among them, thus preventing these units from forcing their way to the Transcaucasian region; this was very effective support rendered to our infantry. As a classic example of the interaction between attack aircraft units and land troops one may cite the breaking of the German defensive 'Blue Line' in the Kuban River area in July 1943. Before the ground troops attacked, attack air divisions sent their Il-2s in columns made up of five-aircraft formations to deal massed blows against the enemy first line of defence and artillery emplacements; we made, each of us, four successive passes, suppressing in the first pass the numerous anti-aircraft weapons of different calibres, and then we were the complete masters of the battlefield, significantly facilitating the breaking of the enemy's heavily fortified defensive line. In the battles in the vicinity of Kerch [in the Crimea] we established particularly close cooperation with the Marines, for example, during attacks intended to capture the dominating ridge of 175.0 in November 1943. This was effected by means of successive

blows struck by pairs of the Il-2s for the purpose of suppressing the enemy's weapon emplacements. When each pair of Il-2s put in their appearance over the battlefield, their action caused the enemy's fire to die down and the Marines rose and speedily advanced without meeting much resistance. This vividly showed the interaction between the Marines and the Il-2 aircraft.

To sum up, here is the assessment by the Russian aviation historians V. Perov and O. Rastrenin, who are noted for their research on the Il-2:

A searching analysis of the Il-2's design features allows us to say that Ilyushin, after all, failed to fulfil his promise to create a 'flying tank' – the aircraft's armour plating could not withstand the impact of cannon shells, and its armament was not on a par with that of a tank. But Ilyushin did succeed in creating a sort of 'flying infantry armoured vehicle', an outstanding aircraft which subsequently became an unsurpassed classic among ground-attack aircraft. The Il-2 and its derivative, the Il-10 (the latter at the closing stage of the

This winter-camouflaged Il-2 bears the somewhat obscure legend *Privet poslantsam Tuvinskovo naroda!* ('Greetings to the delegates of the Tuva people'; Tuva is one of the constituent republics of the Russian Federation). Yefim Gordon archive

Sometimes Il-2s were on the receiving end of air-to-ground attacks. This two-seater example has been knocked out by a German air raid (note the bent propeller blades which mean the aircraft could not possibly have flown and landed in this condition). Yefim Gordon archive

This view of a trio of Il-2s streaking over the battlefield shows how low the attack aircraft would approach the target to avoid detection. The altitude is only about 30m (100ft). Yefim Gordon archive

Mechanics repair battle damage to the rear fuselage and tail unit of an Il-2 after a sortie. The damage was inflicted by ground fire (note how the fragments of skin curl upwards around the holes).
Via AVICO Press

Service pilots on leave from the front have a meeting with S.V. Ilyushin (third from right) and test pilot Vladimir K. Kokkinaki (second from left).
Yefim Gordon archive

war) were the only production ground-attack aircraft in the world during the Second World War period which happily combined good armour protection with sufficiently potent armaments, comprising cannon, machine-guns, rockets projectiles, bombs, incendiary weapons and chemical devices.

In conclusion, one may quote the assessment of the Il-2 by German land force commanders of during the closing stage of the war. Commander of Army Group *Ost-Preussen* Gen von Sauken wrote:

The effectiveness of the actions of Russian aviation in the Danzig area is enormous. Russian aviation in this area has paralysed the manoeuvrability of our troops and interdicted the transfer of reinforcements towards the front by constantly bringing its might to bear on our communications. We have been unable to oppose this air power, whether it be by our own aviation or by a massive anti-aircraft artillery fire.

His words were echoed by Gen Groge, commander of the 1st Heavy Mortar Brigade: 'During the recent battles the Russians have to a large extent resorted to a massive use of attack aircraft. They are an effective weapon for providing support to ground troops . . .

Their moral effect is always exceptionally strong.'

An eloquent testimony to the role played by airmen in attack air units in the course of the war is the following: among Soviet airmen upon whom the title of Hero of the Soviet Union was conferred (2,271 in all), the biggest group (860) is made up of the airmen of attack air units. Ranking second (836) are fighter pilots. Among the sixty-five airmen who were awarded the title twice, twenty-seven were from attack aviation; the number of fighter pilots with the same distinction was twenty-six.

The results of an Il-2's work: this gaping hole was made in the side of a German light tank by a shell from a 37mm cannon. Via AVICO Press

A Soviet infantryman examines a German Pz Kpfw 38 (t) light tank destroyed by an ROFS-132 high-explosive/fragmentation rocket fired by an Il-2. It was not for nothing that the Il-2 was dubbed 'flying tank'. Via AVICO Press

Soft-skinned vehicles stood even fewer chances against the Il-2, as these German vehicle convoys shot up by Il-2s testify. Via AVICO Press

This Il-2 (c/n 301060), originally built as a single-seater, was shot down during the war, subsequently discovered and painstakingly restored in two-seater configuration by the Ilyushin OKB. The AM-38 engine was completely overhauled, enabling the aircraft to taxi under its own power. Here, Il-2 c/n 301060 is seen taxiing at Moscow-Khodynka. After starring in several films the aircraft was donated to the Soviet Air Force Museum in Monino. *Kryl'ya Rodiny*

This well-preserved two-seater Il-2 resides at the *Muzeum Wojska Polskiego* (Polish Armed Forces Museum) in Warsaw in company with other Soviet types. The gunner's station has been closed off with sheet metal to stop rain from getting in. Yefim Gordon

In the early 1990s, the freshly-repainted Il-10 from Monino was part of a one-day display at Frunzenskaya embankment in the centre of Moscow. Yefim Gordon

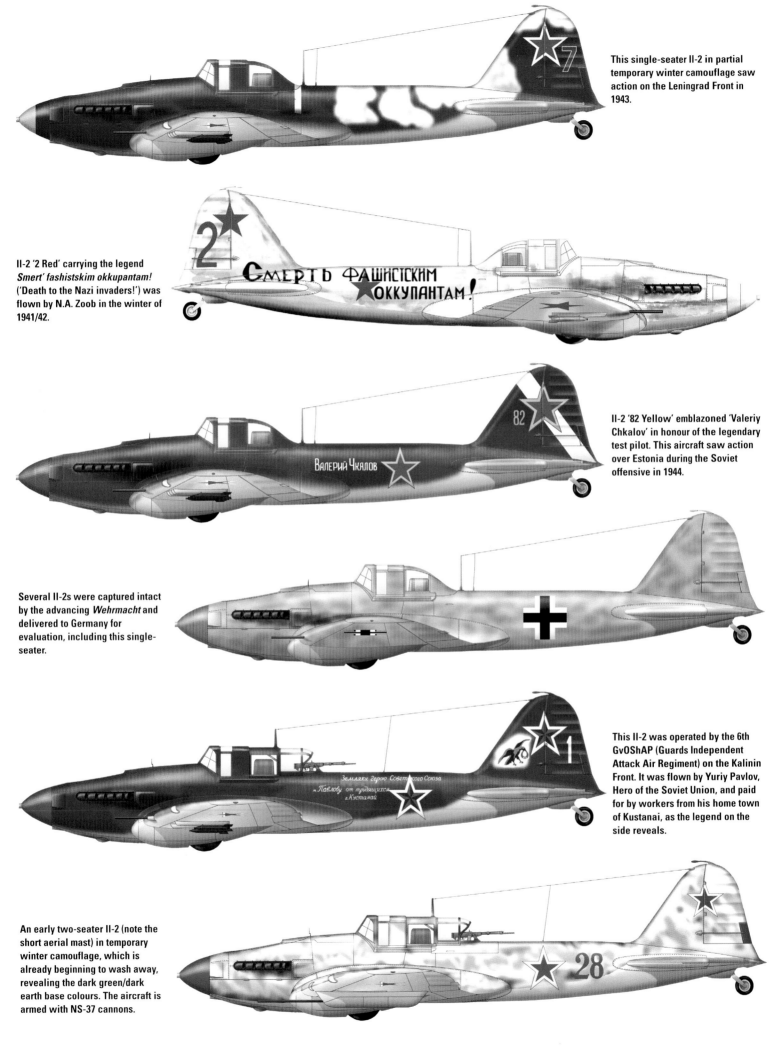

This single-seater Il-2 in partial temporary winter camouflage saw action on the Leningrad Front in 1943.

Il-2 '2 Red' carrying the legend *Smert' fashistskim okkupantam!* ('Death to the Nazi invaders!') was flown by N.A. Zoob in the winter of 1941/42.

Il-2 '82 Yellow' emblazoned 'Valeriy Chkalov' in honour of the legendary test pilot. This aircraft saw action over Estonia during the Soviet offensive in 1944.

Several Il-2s were captured intact by the advancing *Wehrmacht* and delivered to Germany for evaluation, including this single-seater.

This Il-2 was operated by the 6th GvOShAP (Guards Independent Attack Air Regiment) on the Kalinin Front. It was flown by Yuriy Pavlov, Hero of the Soviet Union, and paid for by workers from his home town of Kustanai, as the legend on the side reveals.

An early two-seater Il-2 (note the short aerial mast) in temporary winter camouflage, which is already beginning to wash away, revealing the dark green/dark earth base colours. The aircraft is armed with NS-37 cannons.

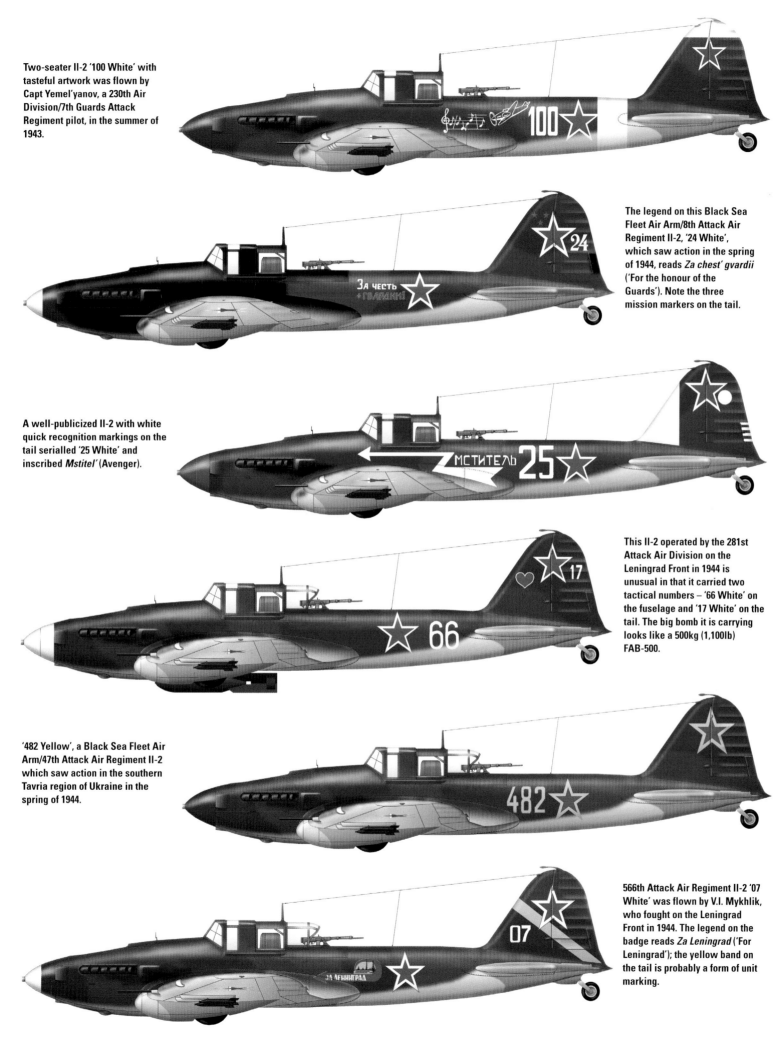

Two-seater Il-2 '100 White' with tasteful artwork was flown by Capt Yemel'yanov, a 230th Air Division/7th Guards Attack Regiment pilot, in the summer of 1943.

The legend on this Black Sea Fleet Air Arm/8th Attack Air Regiment Il-2, '24 White', which saw action in the spring of 1944, reads *Za chest' gvardii* ('For the honour of the Guards'). Note the three mission markers on the tail.

A well-publicized Il-2 with white quick recognition markings on the tail serialled '25 White' and inscribed *Mstitel'* (Avenger).

This Il-2 operated by the 281st Attack Air Division on the Leningrad Front in 1944 is unusual in that it carried two tactical numbers – '66 White' on the fuselage and '17 White' on the tail. The big bomb it is carrying looks like a 500kg (1,100lb) FAB-500.

'482 Yellow', a Black Sea Fleet Air Arm/47th Attack Air Regiment Il-2 which saw action in the southern Tavria region of Ukraine in the spring of 1944.

566th Attack Air Regiment Il-2 '07 White' was flown by V.I. Mykhlik, who fought on the Leningrad Front in 1944. The legend on the badge reads *Za Leningrad* ('For Leningrad'); the yellow band on the tail is probably a form of unit marking.

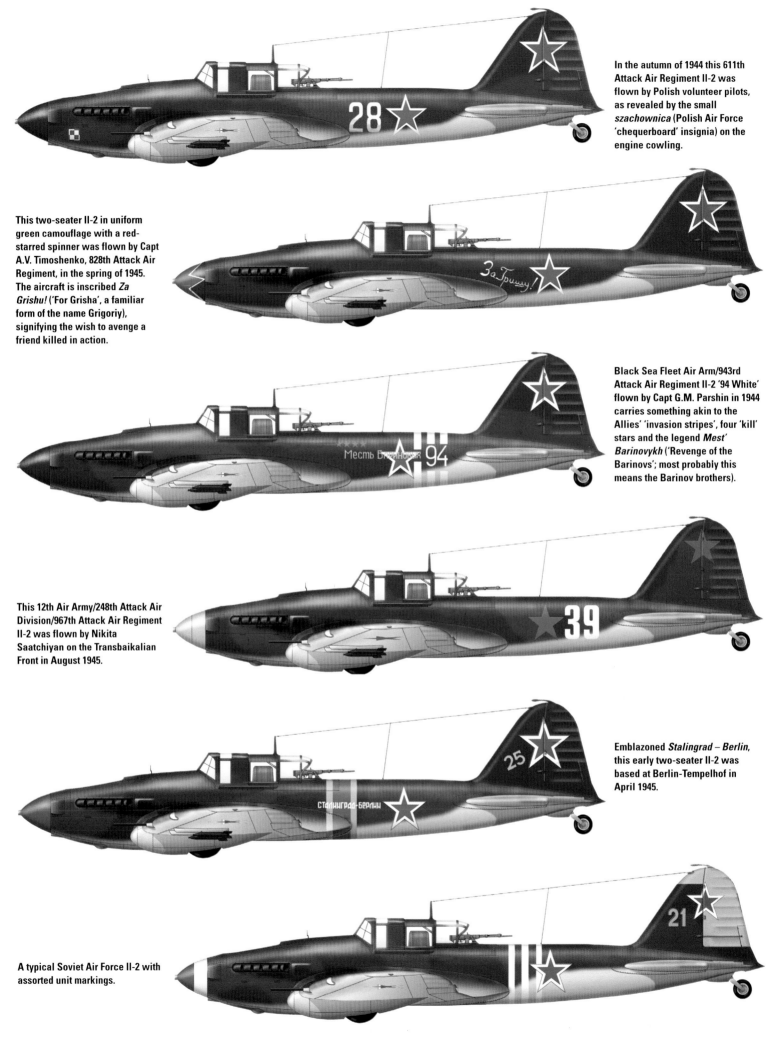

In the autumn of 1944 this 611th Attack Air Regiment Il-2 was flown by Polish volunteer pilots, as revealed by the small *szachownica* (Polish Air Force 'chequerboard' insignia) on the engine cowling.

This two-seater Il-2 in uniform green camouflage with a red-starred spinner was flown by Capt A.V. Timoshenko, 828th Attack Air Regiment, in the spring of 1945. The aircraft is inscribed *Za Grishu!* ('For Grisha', a familiar form of the name Grigoriy), signifying the wish to avenge a friend killed in action.

Black Sea Fleet Air Arm/943rd Attack Air Regiment Il-2 '94 White' flown by Capt G.M. Parshin in 1944 carries something akin to the Allies' 'invasion stripes', four 'kill' stars and the legend *Mest' Barinovykh* ('Revenge of the Barinovs'; most probably this means the Barinov brothers).

This 12th Air Army/248th Attack Air Division/967th Attack Air Regiment Il-2 was flown by Nikita Saatchiyan on the Transbaikalian Front in August 1945.

Emblazoned *Stalingrad – Berlin*, this early two-seater Il-2 was based at Berlin-Tempelhof in April 1945.

A typical Soviet Air Force Il-2 with assorted unit markings.

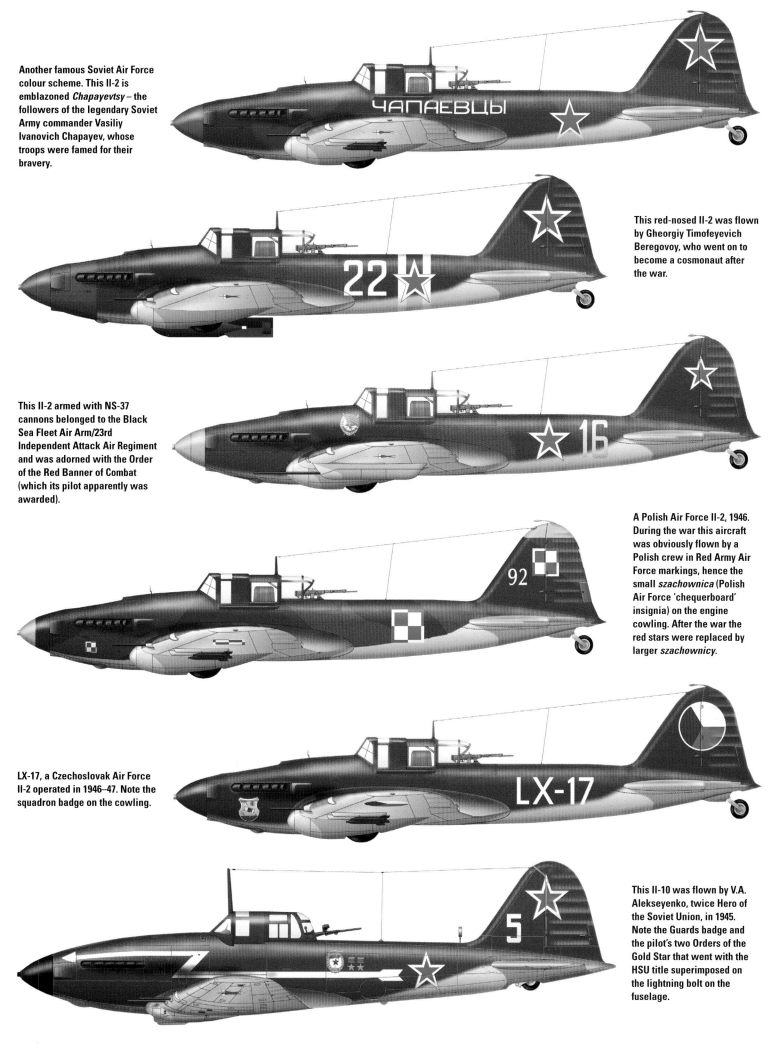

Another famous Soviet Air Force colour scheme. This Il-2 is emblazoned *Chapayevtsy* – the followers of the legendary Soviet Army commander Vasiliy Ivanovich Chapayev, whose troops were famed for their bravery.

ЧАПАЕВЦЫ

This red-nosed Il-2 was flown by Gheorgiy Timofeyevich Beregovoy, who went on to become a cosmonaut after the war.

22

This Il-2 armed with NS-37 cannons belonged to the Black Sea Fleet Air Arm/23rd Independent Attack Air Regiment and was adorned with the Order of the Red Banner of Combat (which its pilot apparently was awarded).

16

A Polish Air Force Il-2, 1946. During the war this aircraft was obviously flown by a Polish crew in Red Army Air Force markings, hence the small *szachownica* (Polish Air Force 'chequerboard' insignia) on the engine cowling. After the war the red stars were replaced by larger *szachownicy*.

92

LX-17, a Czechoslovak Air Force Il-2 operated in 1946–47. Note the squadron badge on the cowling.

LX-17

This Il-10 was flown by V.A. Alekseyenko, twice Hero of the Soviet Union, in 1945. Note the Guards badge and the pilot's two Orders of the Gold Star that went with the HSU title superimposed on the lightning bolt on the fuselage.

5

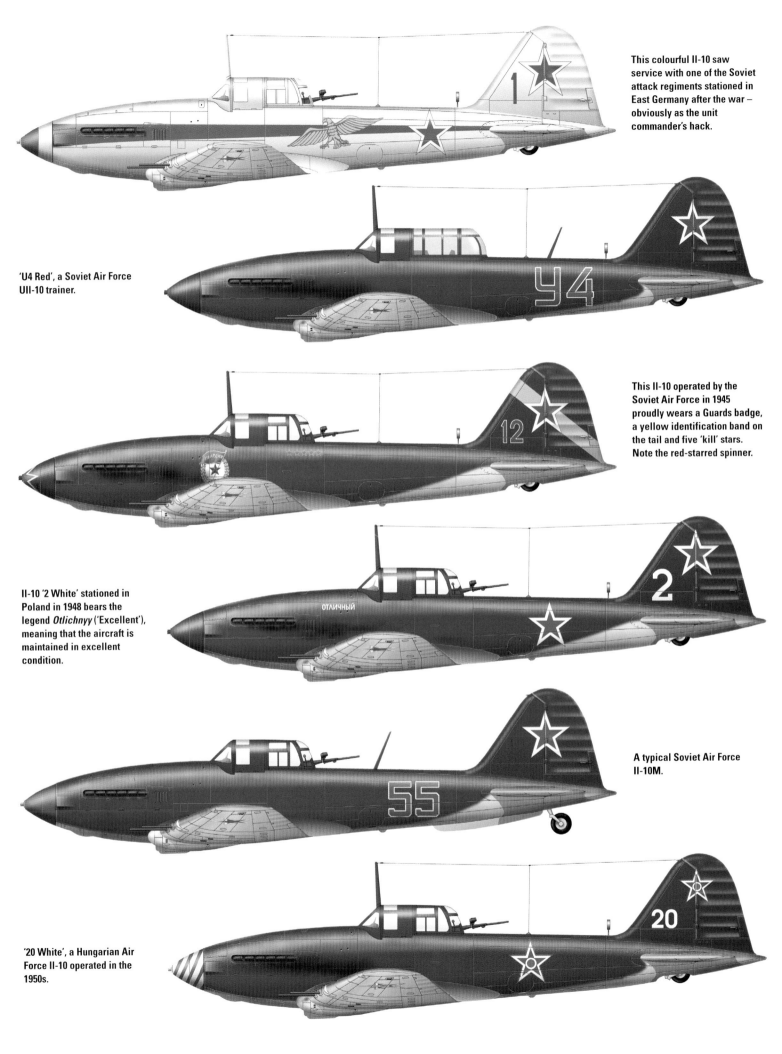

This colourful Il-10 saw service with one of the Soviet attack regiments stationed in East Germany after the war – obviously as the unit commander's hack.

'U4 Red', a Soviet Air Force UIl-10 trainer.

This Il-10 operated by the Soviet Air Force in 1945 proudly wears a Guards badge, a yellow identification band on the tail and five 'kill' stars. Note the red-starred spinner.

Il-10 '2 White' stationed in Poland in 1948 bears the legend *Otlichnyy* ('Excellent'), meaning that the aircraft is maintained in excellent condition.

A typical Soviet Air Force Il-10M.

'20 White', a Hungarian Air Force Il-10 operated in the 1950s.

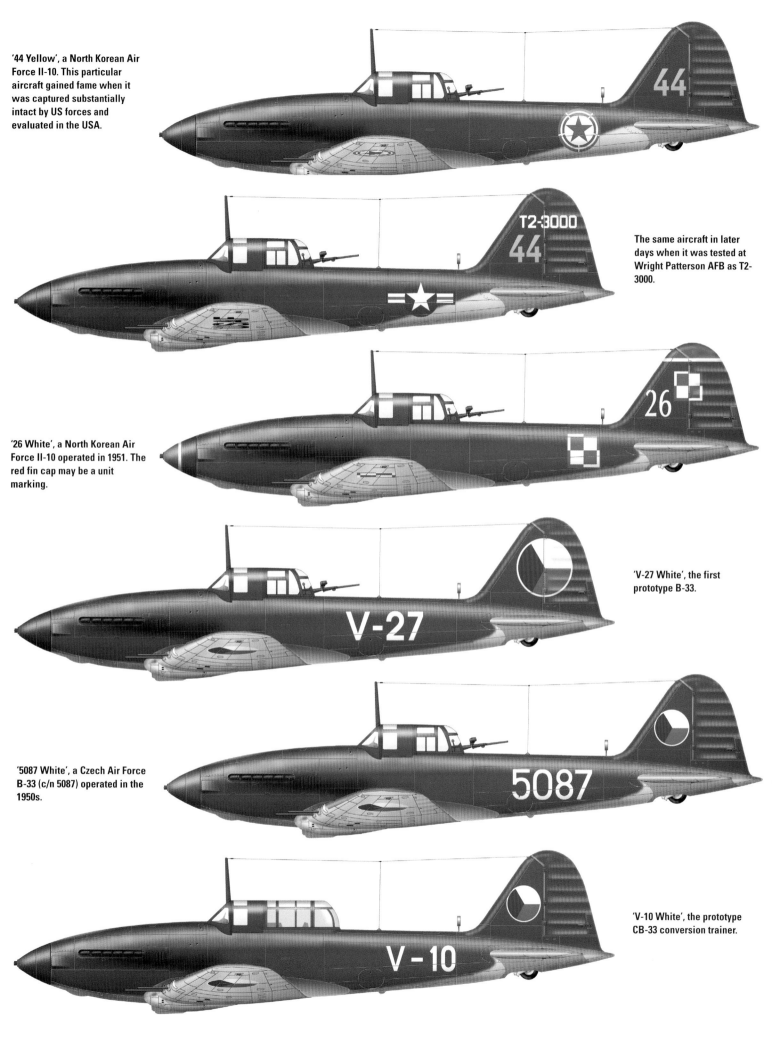

'44 Yellow', a North Korean Air Force Il-10. This particular aircraft gained fame when it was captured substantially intact by US forces and evaluated in the USA.

The same aircraft in later days when it was tested at Wright Patterson AFB as T2-3000.

'26 White', a North Korean Air Force Il-10 operated in 1951. The red fin cap may be a unit marking.

'V-27 White', the first prototype B-33.

'5087 White', a Czech Air Force B-33 (c/n 5087) operated in the 1950s.

'V-10 White', the prototype CB-33 conversion trainer.

Above: The Il-2 at the *Muzeum Wojska Polskiego* has Il-10 (c/n 5542) to keep it company. Yefim Gordon

Left: This Polish Air Force Avia B-33 ('4 White', c/n B33-3061) is preserved at the *Muzeum Lotnictwa I Astronautyki* (Aerospace Museum) in Cracow. Wacław Holyś

Below: The wreckage of this Moscow-built Il-2 (c/n 303561) was discovered in 1983 in Lake Sennagressvannet in northern Norway, south-east of Kirkenes. After recovery in 1984, the aircraft was painstakingly restored in 1988–89 by Russian enthusiasts. Here it is seen in Kirkenes in October 1989 during reassembly. The aircraft is now on display at the local Grensemuseum (Borderland Museum). Sergey Komissarov

CHAPTER FOUR

Veteran Pilots Remember

The story of the Il-2's significant contribution to the Red Army's victory is, above all, the story of the courage and heroism displayed by the pilots and air gunners who flew this aircraft. All too often the damage they inflicted to the enemy was paid for with their lives. Their combat experience was full of dramatic episodes that long remained vivid in the memory of those who survived. After the war some of them wrote and published memoirs in which they shared their recollections with readers. Here are some excerpts from the memoirs, for the most part quoted verbatim, partly condensed and retold.

From the memoirs of P.M. Stefanovskiy, a military test pilot:

The 430th Special Purpose Attack Air Regiment was formed on the basis of the Flight Test Institute of the Red Army Air Force (NII VVS). Lt Col Nikolai Iosifovich Malyshev, former deputy commander of the Air Force Combat Employment Air Unit, was appointed the regiment's commander. Maj Alexander Kuzmich Dolgov, one of the longest-serving test pilots, was appointed his deputy [before the war Dolgov had headed a team of the NII VVS which was engaged in the testing and development of the Il-2, notes Stefanovskiy].

The Combat Employment Air Unit which had been set up at the initiative of Alexander Ivanovich Filin, an outstanding engineer-pilot, had been engaged in developing new methods of using the aircraft that were introduced into squadron service in the Air Force. The 430th Attack Air Regiment started its combat activities in the region of Orsha. The first mission was flown on 5 July. Command of the Western Front received information according to which a large concentration of tanks and motor vehicles had been observed at the airfield of Beshenkovichi. It was impossible to ascertain whose *matériel* it was – ours or the enemy's, because there was no com-

munication with Beshenkovichi. Our tank units, too, were operating somewhere in that area, but the command had no information as to their whereabouts.

Lt Col Malyshev received an order to reconnoitre the mechanized troops concentration and, if these were the enemy's, to strike a blow against them. Maj Dolgov was the leader of the nine aircraft sent on this mission; they were joined by the regiment's commander in the tenth aircraft. In the vicinity of Beshenkovichi the aircraft descended to an extremely low altitude. The machines were flying literally at treetop height. The pilots caught sight of a huge concentration of tanks and armoured vehicles which were arranged in neat rows all over the airfield area. The German *Balkenkreuz* could be easily discerned on the tanks. Soldiers in full combat outfit were rushing about here and there. The airfield's boundaries were lined with red panels – apparently identification signs for the German aviation. The enemy's anti-aircraft artillery was silent: Ilyushin's armoured attack aircraft had not yet been used in combat, and the Germans were not familiar with their recognition features.

The commander was no longer in any doubt. He gave an order to start strafing the airfield. The 100kg [220lb] high-explosive bombs with retarded fuses were dropped, covering almost the whole of the airfield area. Each aircraft was carrying four such bombs. This was followed by launching the heavy-calibre RS-82 rocket projectiles. The airmen made use of their cannon and machine-guns. Belatedly, the enemy anti-aircraft defence crews put into action all their weapons. The situation both on the ground and in the air turned into havoc. The nine attack aircraft set on a course to base.

The regiment's commander, prompted by the desire to check the results of the action, made one more pass over the target. He saw numerous fires that had

broken out on the airfield: the enemy's vehicles, set ablaze, were exploding. The ground was covered with black spots – the bodies of killed and wounded German troops. The enemy's anti-aircraft artillery threw up such a heavy barrage that even a small bird would seem to have no chance of slipping through it. Nevertheless, all the nine attack aircraft returned to base safely. True, some of the aircraft were damaged. For example, Lt Col Malyshev's machine sported more than 200 bullet-holes. And yet, it made it home. The Ilyushins demonstrated their surprising survivability.

[Stefanovsky adds:] The Attack Air Regiment commanded by Lt Col Malyshev helped the formidable armoured attack aircraft to get started on its combat career in the skies of the war . . . The very first experience of combat operations involving the use of the Il-2 showed that the aircraft had to be a two-seater, as originally conceived by S.V. Ilyushin. A.K. Dolgov and other test pilots who were subsequently withdrawn from the front to the NII VVS persistently argued for reinstating the armoured attack aircraft in production in its original two-seat configuration, and eventually obtained a decision to that effect.

From the memoirs of I.I. Pstygo, a wartime Il-2 pilot, later Air Marshal of the Soviet Union:

When we started studying the Il-2 attack aircraft, not a single 'live' example of this aircraft was available in Balashov [where the conversion training was conducted]. We got our perception of the machine from descriptions, drawings and pictures . . . at long last, several Il-2s arrived in Balashov. The aircraft had a pointed nose and a streamlined fuselage, the wings were of metal construction. It was neat and purposeful, its appearance alone was awe-inspiring. We immediately got a liking for it . . . The machine was docile in handling and reacted readily to every input from the pilot. [Pstygo is relating the story of how the 211th Bomber Air Regiment converted to the Il-2 in 1941, after the surrender of Kiyev and Kharkov.]

[There were numerous cases when Il-2 pilots saved their comrades-in-arms at the risk of their own lives. Pstygo recalls a feat accomplished in March 1943 by pilots of the 503th Attack Air Regiment.] When a group led by Lt Demekhin was on its way home after raiding an enemy airfield, the pilots noticed that one of the escorting fighters had made a forced landing in enemy territory. Immediately one of the attack aircraft landed near the fighter to pick up the pilot, but came to grief itself: the Il-2 came under fire and a bullet burst one of the main wheel tyres, making take-off impossible. Now two crews were in trouble. Yet another Il-2 landed nearby, and the crews of the two crippled planes somehow managed to get on board; the two Ilyushin gunners had to accommodate themselves in the main wheel wells of the attack aircraft. The heavily loaded aircraft took off, barely escaping the approaching enemy soldiers. After a short but perilous flight with extended undercarriage it landed safely; all aboard were saved.

[Pstygo relates how the Air Force command issued an order urging the frontline units to use fully the Il-2's potential as a day bomber and to increase its bomb load from 400 to 600kg (880 to 1,300lb).]

Wasn't that rather an abrupt turn? We were in doubts . . . Yet, someone had, after all, to begin flying missions with the new bomb load. The regiment's commander singled out myself, Dokookin, Batrakov and two or three other pilots and said: 'You are to show the example!' And so we did load those 600kg on our mounts. And nothing untoward happened – we went on to fly our missions in much the same way as we had flown them before. When the psychological barrier had thus been overcome, the whole regiment switched over to flying with the heavier bomb load. The enemy came to get a still more telling punch from us.

And then I was involved in an incident which once again demonstrated to me the extraordinary capabilities of the Il-2. When taking off for a combat sortie, I sensed a somewhat unusual behaviour of the aircraft – it reluctantly raised its tail and gathered speed at a slower rate than usual. The centre of gravity posi-

tion also seemed to be unusual. But, since there were no irregularities in the running of the engine and the readings of the instruments, I gathered altitude and proceeded on my course to fulfil the mission. The bombing and strafing duly performed, I returned to base. And then the armourer who loaded my aircraft with ammunition runs up to me, pale-faced, with trembling lips, and says: 'Comrade Senior Lieutenant! Upon my word, it happened accidentally! Believe me, it was a mistake! Comrade Senior Lieutenant! Forgive me . . .'. Frankly, I was surprised: 'Man, what's the matter? Did you make a mess of something? Say it plainly!' As it turned out, he had loaded 740kg [1,630lb] of bombs into the bomb-bays of my aircraft! [On the spur of a moment Pstygo gave a scolding to the armourer, but took no disciplinary action against him – after all, the flight had ended without an incident, he adds:] The aircraft's technician Mikhail Bukin carefully inspected the undercarriage struts. They had suffered no damage.

The Germans tried hard to minimize the casualties inflicted by the Soviet attack aircraft. Pstygo recalls in his memoirs how his group noticed huge trails of dust on the ground – obviously caused by an enemy motorized convoy on the march – during one of the missions. A strafing sortie was undertaken, producing, surprisingly, no return fire from the ground. This prompted Pstygo to descend and take a closer look at what was hiding beneath the dust trail. To his surprise, he discovered that the clouds of dust were produced by huge bundles of tree branches attached by ropes to heavy trucks or tractors. There were next to no combat vehicles in the 'convoy'. Having received a report to this effect, the regiment commander immediately sent the attack aircraft on a new mission, instructing the pilots to make a pass across the path of the 'convoy's' movement. They hit the jackpot. At some distance away from the dust-producing false convoy there were others, moving in parallel courses – this time with not-so-heavy dust trails but consisting of real combat vehicles. The enemy's ploy was revealed, and Soviet pilots were later especially attentive when they saw such trails.

A group of Il-2s led by I. Pstygo on a 'hunt and kill' mission, seeking targets of opportunity, discovered a small lake

surrounded by hundreds of vehicles – trucks, petrol tankers and so on. The water was teeming with the heads of bathing soldiers. Obviously an enemy convoy had halted. The attack aircraft did not miss their chance, attacking the troops first and then destroying the vehicles. The effect was devastating, everything was on fire; the enemy was unable to put up any opposition.

In August 1942 the Air Regiment where Pstygo was serving received an order from T. Khriukin, the 8th Air Army Commander, to destroy a pontoon bridge over the Don River. The bridge was of major importance for German troops on the way towards Stalingrad and had to be destroyed at any cost. The order required all available aircraft of the regiment (twelve to fifteen) to be put into action immediately. However, the battered machines needed major repairs and it proved physically impossible to have them all ready by the stipulated time. Pstygo ventured to fulfil the order with only three aircraft, manned by himself and his trusted friends P. Dokookin and V. Batrakov. He assured the commander that the bridge would definitely be destroyed. The commander had no choice but to give the go-ahead. The attack was crowned with success. To be quite sure, Pstygo dropped his bombs in a very steep dive, close to 60 degrees, the aircraft barely surviving the violent G force when pulling out of the dive. Several pontoons were knocked out by direct hit and the bridge was broken up. When the three pilots returned from the sortie, Khriukin, who had already received a report from ground observers, warmly thanked the airmen for their service. Privately, he asked Pstygo why he had been so sure of the result. The latter intimates that he was ready, as a last resort, to ram the bridge with his aircraft, but fortunately the need had not arisen.

When the troops of our South Western Front were retreating, the enemy captured several trains with Soviet military matériel at Prikolotnoye railway station. Two of these trains were carrying petrol.

Pstygo further relates that Air Maj Gen T. Khriukin, Commander-in-Chief of the 8th Air Army, arrived by air in the 504th Attack Air Regiment where he was serving. Khriukin tasked the regiment with undertaking a raid against Prikolotnoye railway station. The regiment's commander was of the opinion that all available aircraft should be sent on this mission; he appointed Pstygo as the leader of the group. The latter, however, voiced dissent and pleaded his being unable to lead such a big group (ten to twelve aircraft). He argued that in the adverse weather conditions he would run the risk of simply losing sight of his aircraft and being unable to keep the group together. He suggested his own plan: the mission was to be flown by three aircraft only; Pstygo would fly himself together with his trusted friends Dokookin and Batrakov. He was confident that this held a better promise of success. Finally, Khriukin's consent was obtained.

[*Pstygo writes*:] Thus the three of us started on our mission. We approached the station at low altitude. Immediately we caught sight of the trains, looking like long chains. Making use of rocket projectiles was out of the question – the blasts would damage our low-flying planes. I gave the order: 'Bombs!' The bombs were fitted with delayed fuses. They could not possibly miss the target. The station was packed with the trains. Having released the bombs, we went further to the west, made a turn and set a course back to the station. What a sight met our eyes! There were explosions and flames everywhere. The fire at the station was so large that, not only the smoke, but the flames as well reached the low clouds overhanging it.

The 893rd Attack Air Regiment (of which I was the commander) of our 307th Air Division was almost totally equipped with Il-2s with the NS-37 cannon. It was dubbed 'the anti-tank regiment'.

In my capacity of commander I had to test the machine and get my own impressions of its qualities and its armament. I made a flight to the test range and there it became immediately apparent that the precise aiming of the cannon presented a complicated problem. The cannon were mounted in the wings at a considerable distance from the fuselage, from the aircraft's axis, and, consequently, from the CG. When firing, the recoil was so strong that the plane gave a start in the air. What was worse, after aiming and pressing the firing button I noticed that even the first explosions of the shells were not quite simultaneous. The explosions occurred rather close to each other. The

second salvo revealed a still greater discrepancy in the timing of the explosions. The explosions were occurring at an even greater distance from each other. During the third salvo the aircraft rocked so violently that the pilot was thrown about the cockpit from side to side and there was no way of checking this rocking of the aircraft. As a matter of fact, only the first two shells hit the target. The subsequent ones were scattered to great distances and it was impossible to achieve a well-aimed burst . . . There was nothing else to do but to fire as short bursts as possible. However, this posed a problem of its own. It meant that in a diving attack one could take aim only once and fire one short burst. Only experienced pilots could manage to take aim twice, provided the diving was made from high altitude. We did wage com-bat on these machines, but experienced no satisfaction. Soon the industry stopped equipping the Il-2s with the NS-37 cannon.

From the memoirs of Gheorgiy T. Beregovoy, Hero of the Soviet Union, wartime Il-2 pilot, later a Soviet cosmonaut:

Once, a group of four Il-2s of our unit were on their way home after having successfully attacked a German column near Zhitomir. The group was escorted by four fighters. Suddenly the voice of one of the pilots was heard in the earphones: 'Six Messerschmitts to starboard of our course!' And then again: 'Six more, same direction!' . . . Eight German fighters attacked us, the other four engaged the covering group of four fighters. Behind my back sat the gunner/radio operator with his large-calibre machine-gun. I reckoned on his protection. The whole of our group descended to the height of some two dozen metres or, as airmen say, 'lay flat on our bellies' to preclude any possibility of attack from beneath; we undertook manoeuvres, changing our formation all the time so that each aircraft constantly alternated the roles of a wingman or lead aircraft. That helped to ensure the most favourable conditions for our gunners repelling the attacks of the German fighters.

That was far from a simple and easy task, yet we had nothing else to resort to. Should we try to engage in aerial combat on a par with the attacking fighters, given the difference in speeds amounting to 150km/h, this would end up in all the

four Ils being set ablaze within a couple of minutes. On the other hand, by changing formation and ensuring mutual protection we succeeded in engaging the eight enemy fighters while preventing them from coming too close. No matter, from which side the Messerschmitts made a pass for an attack, they were met by machine-gun bursts. The seemingly easy prey turned out to be beyond the German fighters' capacity. All the pilots came safely to base. [Moreover, adds Beregovoi, two Bf 109s were downed by the escort fighters.]

On one of his sorties Beregovoy's Il-2 was attacked by German fighters, which soon set it alight. The obvious choice for him and his gunner – to bail out – was out of the question for the moment, because the aircraft was still above German territory. Two or three minutes were needed to cross the frontline, but they seemed interminably long, the fire getting closer and closer to the airmen in their cockpits. Beregovoy felt as though he were inside an oven; his gunner cried with pain, the flames licking his feet. Mustering all their will and patience, they reached the frontline and then bailed out. Seconds later their Il-2 exploded in mid-air.

[Beregovoi relates the following curious episode connected with the service introduction of the Il-2.]

We received an order to take delivery of the new [Il-2] aircraft and to ferry them to our base at Krapivino . . . The trouble was that . . . it was necessary to transport to base the maintenance personnel as well. And the Il-2s, as is well known, were initially produced as single-seaters . . . What was to be done, how the task could be tackled – no one knew. All of a sudden, we received a directive which had a bewildering effect at first. We were instructed to take 'passengers', accommodating one person in each of the two underwing main undercarriage fairings. The lever operating the retraction system was to be temporarily disconnected to prevent accidents – the pilot might forget about the passengers and retract the wheels as usual . . . Everybody was astounded at first by the seemingly wild scheme; yet, on second thought, the boldness and originality of the idea appealed to the pilots. In addition, it was recommended to open hatches and accommodate two more passengers in the space behind the fuel tank, which was to be fitted with improvised seats made of suspended belts. Thus a single-seater was converted into a five-seat 'airliner' . . . When my Il-2 was gathering speed on the runway before take-off, I did not feel all too confident . . . Still, everything worked out to a perfect satisfaction . . . All the aircraft of the group landed safely, without a hitch.

On the following day we learnt that this method of transporting people on single-seater combat aircraft was developed in the headquarters of the Commander-in Chief of the Air Force. It was the Commander-in-Chief – a participant of the famous rescue expedition to save the crew of the *Cheluskin* steamship in the High North – that conceived the recommendations which at first struck us as exceedingly bold and then as well thought out and reflecting the ability to take a look at things, when needed, from the most unexpected side. 'That man is real clever!' – that was the comment of Yevgeniy Klobukov, our regiment commander. And then he added: 'But please, keep in mind: the Commander-in Chief expressly stipulated that this method be used only in exceptional circumstances. Only in an emergency! This is an order!' Later, throughout the war years, I did not witness a single case of transporting people by air on single-seater attack aircraft . . .

From memoirs of fighter pilot Nikolai Filatov who had flown numerous missions escorting IL-2s (the Fighter Air Regiment in which Filatov served exists to this day; it is now the 159th Guards Novorossiisk Red Banner Fighter Air Regiment):

On 26 June [1944] we were tasked with striking a blow against the retreating German troops and their combat vehicles in the area of Kniazhetsy [30km {17 miles} north of Mogilyov]. One group of eight Il-2s was led by Lt B.S. Levin, flight commander of the 7th Guards Attack Air Regiment. A pair of fighters (myself and A. Samoilov as my wingman) was escorting this group. Soon we discovered large concentrations of enemy troops – hundreds of vehicles, artillery pieces drawn by tractors and so on. When I saw ahead of me a huge 'serpent' made up of vehicles that were on the march on a highway leading towards the Dnepr river, I suggested to Levin that his group should fly a little further to the west and attack there to block the movement of the enemy troops towards the river. The attack aircraft followed this suggestion. One group of four aircraft delivered a blow against a column of vehicles not far from a small bridge. The blow was very precise, and the movement of the enemy came to a standstill. The second group of four went into a banking turn with the intention of starting a strafing attack along the whole of the highway. I also made a turn, accompanying them, and at that moment I saw a large number of vehicles, tractors and artillery pieces that were tightly parked at a forest clearing to the left of the highway. I immediately informed Levin about that. He saw the new target and ordered the second group of four Il-2s to strike a blow at this grouping. The leader of the second group immediately corrected his course and delivered a blow; he did it so masterfully that I was simply amazed. I simply could not resist the temptation to take a closer look at the results of the attack. I reported to Levin that I would lag behind for a while and then catch up, and made a pass over the scene of the attack. The like of such devastation caused to the enemy by a firing pass I had not seen before nor later. That was something fantastic. Words fail me today to describe what I saw. By the way, after this blow a special plane was sent to that place to photograph the scene.

Once we received a very complicated and rather interesting task; it was, as far as I remember, on 29 or 30 September 1944. Intelligence established that the Germans had set up a tank assembly factory and tank repair facilities in the town of Przasnysz, north of Warsaw, some 130km [81 miles] west of the frontline. It was necessary to attack and put out of action these facilities which were of considerable importance to the enemy. This operation was well thought out and executed. To my knowledge, it was one of the few cases in the history of the Great Patriotic War when attack aircraft and not bombers were sent on such a mission. After all, the target was 130km behind the frontline!

Frankly, to this day I have no information about other attack aircraft fulfilling similar tasks. Normally, if, say, fifty attack aircraft were sent on a mission, they required a still bigger number of fighters to ensure cover on the route and in the target area. The command took a decision to block for no less than 30min the airfield of Cechanow situated not far from Przasnysz. This was to be effected by two groups of fighters from our regiment, each numbering twelve aircraft. And so we did. Our fighters prevented the German aircraft from taking to the air. Meanwhile, the attack aircraft that flew unescorted made three passes, as though they were training at a firing range. Everything went according to plan. Our two groups blocked the airfield for 30min (15min for each group). Our group destroyed eight parked aircraft on the airfield. In addition, the fire of two small-calibre flak batteries was suppressed . . . On the following day the airfield of Cechanow was blocked for the same purpose to ensure another blow by attack aircraft.

From memoirs of AM S.A. Krasovskiy, a war-time fighter pilot:

Our friendship with the 'aerial infantrymen' is getting stronger with every passing day. We, a fighter unit, share the same airfield with attack aircraft. This provides good opportunities for personal contact; we often conduct post-flight debriefings jointly at which we discuss in minute detail the questions of interaction on the route and over the target in cases when we are attacked by enemy fighters . . . I remember how attack aircraft pilots expressed their heartfelt gratitude to us for good covering. In our turn we, fighter pilots, said that it was sheer pleasure to escort those who are clever at cooperation . . .

On 12 July [1942] a group of twelve Ilyushins led by Maj Melnikov conducted aerial combat with a big group of the Junkers dive bombers. We, the fighters, in four Yak machines provided the cover for the attack aircraft. When the Ils had dropped their bomb loads on the designated target, the forward air control post radioed to us that several dozen enemy bombers escorted by fighters were approaching our main line of defence. We decided not to give in. The attack aircraft assaulted the Junkers bombers, and our four fighters led by Capt Nikolai Dunayev engaged the escorting enemy fighters. The combat was a bitter one. The air seemed to be boiling with machine-gun and cannon bursts. We scored a victory. The attack aircraft downed eight enemy aircraft, and one more was shot out of the sky by our leader Capt Dunayev. The success was due to the fact that the pilots of the attack aircraft entered the aerial combat not piecemeal, as single aircraft, but as a united group, and to the fact that we did everything to keep the enemy fighters engaged in a combat with us and to prevent them from attacking our brothers-in-arms.

When speaking about the wartime activities of our airmen, one must mention the name of A.L. Shumidub. This attack aircraft pilot contributed many a glorious page to the history of our Army.

Once, a group of nine Il-2s led by Shumidub, escorted by six Yak fighters, on their way to the target area encountered a big group of the Junkers Ju 87s. The enemy bombers formed a circle and tried to bomb our troops from an altitude of 400 to 500m [1,300–1,600ft]. The Yaks cut off the German fighters from the Junkers bombers and engaged the fighters in combat. Two leading flights of the Ju 87 bombers were attacked by the Il-2 aircraft when they were recovering from a dive. One of the bombers caught fire and fell close to the positions of our troops. A fourth flight of the Ju 87s, making a short cut across the circle formation, tried hastily to leave the scene of combat, but Senior Lt Shumidub, the leader of the group, attacked the bombers; in the first firing pass he downed one aircraft and in the second scored a hit on another one. Three destroyed Junkers bombers represented a sizeable success in the combat.

On another occasion a group of six Il-2s led by Shumidub and escorted by six fighters led by Lt Okruzhnov flew a mission with the intention of strafing a column of enemy vehicles. On their way back after fulfilling the task the attack aircraft pilots noticed a large group of the Ju 87s escorted by twelve Fw 190 and Bf 109 fighters. The bombers were flying in a two-tier formation above the positions of our troops. Shumidub radioed to his wingmen: get closer together, gain altitude. The attack aircraft closed in on their leader and the whole formation began approaching the enemy aircraft, while our fighters provided reliable cover for them. Shumidub and his wingman Poosev attacked one of the Ju 87 flights head-on. Opening fire from a distance of 300m [1,000ft], they scored a hit on the flight leader's aircraft setting it ablaze, and then did the same with his starboard-side wingman. Almost simultaneously with the attack aircraft, the escort fighters engaged combat and shot down two Fw 190s.

CHAPTER FIVE

The Il-2 in Detail

The technical manual defines the Il-2 as an armoured ground-attack and bomber aircraft. In the course of 1941 and 1942 the aircraft was manufactured in a single-seater version; from the autumn of 1942 it was equipped with a rear cockpit for the gunner provided with a machine-gun. With regard to dimensions and trimming, the two-seater aircraft did not differ from the single-seater. The introduction of the rear defensive installation led to an increase in the weight of the two-seater, as compared with the single-seater version, from 5,750–5,800kg (12,680–12,790lb) to 6,050–6,100kg (13,340–13,450lb).

Fuselage

The aircraft's fuselage comprised two parts: the all-metal, forward fuselage, which was formed as an armour shell, and the rear fuselage of wooden construction. The armour shell was assembled from some twenty pieces of armour plating joined to each other by steel rivets and bolts with the help of Duralumin sections. Its front part, forming the engine cowling of streamlined shape, comprised two parts: the lower, made undetachable and featuring two hinged inspection hatches, and the upper comprising fifteen separate covers. The cowling also included the air duct of the coolant radiator. The rear fuselage and the wing centre section were attached to the forward fuselage by bolts and rivets. The crew and all the vital assemblies of the aircraft (the engine with its associated equipment, radiators, fuel and oil tanks, as well as the instruments) were housed in the armour shell manufactured from special armour steel plates with a thickness of 4, 5, 6 and 7mm (0.157, 0.196, 0.235 and 0.274in). Placed behind the pilot's back was an armour plate of 12mm (0.47in) thickness; the gunner was accommodated behind an armour bulkhead of 5mm (0.2in) thickness. From the front the pilot was also protected by bullet-proof glass of 55mm thickness (2.2in); the aft-sliding cockpit canopy had its sides manufactured of 8mm (0.3in) armour plates and an 8mm bullet-proof glass panel was placed behind the pilot's head. The cockpit's windshield was made of special armour-glass of 25mm (1in) thickness resting on a 30mm (1.2in) layer of Plexiglass. The rear fuselage was an oval-section body which tapered off into a tail-cone and blended into the integrally-built fin. The skinning was made of *shpon*, strips of

Left: The forward portion of the Il-2's armour **body.** Yefim Gordon archive

Below: A three-view drawing of a late production two-seater Il-2 with increased sweepback on wing leading edges.
Insert: A single-seaer Il-2 side-view

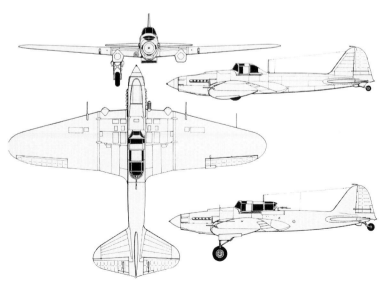

birch wood bonded together with casein glue, with each layer positioned at right angles to its neighbour for extra strength.

The fuselage had a total length of 11.653m (38ft 3in); according to other sources (in some production batches) it was 11.45m (37ft 6²/₃in). The maximum height of the fuselage (without the cockpit canopy) was 1.624m (5ft 4in), the cross-sectional area was 1.76sq m (18.95sq ft). The aircraft's height when resting on the three wheels was 2.95m (9ft 8in); the height tail-up was 4.169m (13ft 8in). The static ground angle was 11 degrees 55min.

Wing and Tail Unit

The wing was a two-spar structure of trapezoidal shape. The wing had two joints, dividing it into three parts:

the wing centre section permanently attached to the fuselage and two outer wing panels attached to the wing centre section by means of four bolts each. The attachment bolts were made of Cromansil alloy and underwent heat treatment. The joints between the outer panels and the wing centre section were covered by a metal strip attached by bolts. The wing utilized the Clark YH aerofoil. The wing had a span of 14.6m (47ft 10⁴/₅in), some sources give the figure as 14.52m (47ft 7²/₃in); its aspect ratio was 5.55. The wing centre section measured 4.2m (13ft 9¹/₃in). The wing root chord (theoretical) was 3.86m (12ft 7⁴/₅in), other sources give the figure as 3.63m (11ft 11in). The mean aerodynamic chord was 2.876m (9ft 5¹/₃in); some sources give the figure as 2.878m. The wing incidence was 0 degrees, the wing dihedral was 4 degrees

45min (3 degrees 55min according to other sources).

The wings were provided with flaps, which were divided into two sections. Of these, one was fitted to the wing centre section and the other to the detachable outer wing panel. Each outer wing panel incorporated a Frise-type aileron, which was divided into two sections. Inboard aileron sections were provided with geared tabs. The aileron area totalled 2.84sq m (30.57sq ft); the flap area was 4.2sq m (45.21sq ft). Flap settings were 45 degrees for landing and 17 for take-off. The two-seater version had a device locking the flaps at take-off in the setting of 17 degrees. The flap setting could be monitored with the help of a mechanical visual indicator placed between the aft ends of ribs No.4 and 5 of the wing centre section on port side. The wing structure comprised two spars, stringers, ribs

The gunner's station of a typical two-seater Il-2. Yefim Gordon archive

The cockpit canopy of an early two-seater Il-2.
Yefim Gordon archive

and skinning. The wing centre section was of all-metal construction. Outer wing panels were manufactured in two versions. In the first the wing panel had ribs, stringers and skinning made of wood and plywood. The wooden framework was attached to metal spars by bolts and rivets. The skinning was bonded by casein glue. In the second version the wing panel had a metal frame to which a plywood skinning was riveted. Two-seater aircraft of late production batches had new outer wing panels of all-metal construction, featuring an increase of the angle of sweep on the leading edge to 15 degrees (6 more than on the preceding model).

The tail surfaces were of a cantilever type. The stabilizer was of all-metal construction, while the fin was made of wood. The elevator and the rudder had metal frames with fabric skinning. Control surfaces were provided with mass balances. The mass balance of the rudder was placed on an outrigger protruding into the airstream. The rudder had a balance tab and the elevator a geared trim tab. The trim tabs were controlled from the pilot's cockpit.

The horizontal tail had a span of 4.9m (16ft 1in); other sources give the figure as 4.8m (15ft 9in). Its area was 7.5sq m (80.74sq ft) and it had a zero dihedral. The elevator had an area of 2.66sq m

(28.63sq ft). The vertical tail had a height (measured from the axis of the aircraft) of 1.9m (6ft 3in); other sources give the figure as 1.83m (6ft). Its area was 2.29sq m (24.65sq ft); the rudder area was 1.035sq m (11.14sq ft); other sources give 1.085sq m (11.68sq ft).

Undercarriage

The main undercarriage units were accommodated in underwing fairings of asymmetrical shape attached to the outer ends of the wing centre section. In flight, the main undercarriage legs swivelled aft and retracted into the wings. When retracted, the undercarriage parts that remained outside the wing were covered by a fairing and only a small portion of the wheel tyre was left uncovered and slightly protruding. The tailwheel was retracted into the rear fuselage. The main wheels measured 800mm × 260mm (31.5in × 10.24in), the tailwheel 400mm × 150mm (15.75in × 5.9in). The wheel track was 3m (11ft 5⁴⁄₅ in); other sources give 3.4m (11ft 2in). In comparison with the single-seater version, the two-seater featured a number of changes in the detailed design of the tail fork, enhancing its shock-absorbing properties.

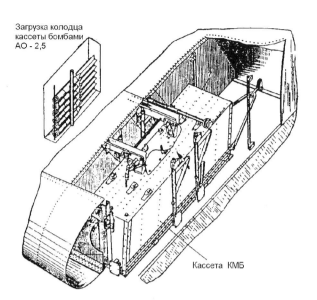

Загрузка колодца
кассеты бомбами
АО - 2,5

Кассета КМБ

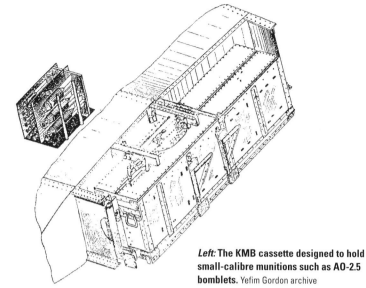

Left: The KMB cassette designed to hold small-calibre munitions such as AO-2.5 bomblets. Yefim Gordon archive

Above: Though of poor quality, this photo clearly shows the reference lines on the Il-2's cowling that were used for ultra-low-level bombing attacks. Yefim Gordon archive

Right: The controls of the VMSh-2 time delay mechanism which dropped the bombs automatically a certain time after the aircraft's nose obscured the target. Yefim Gordon archive

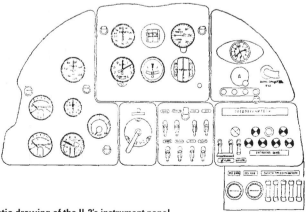

Below: A schematic drawing of the Il-2's instrument panel. Yefim Gordon archive

The PBP-1b collimator sight and reference 'diamond' on the windshield for dive-bombing attacks. Yefim Gordon archive

The VV-1 bead-type gunsight on an Il-2.
Yefim Gordon archive

Powerplant

The two-seater version of the aircraft was powered by the boosted AM-38F engine which was itself a version of the AM-38 engine with an increased take-off rating. It delivered 1,700 to 1,760hp (the AM-38 that initially powered the single-seater Il-2s was rated at 1,600hp) at 2,360rpm and a supercharger pressure of 1,360mm Hg. On the boosted engine the OP-321 oil radiator that had been fitted to the single-seater was replaced by the OP-446 radiator with a cooling area of 10sq m (107.65sq ft).

The two-seaters were fitted with the AV-5L-158 three-bladed, variable-pitch, automatic propeller measuring 3.6m (11ft 9¾ in) in diameter; the single-seaters had a VISh-22T propeller with a diameter of 3.4m (11ft 2in).

The fuel tank capacity was 730ltr (160.6gal) divided as follows: 175ltr (38.5gal) in the upper tank, 269ltr (59.2gal) in the lower tank and 286ltr (62.9gal) in the aft tank. The oil tanks had a total capacity of 81ltr (17.8gal).

Armament

The aircraft was armed with cannon, machine-guns, bombs, unguided rockets and chemical weapons. The cannon and machine-gun armament comprised: two 7.62mm (.30 calibre) ShKAS machine-guns with an ammunition complement of 1,500 rounds; two 23mm (.90 calibre) VYa cannon with a total of 300 rounds (or two 20mm ShVAK cannon with a total of 500 rounds; installation of the ShVAK cannon instead of the VYa reduced the all-up weight of the aircraft by 135kg [298lb]); and a single 12.7mm (.50 calibre) UBT machine-gun with 150 rounds of ammunition. The UBT machine-gun was not installed on single-seater machines.

The cannon were mounted in the wing outer panels between ribs Nos 7 and 8 on two detachable fittings which were attached to the ribs by bolts. Ammunition was fed to the cannon from boxes placed nearby via rigid chutes. The machine-guns were also installed in the wing outer panels, but between ribs Nos 6 and 7. Each gun was mounted on three fittings attached to the wing structure. It was fed from a box attached to the rib web.

A certain number of aircraft were armed with two 11-P-37 cannon (also known as NS-37), each of which weighed 150kg (331lb) – twice as much as the VYa. One 37mm shell weighed 735g (1.6lb). The muzzle velocity of the 11-P-37 was 900m/sec (2,950ft/sec), that is, roughly the same as that of the VYa cannon, but the rate of fire, reaching 250rpm, was lower than that of the VYa. Mounted in underwing fairings immediately outboard of the undercarriage housings, these long-barrelled cannon had an ammunition load of 32rpg. Together with the two ShKAS machine-guns which were retained for aiming, the total weight of the fixed forward-firing armament of the Il-2 armed with the 37mm cannon, including ammunition, amounted to 760kg (1,676lb). In addition to factory-produced machines, some single-seater and two-seater Il-2s armed with the 37mm cannon were converted to this armament configuration in the field by frontline maintenance units.

The bomb armament of the two-seater provided for a load of 300kg (661lb) internally in wing bomb-bays (the normal mode) or of 600kg (1,323lb) in bomb-bays and on external racks under overload conditions. The external bomb racks were fitted under rib No.2 of the wing centre section. In the case of the single-seater, the bomb load amounted to 400 and 600kg (882 and 1,323lb), respectively. The PTAB hollow-charge anti-tank bombs weighed either 1.5 or 2.5kg (3.3 or 5.5lb). Containers holding up to 200 of these bombs could be housed in the four bomb-bays. Bombs weighing up to 15kg (33lb) could also be loaded direct on to bomb-bay doors; on the upper side the bays had easily detachable covers. The armament included also AZh-2 incendiary ampoules with the KS self-inflammable liquid.

In addition, launching rails for the RS-82 or the RS-132 rocket were mounted under the wings. Four such unguided rockets were carried by the two-seater aircraft, while the single-seater could carry twice as many.

Equipment

The aircraft was equipped with the VV-1 gun sight for the pilot, a gun sight for the gunner (the K-8T sight for the UBT machine-gun), as well as with the AGP-1 gyro horizon, the KI-11 compass and other instruments. In the two-seater version the pilot and the gunner communicated via the SPUF-2 intercom and with the help of a three-colour, light-code communication system.

The bomb shackles under the wing of an Il-2. Yefim Gordon archive

Typical Weight Characteristics of the Two-Seater Il-2 Version

Empty weight of the aircraft (with metal wing outer panels)	4,525kg (9,978lb)	2 VYa cannon	142kg (313lb)
		300 rounds of ammunition for the cannon	168kg (370lb)
Useful load	1,536kg (3,387lb)	UBT machine-gun	21kg (46lb)
Including:		150 rounds of ammunition for the UBT	25kg (55lb)
crew	180kg (397lb)	bombs (in the bomb-bays)	300kg (661lb)
fuel	535kg (1,180lb)	4 RS-82 projectiles	27kg (60lb)
oil	65kg (143lb)	Normal all-up weight	6,060kg (13,362lb)
2 ShKAS machine-guns	22kg (48lb)	Overload flight weight with 600kg (1,320lb)	
1,500 rounds of ammunition for the machine-guns	51kg (112lb)	bombs loaded	6,360kg (14,024lb)

Note: wooden wing outer panels increased the aircraft's all-up weight by 100kg (220lb); installation of the ShVAK cannon instead of the VYa reduced the all-up weight by 135kg (298lb).

Typical Weight Characteristics of the Single-Seater Il-2 Version

Empty weight of the aircraft (with metal wing outer panels)	4,253kg (9,379lb)	2 VYa cannon	142kg (313lb)
		300 rounds of ammunition for the cannon	168kg (370lb)
Useful load	1,527kg (3,367lb)	bombs (in the bomb-bays)	400kg (882lb)
Including:		8 RS-82 projectiles	27kg (60lb)
pilot	90kg (199lb)	Normal all-up weight	5,780kg (12,745lb)
fuel	535kg (1,180lb)	Overload all-up weight with 600kg (1,320lb)	
oil	65kg (143lb)	bomb load	5,980kg (13,186lb)
2 ShKAS machine-guns	22kg (49lb)		
1,500 rounds of ammunition for the machine-guns	51kg (112lb)		

Note: wooden wing outer panels increased the aircraft's all-up weight by 100kg (220lb); installation of the ShVAK cannon instead of the VYa reduced all-up weight by 135kg (298lb).

Specification of the Single-Seater Aircraft

Maximum horizontal speeds with engine revs at 2,150rpm

Aircraft	No.2611	No.6522 (average figures for 6 production machines)	
	April 1942	June 1942	
Load	bombs 400kg (882lb)	bombs 400kg	bombs 400kg
	8 RS-82 projectiles	8 RS-82 projectiles	8 RS-82 projectiles
All-up weight	5,720kg (12,613lb)	5,788kg (12,763lb)	n.a.
Speed at sea level	396km/h (246mph) *	380km/h (236mph)	385km/h (239mph)
	404.5km/h (251mph) **	n.a.	396km/h** (246mph)
at 1,000m (3,280ft)	410km/h (255mph)	393km/h (244mph)	400km/h (249mph)
at rated altitude of 2,000–2,500m (6,500–8,200ft)	426km/h (265mph)	406km/h (252mph)	414km/h (257mph)
at 3,000m (9,840ft)	423km/h (263mph)	398km/h (247mph)	409km/h (254mph)
at 4,000m (13,120ft)	414km/h (257mph)	384km/h (239mph)	397km/h (247mph)
at 5,000m (16,400ft)	395km/h (245mph)	364km/h (226mph)	379km/h (236mph)

* speed at nominal power rating of the engine (supercharger pressure at 1,160mm Hg)
** speed at boosted power rating of the engine (supercharger pressure at 1,280mm Hg)

Specification of the Single-Seater Aircraft (*continued*)

Rate of climb with engine revs at 2,080 to 2,150rpm

Aircraft	No.2611	No.1904
Weight of the aircraft	5,720kg (12,613lb)	5,670kg (12,502lb)

Vertical speed
at altitude of:

0m (ft)	7.1m/sec (23.3ft/sec)	6.4m/sec (21ft/sec))
1,000m (3,280ft)	7.1m/sec (23.3ft/sec)	6.6m/sec (21.65ft/sec)
2,000m (6,560ft)	7.1m/sec (23.3ft/sec)	7.1m/sec (23.3ft/sec)
3,000m (9,840ft)	5.8m/sec (19ft/sec)	5.6m/sec (18.4ft/sec)
4,000m (13,120ft)	4.2m/sec (13.8ft/sec)	4.0m/sec (13.1ft/sec)
5,000m (16,400ft)	2.5m/sec (8.2ft/sec)	2.2m/sec (7.2ft/sec)
6,000m (19,690ft)	0.8m/sec (2.6ft/sec)	0.5m/sec (1.6ft sec)

Time to altitude:

1,000m (3,280ft)	2.3min	2.3min
2,000m (6,560ft)	4.3min	4.5min
3,000m (9,840ft)	7.4min	8.0min
4,000m (13,120ft)	10.3min	11.0min
5,000m (16,400ft)	14.7min	16.6min
6,000m (19,690ft)	26.0min	28.0min

Indicated airspeed on climb trajectory

0m (ft)	250km/h (155mph)	244km/h (152mph)
1,000m (3,280ft)	250km/h (155mph)	249km/h (155mph)
2,000m (6,560ft)	250km/h (155mph)	247km/h (153mph)
3,000m (9,840ft)	245km/h (152mph)	243km/h (151mph)
4,000m (13,120ft)	238km/h (148mph)	238km/h (148mph)
5,000m (16,400ft)	n.a.	232km/h (144mph)
6,000m (19,690ft)	n.a.	225km/h (140mph)

Supercharger pressure, mm Hg

0m (ft)	1,170	1,160
1,000m (3,280ft)	1,170	1,160
2,000m (6,560ft)	1,170	1,160
3,000m (9,840ft)	1,080	1,050
4,000m (13,120ft)	970	930
5,000m (16,400ft)	850	820
6,000m (19,690ft)	n.a.	n.a.

Practical ceiling of aircraft No.1904: 6,000m (19,690ft); of aircraft No.2611: 6,200m (20,340ft)

Time of climb to practical ceiling: 28–34min

Airfield performance of single-seater aircraft:
take-off run and take-off

Aircraft	No.1904	No.2611	(average figures for 6 aircraft)
Weight of aircraft	5,690kg (12,546lb)	5,720kg (12,613lb)	

Operation mode: take-off at supercharger pressure: 1,160mm Hg, 2,150rpm

Take-off run	431m (1,414ft)	480m (1,575ft)	460m (1,509ft)
Duration of take-off run	18.0sec	18.6sec	18.3sec
Indicated airspeed at lift-off	150km/h (93mph)	163km/h (101mph)	157km/h (98mph)

Take-off distance to height of 25m (82ft) 1,200m (3,940ft)

Operation mode: take-off at boosted rating, supercharger pressure: 1,280mm Hg, 2,150rpm

Take-off run	409m (1,342ft)	440m (1,444ft)	420m (1,378ft)
Duration of take-off run	16.0sec	17.2sec	17.0sec
Indicated airspeed at lift-off	150km/h (93mph)	162km/h (101mph)	154km/h (96mph)

Take-off distance to height of 25m (82ft) 1,100m (3,610ft)

Landing and landing run

Aircraft	No.1904	No. 2611	(average figures for 6 aircraft)

Operation mode: flaps deflected, use of wheel brakes

Weight of aircraft	5,080kg (11,201lb)	5226kg (11,523lb)	n.a.
Landing run	365m (1,198ft)	365m (1,198ft)	400m (1,312ft)
Duration of landing run	17.5sec	17.5sec	19sec

Landing speed (indicated airspeed) 139km/h (86mph)

Landing distance 825m (2,707ft)

Note: performance figures in the tables are quoted for ISA and zero-wind condition.

Flight mode was to be chosen on basis of special instructions issued by the Directorate of Operation and Maintenance, Red Army Air Force.

Specification of the Two-Seater Aircraft

Aircraft	Production Il-2 c/n. 1874833 Plant No.18, 1942	Production Il-2 c/n. 302399 Plant No.30, 1943	Production Il-2U c/n. 1876152 Plant No.18, 1943
Engine type	AM-38	AM-38F	AM-38F
Engine power, hp			
at take-off	1,665	1,720	1,760
at rated altitude	1,575	1,575	1,575
Length, m (ft)	11.6 (38ft 1in)	11.6 (38ft 1in)	11.6 (38ft 1in)
Wing span, m (ft)	14.6 (47ft 10⅘in)	14.6 (47ft 10⅘in)	14.6 (47ft 10⅘in)
Wing area, sq m (sq ft)	38.5 (414.45)	38.5 (414.45)	38.5 (414.45)
Weights, kg (lb):			
empty	4,427 (9,761)	4,625 (10,198)	4,300 (9,480)
fuel and oil	535+65 (1,180+143)	535+60 (1,180+143)	470+35 (1,180+143)
total load	1,715 (3,782)	1,535 (3,385)	791 (1,744)
All-up weight, kg (lb)	6,142 (13,543)	6,160 (13,583)	5,091 (11,226)
Maximum speed, km/h (mph):			
at sea level	370 (230)	391 (243)	390 (242)
at rated altitude, m(ft)	411 (255)	405 (252)	403 (250)
	at 2,880 (9,450)	at 1,320 (4,330)	at 1,100 (3,610)
Landing speed, km/h (mph)	n.a.	136 (85)	140 (87)
Time to altitude, min			
1,000m (3,280ft)	n.a.	2.2	2.0
5,000m (16,400ft)	16	15	14.8
Range at sea level, km (miles)	685 (426)	685 (426)	n.a.
Take-off run, m (ft)	498 (1,634)	370 (1,214)	385 (1,263)
Landing run, m (ft)	608 (1,995)	500 (1,640)	600 (1,968)
Offensive armament:			
bombs, kg (lb):			
normal bomb load	400 (882)	100 (220)	200 (441)
maximum bomb load	600 (1,323)	200 (441)	–
cannon:	VYa	NS-37	–
number × calibre, mm	2 × 23	2 × 37	–
ammunition load, rounds	300	100	–
machine-guns	ShKAS	ShKAS	ShKAS
number × calibre, mm	2 × 7.62	2 × 7.62	2 × 7.62
ammunition load, rounds	1,500	3,000	1,500
unguided rockets:			
number × calibre	4 × RO-82	–	2 × RO-82
Defensive armament:	UB	UB	–
number × calibre, mm	1 × 12.7	1 × 12.7	–

CHAPTER SIX

Il-2s Abroad

By far the greatest number of the Il-2 attack aircraft were committed to action by the Red Army Air Regiments in 1941–45. During the closing stages of the war a limited number were assigned to air units staffed by Polish and Czechoslovak airmen which later formed the basis of their own air forces after their post-war revival, now as the Soviet Union's allies. The same applies to Yugoslavia. Other recipients of the aircraft included Bulgaria and, interestingly, Mongolia.

Poland

The build-up of the air elements of the Polish armed forces on Soviet territory began in 1943, priority being given to fighter units. It was not until 1944 that the first nominally Polish Attack Air Regiments equipped with the Il-2s made their appearance. It must be borne in mind that most of the experienced Polish airmen who happened to be in the Soviet territory were, in pursuance of agreements between the Allies, sent to the United Kingdom where they flew against Germany. There was a shortage of skilled Polish flying personnel which was only partially alleviated by the extensive training organized at Soviet flying schools. To speed up the formation of a Polish air element, the Soviet leadership decided to assign some Soviet Air Force units to it. Thus in April 1944 the 611th Attack Air Regiment of the Soviet Air Force, equipped with thirty-two Il-2s and a single Polikarpov Po-2, was transferred from the 6th Air Army to the 1st Army of the Polish Armed Forces (Wojsko Polsko) and became the first operational Polish Il-2 unit. In October 1944 the 611th Attack Air Regiment was renamed and became the 3rd Attack Air Regiment, or PLSz (*Pułk Lotniczy Szturmowy*) in the 1st Air Division of the Soviet-sponsored Polish Air Force. It saw action for the first time on 23 August 1944, attacking artillery positions at Mazovsk, near Warsaw. Other Polish units

included the 2nd Attack Air Division (DLSz – *Dywizja Lotnicza Szturmowa*) comprising the 6th, 7th and 8th PLSz (these were based, respectively, on the 658th, the 382nd and the 384th Attack Air Regiments of the Soviet Air Force). The 2nd Air Division was formed at Volchansk (Kharkov Military District) on 30 September. In March 1945 the 2nd Air Division had 102 Il-2s and four UIl-2 trainer versions on strength. To a considerable extent, the nominally Polish units were initially staffed by Russian personnel due, as mentioned above, to the acute shortage of trained Polish pilots and technicians. In addition, the Il-2s were put on the strength of the 14th Separate Reconnaissance and Spotting Air Regiment (*Samodzielny Pułk Rozpoznania Lotniczego i Korygovania Ognia Artylerii*), as well as the 15th Reserve Air Regiment (*Samodzielny Zapasowy Pułk Lotniczy*) and the Military Pilots School (*Woiskowa Szkola Lotnicza*) in Zamoscie. In addition to the combat Il-2s, a number of Il-2U trainers were supplied. The training of the Polish personnel also took place inside the Soviet Union in Kinel (according to other sources in Grechovka) (gunners) and Chkalov (pilots). Polish crews gradually took over from Russian. The Polish Il-2s took part in combat over Germany; notably, they were used to attack the defensive so-called Pomerania Line, and took part in the liberation of the Kolobrzeg harbour from elements of the German army. There the Il-2s of the 3rd PLSz sank a transport vessel and four self-propelled barges. Polish Il-2s also saw action in the Berlin campaign. On 24 April elements of the 2nd Polish Attack Air Division began their attacks against the troops which were trying to force their way to Berlin from the north-west. The Polish attack aircraft thus made a contribution to the complete encirclement of German troops in Berlin, and in the following days they strafed retreating columns. The biggest single mission flown by Polish Il-2s during that operation resulted, it was claimed, in the

destruction of ten tanks and more than a dozen other vehicles. The last combat mission was flown by Polish Il-2s on 3 May. By then the Polish units had to their credit twenty-five knocked-out tanks, more than 1,300 other destroyed vehicles, 290 railway cars and many other pieces of the enemy *matériel*.

After the war, one more Polish unit equipped with the Il-2s – the 2nd PLSz – was formed, but later a reorganization of the air units resulted in the Polish Air Force comprising only three Attack Air Units in 1946 (4th, 5th and 6th PLSz). Well-worn, wartime Il-2s were gradually replaced by factory-new machines of late versions, with increased sweep-back on outer panels. Sometimes the aircraft were put to some rather unorthodox uses in cases of environmental emergency. Thus in March 1947 Il-2s from the 5th and the 6th PLSz took part in the crushing of huge masses of ice that had blocked the flow of the Vistula. They also took part in peacetime military operations against armed groups of Ukrainian nationalists.

Worth mentioning is a curious episode associated with the post-war service of the Il-2s in Poland. In 1948 the maintenance personnel of an attack air regiment stationed at Wroclaw undertook to assemble a complete new Il-2 aircraft from the parts that they hoped to recover at a scrapyard for written-off aircraft in the vicinity of their airfield. The initiative belonged to Viacheslav Budo, a Soviet technician seconded to this regiment. His enthusiasm was shared by Sgt Henryk Bednarkiewicz, Senior Sgt Gustav Czernigiewicz, Sgt Ryszard Fordynacki and Senior Sgt Jan Tumidajewicz. In their spare time they roamed about the yard searching out the necessary parts which often had to be restored to their original condition. Finally, in the summer of 1948 their efforts were crowned with success – an Il-2 assembled from recovered parts was completed. Some problems arose initially with the acceptance formalities, but eventually a special high-level commission

At least three Il-2s captured by the Germans were restored to airworthy condition and evaluated at Flugerprobungsstelle Rechlin. Yefim Gordon archive

In addition to standard 'flying tanks', the Polish Air Force had a small number of Il-2KR artillery spotter/reconnaissance aircraft (note the forward location of the aerial mast). Yefim Gordon archive

A two-seater Il-2 in Polish Air Force markings.
Yefim Gordon archive

from the Air Force command gave its approval and the aircraft was flown and taken into the inventory of the attack air regiment as a training aircraft.

In 1949 the Il-2s began to be phased out and supplanted by Il-10s.

Czechoslovakia

The formation of the first Czechoslovak Attack Air Regiment dates back to September 1944, when the training of Czechoslovak personnel started in the 41st Reconnaissance Air Regiment of the Red Army Air Force. The new unit, named the 3rd Attack Air Regiment, reached its operational strength in the winter of 1944, and in January 1945 it was officially made part of the newly formed 1st Czechoslovak Independent Air Division. It had thirty-three Il-2s and two Il-2Us on strength. The unit took part in combat only to a limited extent, the first sortie being flown on 14 April 1945. The last wartime mission was flown on 2 May against a railway station at Tesine. During its brief operational career, the 3rd Czechoslovak Attack Regiment flew 284 sorties, shooting down one enemy fighter and destroying some forty military vehicles, twenty-two other vehicles, one locomotive, thirty-seven wagons, two fuel depots, three munitions depots, three buildings and sixty-eight anti-aircraft gun sites at the cost of eight Il-2s lost (four shot down and four lost in accidents).

In July 1945, after the end of the war, this Attack Air Regiment, the only of its kind in the Czechoslovak Air Force, was placed under the authority of the country's Ministry of Defence and renamed the 30th Ostrava Attack Air Regiment. The regiment, based at Trenčanske Biskupice, had on strength twenty-four Il-2s and two Il-2Us, which were allocated the Czechoslovak names of B-31 and CB-31, respectively. In 1948–49 these aircraft were phased out. Some Il-2s of the Czechoslovak Air Force underwent upgrades, including the fitting of German radio equipment.

Bulgaria

Being an ally of Germany from 1941, Bulgaria remained neutral towards the Soviet Union; during the closing stages of the war Bulgaria broke her ties with Germany and joined the anti-Hitler coalition, entering into close cooperation with the USSR. Shortly before the end of hostilities, in March 1945, an agreement was signed between the Soviet Union and Bulgaria which provided, *inter alia*, for the delivery of 120

Il-2s and three Il-2Us to the Bulgarian Air Force. Two more of the training version were supplied subsequently (seven, according to other sources). The aircraft reached Bulgaria in several batches over a period of eight months, the last deliveries being made in mid November. The Il-2s were put on the strength of two Mixed Air Divisions based at Sambol and Plovdiv and were retained in service as late as 1954, although they began to be supplanted by the Il-10s at a fairly early stage of their Bulgarian career. Some Bulgarian Il-2s had the wooden sections of their fuselages replaced by all-metal ones received from Yugoslavia.

Yugoslavia

As in the case of Poland and Czechoslovakia, the post-war Yugoslav Air Force, including its attack element, had its origins in war-time events at the Soviet–German front. From 1944 several hundred Yugoslav pilots and technicians underwent training in the Soviet Union at Krasnodar. This was effected with the assistance of personnel of the 10th Guards Attack Air Division of the Red Army; it resulted in the formation of two Attack Air Regiments staffed with Yugoslavs (No.421 and No.422), which were committed to action against German troops and flew some sorties before the end of hostilities. On 10 May 1945, just after Victory Day, pursuant to an agreement between Stalin and Tito, the 10th Guards Attack Air Division received an order to transfer all its equipment to the newly-born Yugoslav Air Force. The transfer ceremony took place on 14 May in Tisa: seventy-eight Il-2s and four Il-2Us changed hands. The latter were subsequently supplemented by two trainer versions converted locally from combat aircraft. Several more batches of Il-2s were delivered to Yugoslavia from the Soviet Union after the end of the war; eighty Il-2s were obtained by the Yugoslavs from Bulgaria in 1947. In all, the number of the Il-2s (including trainer versions) totalled 213. They soldiered on until 1954, as was the case in Bulgaria. The Soviet–Yugoslav discord of 1949 and the severance of all ties between Moscow and Belgrade put an end to the flow of spare parts from the Soviet Union and prompted Yugoslavia to take steps in order to tackle the issue. The Yugoslav industry (Ikarus factory) began producing metal structural elements of the Il-2 airframe to replace the original wooden ones. More than a dozen Il-2s were converted into trainers. Some machines were adapted for night-time operations, receiving black camouflage. The falling-out between the two countries prevented any Il-10s from reaching Yugoslavia as a successor to the Il-2s.

Mongolia

The country possessed only a token air force, comprising several dozen aircraft of different types. Among these were several Il-2s (the precise number is not known). There is a picture showing Il-2s with Mongolian national insignia. No details of their service career are available.

This Il-2 coded '24 White' was operated by the Mongolian People's Republic Air Force. The characteristic *zoyombo* national insignia are clearly visible. Sergey and Dmitriy Komissarov archive

CHAPTER SEVEN

The Il-10 – a Worthy Successor

Blind Alley

The Il-10 attack aircraft, which undoubtedly ranks among the noteworthy successes of the Soviet aircraft industry, was first conceived, curiously enough, not as an attack aircraft but as a fighter. Practically in parallel with the development of the Il-2I fighter version, Ilyushin was ordered to create a single-seater armoured fighter for low and medium altitudes, which received the designation Il-1. It was to have a top speed of 600km/h (372mph) and possess manoeuvrability characteristics that would enable it to fight effectively the latest German fighters: the Messerschmitt Bf 109G-2 and the Focke-Wulf Fw 190F-4. The idea for such

a fighter was suggested by Ilyushin himself in a letter dated 13 April 1943 and addressed to Shakhurin. A response followed in the shape of a directive issued by the State Defence Committee on 17 May which tasked Plant No.18 with producing two examples of the Il-1 armoured fighter powered by the AM-42 engine in a single- and a two-seater version, to be submitted for testing in July. Provision for the construction of a single-seater and a two-seater version was presumably arranged by Ilyushin for the following reason: he, according to some sources, was from the outset extremely sceptical about the viability of the armoured fighter concept and was convinced that the front was much more in need of a high-speed,

manoeuvrable attack aircraft. Therefore he saw to it that the Il-1 be designed with a view to ensuring not only the stipulated fighter performance but also the possibility of using this aircraft later on as a high-speed, agile, attack aircraft.

The Il-1 was designed around a new powerplant – the Mikulin AM-42 liquid-cooled V-12 engine rated at 1,471kW (2,000hp) for take-off. The engineers obtained a high lift/drag ratio by using new wings with a higher wing loading and, accordingly, reduced area as compared to the Il-2I. The shape of the armoured body was improved by placing the water radiator and the oil cooler entirely within the armoured body behind the centre section's front spar. Cooling air was supplied by two intakes in the wing roots and air ducts around the engine; after passing through the radiators it escaped through a slot on the underside of the armoured body, regulated by a flexible piece of armour plate. As a result, the fuselage contours were more streamlined than the Il-2's.

Two views of the Il-1 heavy armoured fighter. The aircraft differed considerably from the Il-2; the forward fuselage, tail unit and landing gear design were almost identical to those of the later Il-10. The small canopy is noteworthy. Yefim Gordon archive

The undercarriage layout was also new. The single-strut main legs retracted aft into the wing centre section, the wheels turning 86 degrees to lie flat, completely buried in the wings. The armament comprised two 23mm VYa cannon in the wing outer panels outside the propeller disc area. There was no provision for bombs in the normal configuration, but 200kg (441lb) could be carried externally in the overload version. To cater for protection in the rear, a cassette with ten AG-2 aerial grenades was carried.

New Start

Work on the Il-1 proceeded slowly because the OKB was overburdened with urgent matters concerning the manufacture of production Il-2s and their current improvement. The stipulated dates for the completion of the prototypes had to be revised and postponed several times. On 19 May 1944 the test pilot V. Kokkinaki took the Il-1 to the air for the first time. A maximum speed of 580km/h (360mph) was reached during manufacturer's trials.

Even before the Il-1 fighter had completed its tests, Ilyushin realized that it had no future and it was decided not to submit it for State acceptance trials. This was because the Air Force had gained air superiority in the middle of 1944 and there was no further need for an armoured fighter. Therefore, concurrently with the work on the fighter, Ilyushin started designing a two-seater, high-speed,

manoeuvrable, armoured attack aircraft based on the Il-1's structure. Initially, the new aircraft was also designated Il-1 and this project was soon given the highest priority – so much so that the two-seater version was actually completed before the single-seater. Factory testing of the two-seater Il-1 began on 18 or 20 April 1944.

As on the TsKB-55 prototype, the armoured fuselage of the new attack aircraft contained not only the engine and pilot's cockpit but also the gunner's. Unlike the Il-2, the gunner was seated just aft of the pilot's armoured backrest. He was protected from the rear by an armoured bulkhead, which also served as a part of the fuselage primary structure. This compact cockpit layout avoided a great longitudinal distribution of mass, thus improving manoeuvrability and handling. The engineering team headed by Ilyushin designed a more rational system of armour, reinforced in the lower part of the cowling and made thinner on the sides of the cockpits. Building on operational experience with the Il-2, the engineers concluded that no armour was needed on the upper forward fuselage section. This area had aluminium skins. The Il-1 had newly developed double armouring of vital structural members, comprising two 8mm (³⁄₈in) armour plates with a space in between. This protected the crew not only from machine-gun bullets but also from 20mm (.78 calibre) cannon shells. In keeping with the OKB's tradition, the armoured shell was integrated into the fuselage primary structure.

The Il-1 two-seater attack aircraft had the same dimensions and structural features as its single-seater precursor, but its structure was all-metal. The offensive armament was similar to that of the Il-2, comprising two 23mm VYa guns with 300 rounds, and two ShKAS machine-guns with 1,500 rounds (provision was made for the eventual replacement of the VYa canon with the 11-P37, or NS-37 cannon, but there is no evidence that this happened). Like the Il-2, its normal bomb load was 400kg (880lb); in overload configuration it could carry up to 600kg (1,320lb). The Il-1 had only two bombbays (four on the Il-2), but they were designed so that small bombs weighing up to 50kg (110lb) could be loaded direct, without bomb cassettes. This speeded up the loading of bombs, reducing mission preparation time. External bomb racks were used to carry two 100 or 250kg (220, 550lb) bombs. Four RO-82 launch rails for unguided rockets were mounted under the wings. The defensive armament was considerably increased. The Il-1 had an experimental 20mm Shpital'nyi Sh-20 gun with 150 rounds installed in a VU-7 turret, and the tail was protected by a DAG cassette with ten 2kg (4.4lb) aerial grenades (a special defensive installation comprising the 20mm BT-20 cannon was designed for the two-seater Il-1, but it was installed on only a later version).

Close-up of the VU-7 ball turret with a Sh-20 cannon. Yefim Gordon archive

In April 1944 the manufacture of the two-seater Il-1 prototype was completed at the Kuibyshev aircraft factory's experimental shop. It was transferred for final assembly to Plant No.240 in Moscow. Following the VVS's tradition of allocating even type numbers to attack aircraft and bombers, it received a new designation under which it would enter production and service, becoming the Il-10.

On 18 April, after the installation of the Mikulin AM-42 prototype engine and the completion of systems tests, the Il-10 made its maiden flight with Vladimir K. Kokkinaki at the controls. Kokkinaki soon completed the initial flight tests and on 13 May the aircraft was transferred to NII VVS for State acceptance trials which lasted till 27 May. These included forty-three flights, most of them performed by Lt Col A. Dolgov. He was well pleased with the aircraft, noting its high stability, controllability and performance. He also stated that the Il-10's piloting techniques were no different from those of the production Il-2. According to some sources, as many as three Il-10 prototypes were built and simultaneously presented for acceptance trials, which made it possible to complete them in a mere two weeks.

At a 6,335kg (13,966lb) AUW the Il-10 had a top speed of 507km/h (315mph) at S/L and 551km/h (342mph) at 2,800m (9,000ft) – 150km/h (93mph) greater than that of a production Il-2. It climbed to 5,000m (16,404ft) in 5min, compared to 8min for the Il-2. Its practical ceiling was 7,300m (23,940ft), and the range was 800km (497 miles) with a bomb load of 400kg (880lb). Although its range was adequate and field performance was good, the take-off run was somewhat longer than the Il-2's. There were also some deficiencies, mostly concerned with the unreliability of the new AM-42 engine, which obviously required much more development. Generally, however, the test results proved the soundness of the concept. The optimum combination of powerful offensive and defensive armament in an armoured attack aircraft with high speed and good agility not only allowed effective, multiple missions to be flown, but enabled the Il-10 to engage all types of enemy fighter. In a fly-off between three attack aircraft types powered by the AM-42 – the Sukhoi Su-6, the Il-8 and the Il-10 – the last emerged as the winner.

The first prototype of the Il-10 attack aircraft seen during State acceptance trials. These views illustrate the new main-gear design, the completely enclosed cockpit and the large rudder horn balance. Note that the prototype had a Shpital'nyi Sh-20 cannon in the ball turret. Yefim Gordon archive

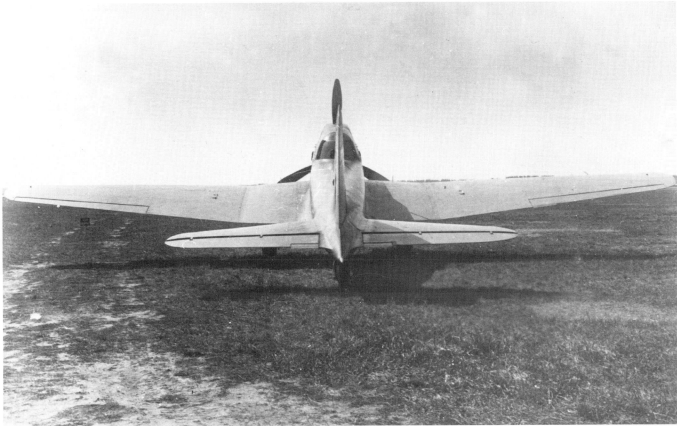

Two more views of the first prototype Il-10. Yefim Gordon archive

An Il-10 undergoing static tests at TsAGI. Yefim Gordon archive

A pre-production Il-10 pictured during trials. Note the high-gloss surface finish, the absence of the DF loop aerial ahead of the fin, and the machine-gun in the ball turret. Yefim Gordon archive

Into Production

A technical report on prototype construction in 1944, issued at the beginning of 1945, stated:

In 1944 a major breakthrough was achieved in the matter of a serious improvement of the performance of our attack aircraft. The AM-42-powered Il-10 attack aircraft fully meets all the requirements and surpasses the AM-38F-powered Il-2 in speed by more than 100km/h at ground level and by nearly 150km/h at altitude.

Series production of the type began in August 1944, but it took some time before it gained momentum. There are conflicting statements concerning the planned figures and the actual output in the closing months of the year. According to some, the original plans called for 100 Il-10s to be manufactured by then, while in reality aircraft plants Nos 1 and 18 'did even better, producing 125 Il-10s by January 1945'. However, some documents present a different picture. On 29 August the NKAP issued order No.476ss, which tasked the two plants with organizing series manufacture of the Il-10 and set target production figures for them. Total production of the Il-10 by the two plants in the course of 1944 was to amount to 450 machines. The rate of production was to grow from month to month, the target figure for December being 125 from each plant. Reality proved to be somewhat different. Plants No.1 and 18 turned out initial batches of five machines each by 1 October. Production during the following three months was as follows: Plant No.1 manufactured twenty-five machines in October, seventy-three in November and forty-six in December. Plant No.18 produced five, thirty and thirty-three machines. That gives a total output of 212 from the two plants during the last three months of 1944, falling short of the planned figure of 450 (212 seems actually to be too high – a source states that combat units received only forty-one Il-10s from Plants No.1 and No.18 in the last three months of 1944). Mastering the Il-10 in production was far from trouble-free. The testing of several machines from the first production batches revealed a number of design faults both in the airframe and the engine; rectifying them led to the slowing down of the tempo of production, and even to halting it altogether for a while in December 1944, when an

Il-10 suffered a fatal crash caused by engine fire. Production was resumed on 26 December and proceeded at an ever-increasing tempo; by 1 May 1945 Plants No.1 and No.18 delivered 785 Il-10s to the Air Force (not all reached the frontline units, though).

The 108th GvShAP, part of the 2nd Air Army, was the first unit to receive these formidable aircraft. Production machines differed slightly from the prototype. For instance, the experimental Sh-20 movable gun was replaced by a series-produced 12.7mm (.50 calibre) Berezin UBT machine-gun and later by the Berezin UB-20. The VU-7 turret was replaced by the broadly similar VU-8, previously used on Il-8 experimental attack aircraft. The armament fit of the Il-10 was subject to several upgrades and modifications in the course of production. For example, an order issued by NKAP on 12 February 1945 required Ilyushin to design guide rails for the Il-10 intended for M-13 rockets (an improved version of the RS-132). Simultaneously, production plants No.1 and 18 were tasked with beginning the manufacture of these devices, so that from 20 March 1945 onwards all Il-10s should be equipped with launching rails permitting the carriage of four RS-82 or four M-13 rockets.

Initial batches of the Il-10s, as can be gleaned from documents, lacked dust filters (presumably because these were not needed during winter months). On 30 April NKAP issued an order requiring Plants No.1 and 18 to manufacture all Il-10s with dust filters of the type which had been developed and tested by Plant No.18 on an Il-10, No.404. Special teams sent from these plants were to retrofit all the previously manufactured Il-10s with dust filters in a modified version, suitable for installation in field conditions.

Into Action and After the War

The Il-10s were committed to action for the first time on 2 February 1945; alongside their more numerous stablemates, the Il-2s, they made their contribution to the effort that resulted in final victory. After a few months' respite, they joined combat again when the Soviet Union declared war on Japan in August. The operational career and combat experiences of the Il-10 are described in the next chapter. When the war with Japan ended, all

Soviet Air Force attack air regiments converted to the Il-10.

The post-war history of its development is marked by efforts designed to further enhance performance and serviceability and widen the scope of its use. Much attention was also paid to rectifying numerous faults and defects that were revealed during the aircraft's operational life.

In 1946 steps were taken to improve the Il-10's armament fit. On 21 May the People's Commissariat of the Aircraft Industry issued Order No.313s, tasking the Ilyushin OKB and Plant No.18 with producing a version of the Il-10 armed with four NS-23 cannon. The machine was to be submitted for factory tests by 1 September. Accordingly, the two 23mm VYa cannon and two 7.62mm ShKAS machine-guns were replaced by four wing-mounted NS-23 cannon with 150rpg. These newly-developed cannon weighed barely more than half of their predecessors and their recoil was 1.6 times less, allowing a simple, light and easily serviced gun mount to be designed. They gave an increased weight of fire and higher accuracy because shell scatter decreased to between 50 and 30 per ecnt of the former value. The four NS-23 cannon were supplemented by a B-20T cannon on the VU-9 flexible mount. This version was produced in quantity.

The same NKAP order envisaged the construction of a prototype Il-10 with a modified bombing armament, permitting the attachment of bombs direct to their shackles, without cable girdles supporting the bombs from beneath. This prototype, also featuring pneumatic control of the bomb-bay doors, was to be submitted for testing in the NII VVS by 15 June. Another three prototypes thus modified were to have, additionally, the new VU-9 turret equipped with the 20mm Berezin cannon (BT-20) instead of the VU-8 turret equipped with the 12.7mm Berezin UBT machine-gun. In November the Il-10s incorporating these features successfully passed State acceptance trials, and the modified bombing armament was introduced into series production starting with the thirtieth production batch. The weapons range was expanded to include new powerful PTAB bombs and improved rockets capable of destroying heavy tanks and other armoured vehicles. As for the VU turret with the BT-20 cannon, this installation was first ground-tested on the

An early-production Il-10 at NII VVS during check-out trials. Yefim Gordon archive

Another early-production Il-10 on the apron at NII VVS (Shcholkovo AB). The water radiator inlets in the wing roots are easily visible. Yefim Gordon archive

This Il-10 is interesting in that it has a raked aerial mast mounted further aft and a gun camera on the defensive machine-gun. Yefim Gordon archive

Il-2 as early as January 1945, and Ilyushin suggested that it be introduced into series production as early as February, without waiting for the final results of the State tests. However, it took more time than he had expected. The State acceptance tests of two Il-10s equipped with these turrets (c/n 1896306 and 105123, Plants No.18 and No.1, respectively) were duly conducted and completed with positive results. After the final report on the results of the tests had been endorsed on 6 September 1945, the Air Force Command issued a request for 100 Il-10s with the VU-9 turret and the BT-20 cannon to be manufactured and delivered for service tests.

A trainer version, designated UIl-10 or Il-10U (Il-10UT) (*uchebno-trenirovochnyi* – for instruction and training), was also manufactured on a small scale. Specifications for this version were endorsed by deputy Commander-in-Chief of the Air Force F.Ya. Falaleyev on 21 April 1945. But as early as 26 February the OKB had been ordered to produce production drawings for this version. The drawings were to be transferred to Plant No.1 before 15 March, and the first production UIl-10 was to be submitted for State acceptance tests on 1 May at the latest. On 16 May an example of the UIl-10 arrived at the NII VVS for testing, which started on 20 May and was successfully completed at the beginning of June. The document (Act) presenting the results of State trials of the UIl-10 was endorsed by Commander-in-Chief of the Air Force, Chief AM A.A. Novikov on 4 June.

The example tested was a production UIl-10, c/n 106085, manufactured by Plant No.1. It had the gunner's station fitted out as a second cockpit for the instructor. The defensive armament was deleted and the offensive armament was slightly simplified. Also removed was the armour bulkhead between the cockpits of the pilot and the gunner. The aircraft was stripped of the VYa-23 cannon but retained the ShKAS machine-guns; also removed were the DAG cassette for aerial grenades and two of the four rocket launch rails. However, some examples had a full complement of cannon and machine-guns. In some sources the armament of the UIl-10 is said to comprise two VYa cannon, later replaced by the NS-23 cannon, and two launch rails for rockets, with the ShKAS machine-guns deleted.

Some examples of the Il-10U in foreign service lacked the armament altogether. Machines from different batches featured different types of rear cockpit glazing. The first production version of the Il-10U was deficient in certain respects and required some improvements. The instructor's cockpit provided a poor view and generally fell short of the requirements introduced in 1945. The opening and the closing of the cockpit canopy presented some difficulties and the instructor lacked radio contact with the ground. Thus Plant No.18 was tasked with presenting a modified example of the Il-10U for State acceptance trials to the NII VVS by 25

Close-up of the aft end of an Il-10 modified for spinning trials. A spin recovery parachute is installed on a special truss attached to the rear fuselage. Yefim Gordon archive

June 1946. No information is available as to the nature of the modifications. The UIl-10 was manufactured by Plants Nos 1 and 18, production totalling 280. Plant No.1 produced 268 of these aircraft, 227 in 1945.

Further Changes

In 1949 several Il-10s were experimentally fitted with reversible AV-15 propellers, which made it possible to reduce the landing run considerably. The pilots who conducted trials of the machines were pleased with this new feature and

The prototype of the Il-10U (UIl-10) conversion trainer at NII VVS. The redesigned cockpit canopy is clearly visible. Yefim Gordon archive

recommended that the new propellers be put into series production. However, the Ministry of the Aircraft Industry was opposed and effectively blocked it by asserting that the use of reversible propellers during the landing run would be accompanied by increased engine ingestion of dust, thus curtailing its service life. As a result, the propellers were consigned to oblivion.

The Il-10 was adapted to some other duties in addition to its role as a combat aircraft. Thus on 2 September 1946 the Ministry of the Aircraft Industry tasked Ilyushin's OKB with producing a target-towing version. A prototype was to be submitted for State acceptance tests within two months. The appropriately equipped Il-10 had a towing cable drum fitted under the fuselage just aft of the wing. A more unorthodox way of using the Il-10 for gunnery training purposes envisaged converting it into a piloted target aircraft. Protected by appropriate armour plating, it was expected to withstand being shot at with frangible bullets. Development of this version was included into the plan for prototype construction for 1946–47; no information is available as to the results.

In May 1946 Ilyushin's OKB was ordered to produce a prototype of the Il-10 version powered by the AM-43 engine. It was a further development of the AM-42 engine, boosted in rpm. The AM-43 engine with direct injection had a take-off rating of 2,300hp and a nominal rating of 2,000hp at 2,300m (7,540ft). The order, No.313 issued by the Ministry of the Aircraft Industry on 21 May, stipulated that the prototype should pass factory tests by 1 September. However, on 6 September the Ministry issued order No.607s which cancelled the task for the AM-43-powered version of the Il-10, citing the termination of manufacture of the AM-43 engine. No mention is made of any prototype having been built. Curiously, some researchers have produced a somewhat different version of these events. The Il-10 powered by the AM-43 with the AV-5L-24 propeller was allegedly built in December 1945 at Plant No.18 and tested, although no record has been found. It is assumed that the tests did not proceed beyond taxiing runs and hops because of the troublesome functioning of the engine. It may well be that the construction of the prototype actually did take place in December as the OKB's

'private venture' and was 'legalized' at a later stage through a formal NKAP order.

New Lease of Life

The Il-10 was manufactured until 1948, by which time 4,540 had been built. Two years later, when the Korean War broke out, the Il-10s operated by North Korea went into action and their operations at the start of the war were regarded as successful. The Soviet Air Force Command came to the conclusion that the Il-10 could still be useful and should be reinstated in production. On the 12 January 1951 the Soviet government issued a directive stipulating that the manufacture of the Il-10 be organized at Plant No.168 at Rostov-on-Don. A massive redesign undertaken in this connection by the OKB resulted in the Il-10M (*modifitsirovannyi* – updated). The new version differed from the older one mainly in having new wings with a 3sq m (32.25sq ft) bigger area and characteristically squared-off wingtips instead of rounded ones. The wings featured a uniform dihedral all along their span, as distinct from the original Il-10 wings with their combination

A production UIl-10 runs up its engine on a tactical airfield. The hinged portion of the instructor's canopy has been removed. Yefim Gordon archive

of a level wing centre section and dihedralled wing outer panels. New slotted flaps with better lift properties were installed on the underside of the wings. The horizontal tail, also altered in plan form, was raised 75mm (3in) to move it out of the wing slipstream. The area of all control surfaces was increased considerably and modified flaps were introduced. The aircraft's total length increased by 750mm (2ft 5½in), starting with the second prototype (the first being a kind of a transitional type, featuring the 'old' short fuselage in combination with the 'new' wing). The tailwheel was moved 700 mm (2ft 3½in) to aft. The higher gross weight required the main undercarriage legs to be reinforced and equipped with bigger wheels. Changes were also made to the armament, the NS-23 cannons giving way to new Nudelman/Rikhter NR-23 cannon of the same calibre but with an increased rate of fire, each with 600rpg. The bombing armament was supplemented by racks under the detachable outer wings, permitting the carriage of 250kg (550lb) bombs and 300ltr (66gal) auxiliary fuel tanks. An electrically-powered VU-9M gun turret was installed, enabling the flexible cannon to move faster; it was equipped with the 20mm BT-20EN cannon with 150 rounds.

The first production Il-10Ms displayed insufficient directional stability. Its cause was traced to the gussets fitted to the rudder in order to eliminate previously revealed self-oscillations. The fault was remedied by mounting a ventral strake beneath the rear fuselage; this became a standard feature on all production Il-10Ms. Another problem revealed itself in the course of the service introduction of the Il-10M; it may best be described by quoting a passage from the memoirs of Marina Popovich, a well-known woman test pilot:

At one time reports started coming in from service units to the effect that the Il-10M was 'misbehaving' in spin. A need arose to test this aircraft urgently. This testing was entrusted to Mikhail Stepanovich [Tvelenev]. He was to establish precisely what happened when this otherwise rather docile aircraft entered a spin, and then to work out authoritative recommendations for service units.

Popovich gives the following account of a situation which arose in one of Tvelenev's test flights:

It is time to recover from the spin. But the control surfaces resist, as if they were blocked. The heavy machine continued its rapid rotation. Ivan Stepanovich pressed the right pedal with all the force he was capable of, and then, using his both hands, tried to push the control stick energetically forward. However, it would not move. At the cost of an extreme exertion he succeeded in pushing the stick forward and retaining it in this position. The aircraft reluctantly recovered from the spin . . . That's what appears to be the reason for alarming reports from the service units . . . The pilots simply lack the physical force to overcome the resistance of the control surfaces . . . The decoding of the test equipment recordings revealed the level of control forces: on the pedals they reached 100kg [220lb], on the control stick – more than 50kg [110lb].

Aircraft of this type were immediately grounded pending the elimination of the faults.

There is evidence that the Il-10M was used for target towing. The drum for the towing cable was mounted under the fuselage just aft of the wing; the fuselage tail-cone was cut down. One production Il-10M was experimentally fitted with a liquid-fuel rocket booster in the aft fuselage. The fuselage tail-cone was cut down immediately behind the empennage to provide the opening for the rocket engine nozzle.

The Il-10M was in production from 1952 till 1954. During that period Plant No.168 manufactured 136 (a figure of 146 is quoted in some sources).

The Il-10M prototype at Moscow's central airfield (Khodynka), showing the twin cannons and rocket launch rails. Yefim Gordon archive

This Il-10M features a rocket booster in the cropped tail-cone; a large ventral fin has been added for better directional stability. Yefim Gordon archive

CHAPTER EIGHT

The Il-10 in Combat

The first 125 production-standard Il-10s were manufactured by Plants No.1 and No.18 in January 1945. The 108th GvShAP, part of the 2nd Air Army advancing towards Berlin, was the first unit to receive these formidable aircraft. The forty-five machines delivered to it were intended for service trials.

The Il-10 got its baptism of fire on 2 February 1945, when a squadron of the 108th GvShAP led by F. Zhigarin (Hero of the Soviet Union) attacked tanks and motorized infantry near the Neisse river in the region of Sprottau airfield, the unit's base. Despite AA fire and the activity of German fighters, the Il-10s successfully accomplished their mission, returning home unscathed. In the course of the service tests, airmen of the 108th GvShAP destroyed or damaged six armoured vehicles, sixty trucks and a hundred cartloads of the supplies. A report on the results of the service tests stated:

Availability of a greater range of speeds and better manoeuvrability make the task of escort fighters easier and enable the aircraft to engage in an aerial combat with the enemy. Complete armour protection of the crew cockpits enhances the aircraft's survivability . . . Ease of handling and relatively easy conversion of both flying and ground personnel make it possible to introduce this aircraft into squadron service within the shortest time possible.

Fighting in the Skies

During a short respite at the front, Lt Col O. Topilin, commander of the 108th GvShAP, made the pilots of his unit undergo training in the use of the Il-10 against ground targets. In addition, some training was given in the tactics of aerial combat. For this purpose, at the commander's initiative, a mock fight was staged in which a La-5FN fighter from the 5th GvIAP (Guards Fighter Air Regiment), also stationed at Sprottau, was pitted against the new aircraft. The Il-10 was piloted by Capt Sirotkin, and the La-5FN by Capt V. Popkov, Hero of the Soviet Union, one of the acknowledged fighter aces who had thirty-seven victories to his credit (by the end of the war this number would reach forty-one and he would be awarded a second Gold Star of Hero of the Soviet Union). The 'combat' was conducted at low and medium altitude and included the use of banking turns and complicated aerobatic figures. Only after a number of violent and resolute manoeuvres did the fighter succeed in getting on

A rare wartime shot of a flight of operational Il-10s. Note that all aircraft have additional raked aerial masts on the rear fuselage and UBT machine-guns in the turrets. Yefim Gordon archive

the tail of the attack aircraft (at the same time the gun camera film registered the La-5FN several times as being caught in the tail-gunner's sight). After landing Popkov said, 'This is a good attack aircraft, almost a fighter and a worthy opponent to a Lavochkin.' Interestingly, when Ilyushin became aware of a tendency by pilots to engage in aerial combat, thus turning the Il-10 into a fighter, he was somewhat concerned about the possible consequences. He found it necessary to emphasize that the Il-10 was not stressed

for aerial combat and that a restressing might be needed, should the aircraft also be required to fulfil this role.

Standing Comparison

The Il-10 makes an interesting comparison with the Fw 190F, which was in widespread use as an attack aircraft by the end of the war. When the German fighter was carrying a 250kg (550lb) bomb externally (the Fw 190 had no

internal bomb-bays), its speed at low altitude, where it was best compared with Ilyushin's attack aircraft, was 15 to 20km/h (9.3 to 12.4mph) higher. After dropping its bombs the Il-10 was almost equal to the Fw 190F in horizontal manoeuvrability, although it was inferior in vertical manoeuvres. On the other hand, the Il-10 was a two-seater and hence better protected. At 1,010kg (2,226lb), its armour made up 15.8 per cent of the AUW, while the Fw 190F's armour weighed only 360kg (793lb) or 8.2 per cent of its AUW. The German aircraft was also more lightly armed; for instance, tests showed that the Il-10's weight of fire was 1.61 times greater than that of a production Fw 190F without underwing 30mm (1.18 calibre) gun packs, according to tests conducted in the NIP AV (Scientific Research Test Range of Aviation Armaments) of the

Three Il-10s over the frontline. Note how the sun brings out the structure of the rudder showing through the skin. Yefim Gordon archive

Increasing the Inventory

In the meantime, the new aircraft were turned out in steadily increasing numbers. During the first four months of 1945, Plant No.8 produced 301 Il-10s and Plant No.1 another 389. This allowed more regiments to re-equip with the Il-10. When Germany capitulated, 146 Il-10s remained operational; of these 120 were combat-ready. Another twelve Il-10s remained in the inventory of the Naval Air Arm.

The Il-10 made up 4 per cent of the Soviet Air Force's attack aircraft fleet. The majority of the Il-10s had been delivered to the 3rd, 15th, 16th and 8th Air Armies, all in active service at the end of the war.

In May 1945 the Il-10s supplanted the Il-2s in the inventory of the 6th Guards Attack Air Division (GvShAD), which included the 108th GvShAP as one of its units. From the end of April, among the units operating the Il-10 was the 118th GvShAP (commanded by V. Vereshchinskiy), which was the first to undertake ground attack sorties without fighter escort. On the eve of Germany's capitulation the crew headed by Sqn Cdr P. Odnobokov downed two Bf 109 fighters during one sortie. Having noticed in time a fighter making a diving attack against his machine, the pilot of the Il-10 slowed down by throttling back the engine. The lead aircraft of the German pair rushed by, only to be hit by the fire of the wing-mounted cannon, and his wingman was downed by Averkov, the gunner.

Before the end of the Great Patriotic War twelve Soviet Air Regiments were converted to the Il-10; among these were some regiments of the Naval Air Arm. Yet, there were also regiments – such as the 7th GvShAP that had been engaged in ground attacks throughout the war – which received the Il-10s, but did not have the chance to make a single sortie with them.

Problems

The operational service of the Il-10 was not free from technical problems. In the course of the initial stages of series production of the Il-10 serious defects came to light, some due to faulty design stemming from the hectic tempo of design work under wartime conditions. During

---

Red Army. In summary, by the end of the war the Soviet Air Force had an excellent attack aircraft.

It is interesting to note the appraisal given to the Il-10 in a report dated 15 October 1944, prepared by Chief Engineer of the Red Army Air Force A. Repin for the Air Force Commander AM Novikov. Drawing a comparison between Soviet and foreign aircraft, Repin wrote that among attack aircraft 'the Il-10 is the best type in this category of aircraft, having no equal abroad'. Service pilots noted the Il-10 had considerable advantages over the Il-2. Its wide speed envelope and greater agility made it easier for escort fighters to do their job

and allowed it to take on enemy fighters if necessary. The Il-10 was capable of steeper diving angles as compared to the Il-2 (50 degrees as against 30); this enhanced the effectiveness of the Il-10 as an anti-tank weapon when used by skilled pilots (diving at steep angles was beyond the capacity of young pilots). The all-round crew armour increased survivability. The Il-10's easy handling and relatively simple maintenance allowed both air and ground crews to convert to the type in the shortest possible time. Unfortunately, the defects of the new AM-42 engine noted during State trials persisted. The designers did not manage to eliminate them until the war's end.

This Il-10 with the tail number '1 Red' wears a highly unusual colour scheme (silver overall with a red side flash). Yefim Gordon archive

Soviet Army soldiers inspect the scene of an Il-10's forced landing. Yefim Gordon archive

Flight upon flight of Il-10s armed with rockets cruises to the target. Note the pattern of the exhaust stains on the fuselage. Yefim Gordon archive

A senior political officer gives a run down on current events to the technical staff of an Il-10 unit. The two-tone camouflage on this aircraft is noteworthy, as is the cloth cover over the engine section. Yefim Gordon archive

one of the acceptance flights performed by Lomakin, a pilot of Plant No.18, a fire broke out in the engine. The exact cause could not be established, but, to be on the safe side, the so-called 'anti-flaming net' (the Russian term) was mounted at the carburettor air intake in order to prevent exhaust gases from reaching the carburettor. This was to no avail: only when the air duct was fitted with a shutter connected mechanically to the throttle did the fires ceased to occur.

A story about another defect which at one time grounded 300 aircraft was related by V.N. Bugaiskii, who at that time held the posts of chief designer of Plant No.18 and Ilyushin's deputy:

On some machines, their landing gear failed to extend when they were coming in for landing. Leading engineers from the OKB-240 [Ilyushin's bureau] ascribed the fault to a poor production standard of the locks keeping the undercarriage struts in the retracted position. Inspection showed, however, that the locks had been brought to a perfect condition. Everything had been polished and greased, yet the undercarriage would not extend. A general entrusted with the preparations for the Victory Parade summoned me to the airfield's command post and declared that he would report to Stalin that the Il-10 aircraft were unable to take part. I asked him to grant me a couple of days; then I invited the designers to a meeting and informed them about the situation. No

worthwhile suggestions were offered, and then I somehow came to think of the shackles for the suspension of bombs – I was positively informed that they never failed. A comparison was made, and it revealed that the hook of the undercarriage lock, when engaged, enclosed more than 300 degrees of the circular section of a bracket cam on the undercarriage strut, whereas on the bomb shackle this figure was nearly half as big, thanks to which there were no additional frictional forces during the release. Workers urgently made the necessary modifications to the locks on all the machines, thus eliminating the defect, but the Il-10s, nevertheless, failed to take part in the Victory Parade due to bad weather.

There were numerous other faults to be rectified. The main defects which had to be eliminated or remedied during the aircraft's operational service and the improvements introduced in the course of production were:

- Surface finishing was improved so as to enhance aerodynamic qualities of the aircraft.
- The structure of the wing centre section and of the outer wing panels (the spars and the skinning) was strengthened.

The crew of an Il-10 pose on the wing of their aircraft on a snow-covered airfield. Note the absence of wing cannons and main-gear doors. Yefim Gordon archive

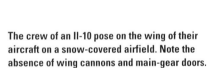

A post-war shot of the flight line at a Soviet air base hosting an Il-10 unit. Yefim Gordon archive

- Similar strengthening was undertaken as regards the rear fuselage, stabilizer, undercarriage retraction struts.
- A dust filter was introduced on the engine carburettor air duct, and many Il-10s had to be retrofitted with the filter in the field (absence of filters had considerably shortened the service life of the engines).
- Excessive heat in the cockpit necessitated modifying the ventilation system.
- The crew cockpit interior was rearranged to improve visibility and create better working conditions.
- Bomb-bays were strengthened and faults in the bomb-bay door mechanism eliminated.
- Sturdier engine exhaust stubs were introduced.
- Corrosion of water piping in the cooling system had to be dealt with by using stainless steel.
- The oil radiator had to be modified.
- Complaints were made about the quality of the armour shells used on the Il-10s.
- Much nuisance was caused by the main undercarriage wheels, the tyres of which proved unsuitable for

operations from concrete runways and had a short service life.
- The wheels themselves called for a redesign.
- Defects revealed on the Il-10s seriously hampered their operational use, many aircraft being grounded. To remedy the situation, special repair teams were sent from Plants No.1 and No.18 to attack air units of the Air Force.
- A special problem arose concerning the quality of the steel used in the armour shells of the Il-10; the AV-2 steel that had been used both on the Il-2 and the Il-10 throughout the war was found to no longer match the more stringent requirements intro-

duced after the war. The armour was to possess higher tensile qualities enabling it to withstand the impact not only of 7.62mm bullets, but of 12.7mm bullets as well.
- Special problems were posed by the AM-42 engine which proved very unreliable; cases were recorded of the main bearings and connecting rods disintegrating.
- Engine defects comprised also reduction gear failures, crankshaft failures, the burn-out of cylinder valves. The consequences could be serious.

Thus numerous engine failures which occurred in the 10th Guards Attack Air Division in February and March 1946

This Il-10 was displayed at a military hardware exhibition near Riga, Latvia, in the immediate post-war years. The bomb shackles under the wing roots are clearly visible. Yefim Gordon archive

A shot of a UII-10 based in East Germany after the war. Note the serial Y4 (i.e., U4 in Cyrillic, the U standing for *uchebnyi samolyot* – trainer). The raked additional aerial is also noteworthy. Sergey and Dmitriy Komissarov archive

resulted in several crashes and the loss of pilots. At the end of 1946 the Naval Air Force took delivery of forty Il-10 aircraft. During ferrying flights three crashes occurred caused by the failure of the crankshaft balance weight and of the bolts of the main connecting rod cover. On 29 December 1949 an UIl-10 trainer crashed at the airfield of Plant No.301 in Khimki (near Moscow); it was caused by the dis-integration of the bushing of a crankshaft bearing. It must be noted, however, that some engine failures were traced to faulty maintenance in the service units.

Against Japan

The Il-10 aircraft were used in some numbers in the war against Japan. When attacking enemy ships the Il-10s not only performed bombing strikes in level flight or shallow glide, but also widely practised mast-top bombing (in the Soviet parlance of the day). Two FAB-250 bombs were carried externally by the Il-10s on such occasions. On 10 August 1945 a group of six Il-10s commanded by Capt I.F. Voronin attacked Japanese ships stationed in Rasin harbour. Voronin himself, forcing

Left: A typical production UIl-10 begins its take-off run as a signal man gives clearance to take off.
Sergey and Dmitriy Komissarov archive

Below: A flurry of pre-flight activity around an Il-10M as armourers hook up bombs and load ammunition belts.
Yefim Gordon archive

his way through a wall of anti-aircraft fire, hit a destroyer and sank it; a Japanese fighter which approached the attack aircraft was downed by A. Ivanov, the tail gunner. Maj A. Nikolayev, commander of the 26th ShAP of the Pacific Fleet Air Force, was also piloting his Il-10 over the harbour on that day. His piloting was skilful, masterly and full of daring; he personally sank two Japanese transports. For these exploits Nikolayev and Voronin were awarded the titles of Hero of the Soviet Union. Several days later, on 17 August, the pilots of the 26th ShAP flew a mission involving the destruction of Japanese trains and railway lines in the vicinity of Seisin; in particular, a railway tunnel was to be destroyed. The latter objective was fulfilled through the use of skip-bombing – an ingenious way of getting bombs into a tunnel.

After the War

As noted in the previous chapter, after the war the remaining attack air regiments of the Soviet Air Force were re-equipped with the Il-10 aircraft. However, this took some time during which the veteran Il-2s soldiered on alongside their junior stablemates. Some figures will give an idea of the scale of series manufacture of the Il-10: in 1945, 2,555 Il-10s were manufactured by Plants No.1, 18 and 30; of these, 227 were the Il-10U trainer versions (according to another source the figures were, respectively, 2,603 and 186; the difference may be due to the method of calculation). In March 1946 a draft resolution of the government for deliveries of military aircraft in that year was submitted to Stalin for consideration; it envisaged the manufacture of 2,000 Il-10

attack aircraft, including 250 trainer versions; in a later document, dated 21 December, a figure of 1,900 appears as the estimated actual deliveries, including some 200 trainer versions; interestingly, this volume of deliveries was considered as falling short of the Air Force requirements.

As mentioned above, the Il-10 and its trainer version – the UIl-10 – were in production until 1948, by which time 4,540 machines had been manufactured; they were supplemented by a relatively small number of the Il-10M which was developed and produced between 1951 and 1954. The post-war career of the Il-10 in Soviet service was uneventful, but it had the chance to fire its guns in anger in the service in the air forces of North Korea and Communist China.

Rather grim-faced Soviet Air Force pilots pose before a line-up of Il-10Ms. The picture was taken in the early 1950s, as indicated by the new style of the airmen's attire. Yefim Gordon archive

CHAPTER NINE

The Il-10 in Detail

The Il-10 powered by the AM-42 engine was a two-seat armoured ground-attack aircraft. It was a cantilever, low-wing monoplane with retractable tailwheel undercarriage. The aircraft was provided with potent machine-gun, cannon and bomb armament; all vital assemblies and the crew were protected by armour.

Fuselage

The aircraft's fuselage comprised two sections: the forward fuselage and the rear fuselage. The forward fuselage, which also included the cockpit, was manufactured as an armour shell made of special armour steel plates with a thickness ranging from 4 to 8mm (0.16 to 0.31in). The armour shell housed all the main assemblies of the powerplant, controls and cockpits. The rear fuselage was of metal construction, its structure made up of frames and stringers. To eliminate drag caused by air flow within the fuselage, all openings and gaps permitting such flow were hermetically sealed; special bulkheads dividing the aircraft into sections were provided.

The rear fuselage was flush-riveted. Placed in its underside was a window for the AFA-IM camera, provided with two doors. The opening for the tailwheel was topped by a dome-shaped, stamped Duralumin cover. The canopy of the pilot's cockpit comprised a windshield with quarterlights and two hinged, glazed sections. They opened sideways, which enabled the pilot to abandon the aircraft in an emergency, even in the case of a complete nose-over. The hinged glazed sections had sliding clear-view windows. The gunner's cockpit canopy had a sliding clear-view window on the port side and was hinged to starboard. The pilot's cockpit was hermetically sealed and provided with ventilation; in addition, the pilot and the gunner were equipped with gas masks. The pilot's seat and the gunner's tip-up seat were stamped from Duralumin. The gunner's cockpit was also provided with a belt seat intended for use when firing the machine-gun.

The aircraft's length was 11.12m (36ft 6in); according to other sources, the fuselage, that is, the aircraft as such, was 11.057m (36ft 3⅓in) in length. The aircraft's height tail-up was 4.18 m (13ft 1⅓in). The ground clearance of the propeller in the tail-up attitude was 300mm (11.8in).

Wing and Tail Unit

The aircraft's wing was a two-spar, all-metal structure comprising the centre section and outer wings. It featured a variable airfoil: at the root it was the NACA-0018 with a thickness/chord ratio of 18 per cent; further on it was the NACA-230 and the wingtip airfoil was the NACA-044 (NACA-4410, according to some sources). A smooth transition from the wing centre section to the fuselage was achieved with the help of small fairings. The wings were provided with Frise ailerons and Schrenk flaps which had a setting of 17 degrees at take-off and 45 during landing. The flaps were attached on hinge brackets to the wing centre section and outer panels. The ailerons were 100 per cent mass-balanced and aerodynamically balanced; their angles of deflection were 22 degrees upwards and 15 downwards. The leading edge of the aileron up to the spar had Duralumin skinning of 0.8mm thickness; the whole of the aileron frame had a fabric covering. The starboard aileron had a fixed trim tab for counteracting propeller torque. The starboard outer panel was fitted with a landing light, and the port one with a Pitot head. On the parked aircraft the Pitot head was protected by a cover carrying a red pennant. Tie-down brackets for the snap-hooks of the arresting cables were mounted on the underside of the wing panels at the intersection of the aft spar and rib No.14. The ailerons and control surfaces had fabric covering.

The wings had a span of 13.40m (43ft 11⅔in) and an area of 30sq m (323sq ft). The wing centre section had a span of 3.80m (12ft 5⅔in). The wing root chord measured 3.22m (10ft 7in), the wingtip chord 1.29m (4ft 3in). The wing incidence was 2 degrees 30min and the wing dihedral 5 degrees.

The tail unit featured all-metal cantilever tail surfaces. The rudder and the elevators had tubular Duralumin spars, stamped Duralumin ribs and fabric covering. Both sections of the elevator and the rudder incorporated trim tabs, controlled from the cockpit. The control surfaces were 100 per cent mass-balanced. The horizontal tail had a span of 4.94m (16ft 2½in), the stabilizer had an incidence of 1 degree. The stabilizer's spars were attached to the fuselage by adjustable steel fittings. The joint line between the stabilizer surface and the fuselage was covered by a Duralumin fairing, which was attached by bolts to the fuselage and the stabilizer skinning. The stabilizer incidence could be adjusted on the ground within a margin of 2 degrees up or down; for this purpose a special fitting was mounted on frame No.11 of the fuselage. The control linkages to the elevators were rigid, while the ailerons had combined rigid and cable controls; the rudder and trim tabs on other surfaces had cable controls and the rudder trim tab was electrically controlled. The rudder had a horn balance; a mass balance was placed at the forward end of the horn.

Undercarriage

The undercarriage featured single-strut units. The main unit struts with wheels, measuring 800mm × 260mm (31½in × 10¼in), had oleo-pneumatic shock absorbers and were retracted into the wing centre section, swivelling aft and turning through 86 degrees to lie flat in the wing. The main-wheel legs had folding drag struts connected to the wheel-retraction

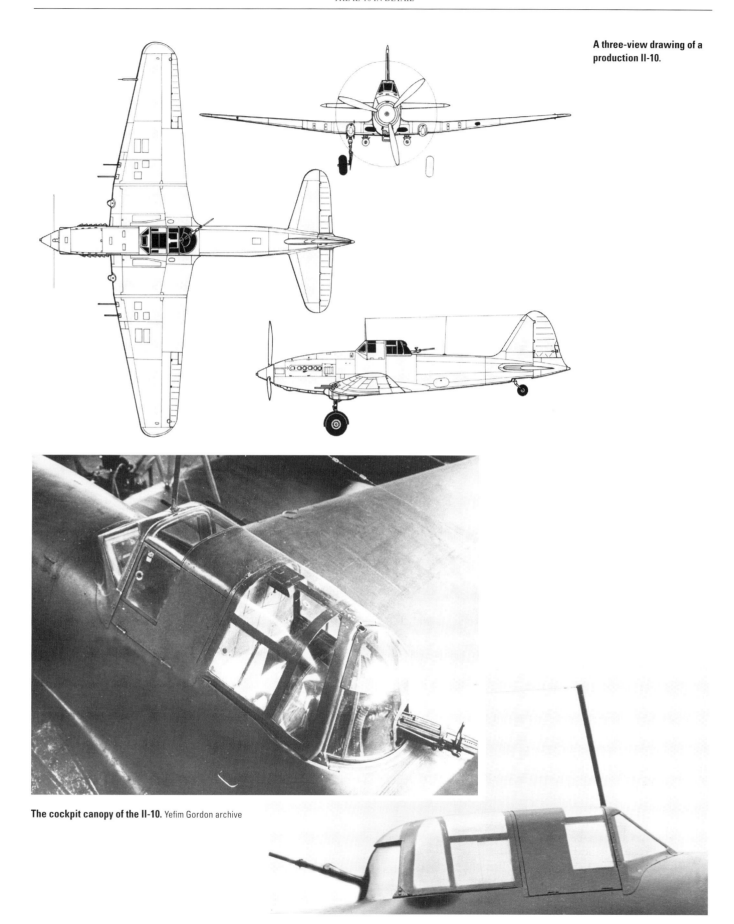

A three-view drawing of a production Il-10.

The cockpit canopy of the Il-10. Yefim Gordon archive

mechanism. The undercarriage was maintained in the extended position by a downlock placed at the centre of the folding strut; in the retracted position it was maintained by the uplatch placed on the wing. The tailwheel, measuring 400mm × 150mm (15.9in × 5.9in), was retracted backwards into the fuselage. The wheel track was 3m (9ft 10in). Retraction and extension of the undercarriage were effected pneumatically. The undercarriage control lever was placed in the pilot's cockpit. The undercarriage units had oleopneumatic shock absorbers. The compression of the main unit shock absorbers amounted normally to 40–60mm (1.6–2.4in), with a maximum of 200mm (7.9in). The main-wheel tyres were compressed by 55–65mm (2.2–2.6in), the tailwheel tyre by 35–55mm (1.4–2.2in).

There were two methods of indicating the position of the undercarriage – an electric system using indicator lamps and a mechanical one using visual undercarriage-position indicators on the upper surface of the wing centre section. The position of the tailwheel was indicated only electrically.

A system for the emergency extension of the undercarriage comprised a lever, a cable system and a winch mounted on the sidewall of the pilot's cockpit. There was no provision for an emergency extension of the tailwheel.

Powerplant

The aircraft was powered by the AM-42 in-line, liquid-cooled engine with a nominal rating of 1,750hp at sea level. The AV-5L-24 propeller, measuring 3.6m (11ft 9⅗in) in diameter, was equipped with the R-7A speed governor. The engine was attached to the engine mount by sixteen bolts. The gap between the exhaust stubs and the edges of the armour plates was covered by steel deflectors cut to shape.

The carburettor air intake was provided with a shutter geared to the undercarriage; it opened when the undercarriage was retracted, so as to afford unobstructed passage of the air and closed when the undercarriage was extended, ensuring that the air passed through filters. Normal throttle control, boost control and operation of the fire-extinguisher valve were effected via flexible cables encased in tubes. The air required for the engine was fed through an air intake placed under the engine cowling. The aircraft utilized the VS-50B engine-starter system incorporating the PN-1 starter pump. The engine's cooling system comprised an expansion tank with a capacity of 20ltr (4.4gal) mounted above the engine's reduction gear, and a tubular finned water radiator installed side-by-side with the oil radiator. The intakes of the water radiator air ducts were located in the wing centre section leading edge, on either side of the engine.

The outer and inner faces of the Il-10's port main-gear unit. Yefim Gordon archive

The aircraft's fuel system comprised two self-sealing fuel tanks with a total capacity of 720ltr (158.4gal). The venting of the lower fuel tank was effected through the upper tank, which had an outlet into the atmosphere. A service tank with a capacity of 165ltr (36.3gal) was placed in the upper fuel tank. The engine's oil supply came from two tanks placed close to the cylinder banks and connected by piping. The oil intake was through a pipe connected to the left tank. The total capacity of the oil system was 94ltr (20.7gal), 47ltr (10.3gal) in each tank. The air intake of the duct leading to the oil radiator was located in the wing centre section leading edge, close to the port side of the engine cowling. The temperature of the water and the oil were regulated by shutters mounted at the exit of the radiator ducts.

Armament

Forward-firing, wing-mounted armament comprised two 23mm (.90 calibre) VYa cannon with a total ammunition complement of 300 rounds, and two 7.62mm (.30 calibre) ShKAS machine-guns with a total complement of 1,500 rounds. The VYa cannon were mounted in the wing outer panels on two detachable fittings in a fashion similar to that on the Il-2; the fittings were attached to the wing ribs by bolts. The machine-guns were mounted in the wing outer panels between the ribs No.1 and 2. The gun was attached to the wing ribs at three points. Provision was made for replacing the wing outer panels incorporating the VYa cannon with new ones, incorporating the 37mm (1.46 calibre) 11-P cannon.

The firing of the wing-mounted cannon and machine-guns was controlled electrically, by a button placed on the control stick and two switches on a panel in the cockpit. To put the weaponry into action it was necessary first to turn on the switch of either the cannon or the machine-guns and then to start firing by pressing the button on the control stick. Both switches had to be turned on if the simultaneous firing of both types of weapon was required.

For rear defence the prototype Il-10 was provided with the VU-7 flexible mount, carrying the 20mm (.78 calibre) Sh-20 cannon with 150 rounds. Production aircraft were fitted with the VU-8 flexible mount carrying the 12.7mm UBK machine-gun; its ammunition load included 150 rounds in three ammunition

Left: **The propeller spinner of the Il-10, showing the Hucks starter dog.** Yefim Gordon archive

Bottom left: **The cooling air intake in the port wing root was divided into channels for the port water radiator and the oil cooler.** Yefim Gordon archive

Bottom right: **The starboard cooling air intake served the water radiator only.** Yefim Gordon archive

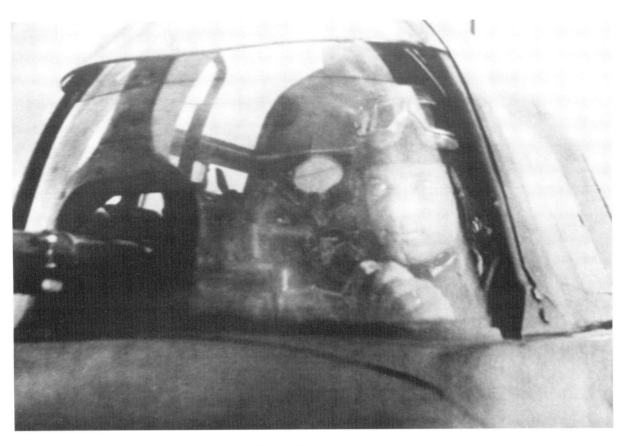

The gunner's position of an Il-10 equipped with a UBT machine-gun. Yefim Gordon archive

The port VYa cannon and ShKAS machine-gun of an Il-10. Yefim Gordon archive

boxes. The VU-8 mount afforded the following angles of fire to the rear: 50 degrees upwards, 18 downwards, 45 to starboard from the gunner and 55 to port. Defensive armament also included ten AG-2 aviation grenades in a DAG-10 container, installed in the aft fuselage. For training purposes and for checking the results of combat fire, provision was made for the installation of PAU-22 gun cameras on the starboard side of the UBK machine-gun mount and in the wings. Two bombs of either the FAB-100 or the FAB-250 type (HE bombs weighing, respectively, 100kg [220lb] and 250kg [550lb]) and four RS-132 unguided rockets could be carried on external underwing shackles; the bomb-bays housed the FAB-50 and FAB-100 bombs to a total weight of not more than 200kg (440lb). Fragmentation and incendiary bombs weighing from 1 to 25kg (2.2 to 55lb) apiece, as well as AZh-2 incendiary ampoules, could be laid direct on the hinged doors of the bomb-bays, which were retained in place by chain links connected to the DER-21 shackles. The bombs were released by pressing a button on the control stick,

which actuated the electrical ESBR-3P bomb-release device. In addition, the VMSh-10 time-setting release device could be used. Four launching rails were mounted under the wings (two under each wing panel; they could carry unguided rockets of three types: RS-132, ROFS-132 and RS-82).

Equipment

The Il-10's equipment comprised a set of standard piloting and navigation instruments and gauges intended for the powerplant control. These were supplemented by the RPK radio compass, the RSI-4 radio receiver, the RSI-3 radio transmitter and the AFA-IM camera for aerial photography.

Pneumatic System

The aircraft's pneumatic system comprised two compressed air bottles (the main one and the one for starting the engine), pressure-reducing regulators,

undercarriage and flap control valves, shut-off valves and a non-return valve, and piping with pressure gauges. The air bottles were placed in the rear fuselage. The main air bottle's capacity was 12ltr (2.64gal) and the upper limit of its pressure was 50kg/sq cm (711lb/sq in). The normal pressure in the air system was 40 kg/sq cm (569lb/sq in). Pressure reducing regulators, pressure gauges, undercarriage and flap control valves and shut-off valves were placed in the pilot's cockpit.

Differences between Original Production Il-10 and the Il-10M; Technical Description of the Il-10M

The main differences between the two (for the first production batches of the Il-10M, according to technical descriptions) were:

- New wing introduced, featuring a new airfoil and a 10 per cent increase in area, 33sq m (365.2sq ft) – 3sq m (32.3sq ft) more than previously;

FAB-250 bombs under the inner wings of an Il-10. The fairing in between is for the carburettor inlet/filter; the hinged cover at the front opens as the gear retracts, allowing direct air access. Yefim Gordon archive

- Forward fuselage lengthened by 250mm (9.84in);
- Rear fuselage lengthened by 500mm (19.68in), the tailwheel moved rearwards by 770mm (30.3in);
- Horizontal tail raised by 75mm (2.95in);
- Some detail changes in the undercarriage: the wheels measuring 800mm × 260mm (31.5in × 10.24in) replaced by new ones measuring 900mm × 300mm (35.43in × 11.81in);
- Pilot's cockpit received improved fire-prevention insulation from the powerplant; a fire-extinguishing unit introduced;
- Duplicate rigid control linkage to the elevator added;

- Mechanical system for emergency undercarriage extension replaced by a pneumatic system; a pneumatic emergency braking system introduced.
- OSP-48 blind-landing equipment installed, comprising the ARK-5 radio compass, the MRP-48P marker radio, the GPK-48 directional gyro, the DGMK-3 remote-reading, magnetic, directional gyroscope; the RPKO-10M radio compass and the PDK-45 compass deleted;
- RSI-6 radio replaced by the RSIU-3M;
- The SRO 'Bariy-M' IFF transponder installed instead of the SCh-3.

- GS-350 batteries replaced by those of the GSK-1500 type; the 12A-10 storage battery replaced by the 12F-30;
- Fuses of the automatic circuit protection device replaced by those of a new type;
- Fluid anti-icers installed on the windshield and the propeller;
- NS-23 cannon replaced by the NR-23;
- Additional shackles for the carriage of bombs installed under the wing centre section and the outer wings;
- Provision made for the carriage of external fuel tanks on shackles under the wing outer panels;
- Shackles for the carriage of the DAG-10 aviation grenades removed;

Specification of the Il-10			
Aircraft	Il-10 prototype State acceptance trials, 27.05.44	production Il-10 c/n 1894915, 09.45	production UIl-10 c/n 106085, 06.45
Crew	2	2	2
Engine type	AM-42	AM-42	AM-42
Power:			
max, hp nominal	2,000	2,000	2,000
at rated altitude, hp	1,750	1,750	1,750
Length, m (ft)	11.12 (36ft 6in)	11.12 (36ft 6in)	11.12 (36ft 6in)
Wing span, m (ft)	13.4 (43ft 11⅔in)	13.4 (43ft 11⅔in)	13.4 (43ft 11⅔in)
Wing area, sq m (sq ft)	30.0 (323)	30.0 (323)	30.0 (323)
Empty weight, kg (lb)	5,050 (11,135)	4,723 (10,414)	4,571 (10,079)
All-up weight, kg (lb)	6,335 (13,969)	6,385 (14,079)	5,680 (12,524)
Maximum speed:			
at sea level, km/h (mph)	507 (315)	493 (306)	502 (312)
at altitude, km/h (mph) at m (ft)	551 (342) at 2,800 (9,190)	543 (337) at 2,600 (8,530)	560 (348) at 2,500 (8,200)
Landing speed, km/h (mph)	148 (92)	149 (92.6)	145 (90)
Time to altitude, min			
1,000m (3,280ft)	1.6	n.a	1.5
3,000m (9,840ft)	5.0	5.8	4.8
5,000m (16,400ft)	9.7	n.a	9.6
Range, km (miles)	800 (497)	n.a.	n.a.
Take-off run, m (ft)	475 (1,560)	470 (1,540)	485 (1,590)
Landing run, m (ft)	460 (1,510)	n.a.	520 (1,700)
Offensive armament:			
bomb load, kg (lb)			
normal	400 (880)	400 (880)	200 (440)
maximum	600 (1,320)	600 (1,320)	n.a.
cannon:			
number × calibre, mm	2 × 23, VYa-23	2 × 23, VYa-23	2 × 23, VYa-23
ammunition, rounds	300	300	300
machine-guns:			
number × calibre, mm	2 × 7.62, ShKAS	2 × 7.62, ShKAS	2 × 7.62, ShKAS
ammunition, rounds	1,500	1,500	1,500
unguided rockets:			
number × type	4 × RO-82	4 × RO-82	4 × RO-82
calibre, mm	(RO-132)	(RO-132)	(RO-132)
Defensive armament:			
number × calibre, mm	1 × 20, Sh-20	1 × 12.7, UBK	–
ammunition, rounds	150	150	–
AG-2 aviation grenade, number	10	10	–

- Counterbalance introduced into the elevator controls;
- Slotted flap installed;
- AFA-IM aerial photography camera installed (only in initial batches of the Il-10M);
- Area of the ailerons increased by 31 per cent, the area of the elevator by 22 per cent.

The basic technical features of the Il-10M were:

Fuselage

The airframe comprised the armour shell, the rear fuselage and outer wing panels. The forward fuselage (engine cowling) and the centre fuselage (cockpit) made up the armour shell, manufactured from special armour steel plates. The cockpit canopy visor incorporated the windshield made of bulletproof glass. The armour shell housed all the main assemblies of the powerplant, control systems and cockpits. The rear fuselage was of metal construction. The fuselage had a length of 11.89m (39ft) (sometimes a figure of 11.87m is cited); the aircraft's height tail-up was 4.22m (13ft 10in).

Wing and Tail Unit

The wing had a trapezoidal planform. The tail-unit control surfaces and ailerons had fabric skinning. The slotted flap comprised two halves and was placed partly under the fuselage and partly under the trailing edge area of the wing panels, occupying a part of the wingspan. The wingspan was 14.0m (45ft 11in) with an area of 33.0sq m (355.2sq ft); it had an aspect ratio of 5.95 and a taper of 2.15. The thickness/chord ratio was 18 per cent at the root and 12 at the wingtip, the wing's dihedral was 4 degrees. The stabilizer comprised two halves; its incidence could be adjusted on the ground. The horizontal tail had a span of 4.94m (16ft 2½in) and an area of 6.6sq m (71sq ft); it had zero dihedral. The vertical tail area was 2.29sq m (24.65sq ft).

Powerplant

The Il-10M was powered by the AM-42 water-cooled engine with a nominal power rating of 1,750hp at sea level. The AV-5L-24, measuring 3.6m (11ft 9¾in), had a speed governor. The fuel was housed in two fuselage tanks with a total capacity of 800ltr (176gal). Additionally, a total of 300ltr (66gal) were held in two underwing drop tanks.

Undercarriage

The undercarriage was retracted into the wing centre section. The wheels had the following dimensions: main wheels, 900mm × 300mm (35.4in × 11.8in); tail-wheel, 400mm × 150mm (15.75in × 5.9in). The wheel track was 3.26m (10ft 8.4in).

Equipment

Electric equipment comprised the GSK-1500 generator and the 12A-30 storage battery. The radio equipment comprised the RSIU-3M VHF radio, the ARK-5 automatic radio compass, the MRP-48P marker radio, the RV-2 radio altimeter, the SPU-2 intercom and the SRO 'Bariy-M' IFF transponder.

Navigational equipment enabled the aircraft to operate in all weather conditions and at night.

Photographic equipment consisted of the AFA-BA/21 camera, accommodated in the rear fuselage.

Armament

Cannon armament comprised four 23mm (.90 calibre) NR-23 cannon in the wings (two in each wing panel) and one rearward-firing 20mm (.80 calibre) B20-EN cannon on a flexible mount in the gunner's cockpit. The total ammunition complement for the NR-23 cannon was 600 rounds; the B20-EN was provided with 150 rounds. The pilot had the PBP-1b gunsight and the gunner the OMP-13s gunsight. Bombs could be carried in the following combinations: 2 × FAB-250; 18 × AO-15; 6 × FAB-100; 54 × AO-10; 8 × AO-25-35; 190 × AO-2.5; and 152 × PTAB-2.5. They could be carried externally on shackles under the wing centre section (for bombs weighing up to 100kg [220lb]) and on two shackles under the outer wing panels (these were suitable for bombs weighing up to 250kg [551lb], or for the UKhAP-250 chemical weapon containers, or for drop tanks). Four launch rails for unguided rockets could be mounted under the wings.

Specification of the Il-10M		
Aircraft	Il-10M prototype	production Il-10M
Wing span, m (ft)	14 (45ft 11in)	14 (45ft 11in)
Length, m (ft)	11.64 (38ft 2¼in)	11.87 (38ft 11²/₅in)
Wing area, sq m (sq ft)	33.0 (355.24)	33.0 (355.24)
Empty weight, kg (lb)	5,588 (12,322)	5,353 (11,803)
Fuel load, kg (lb)	589 (1,300)	549 (1,211)
All-up weight, kg (lb):		
normal	7,120 (15,700)	7,100 (15,655)
overload	7,380 (16,273)	7,320 (16,140)
Maximum speed:		
at sea level, km/h (mph)	475 (295)	476 (295.8)*
at rated altitude, km/h (mph), at m (ft)	516 (321) at 2,600 (8,530)	512 (318) at 2,650 (8,690)
Time to altitude, min:		
1,000 m (3,280ft)	2.0	2.2*
3,000 m (9,840ft)	6.1	6.4*
Practical ceiling, m (ft)	n.a.	7,000 (22,970)
Range at 500m (1,640ft) altitude with 400kg (880lb) bomb load km (miles):		
without drop tanks	830 (516)	805 (500)
with drop tanks	1,005 (625)	n.a.
Take-off run, m (ft)	n.a.	410 (1,345)
Landing run, m (ft)	388 (1,273)	500 (1,640)
* At an all-up weight of 6,875kg (15,160lb)		

CHAPTER TEN

The Il-10 Abroad

The Il-10 had a more prominent and eventful career in foreign service than its progenitor, the Il-2. Not only did it come as a natural successor to the Il-2s that were on the strength of the Air Forces of Poland, Czechoslovakia and Bulgaria (Yugoslavia being excepted due to the conflict between Stalin and Tito), it also found its way into the arsenals of a number of other countries, both in the Communist bloc and outside it, in Europe as well as Asia. After the end of the Second World War it fell to its lot to be commit-

ted to action in several local conflicts. It had also the distinction of being produced outside the Soviet Union, namely, in Czechoslovakia, which makes it logical to choose it for opening a country-by-country review.

Czechoslovakia

At the end of summer 1950 the Czechoslovak Air Force received its first batch of Il-10s from the Soviet Union; it

comprised eighty combat machines armed with VYa-23 cannon, and four to six trainer versions. In 1951 the Soviet Union and Czechoslovakia reached an agreement providing for the manufacture of the Il-10 in Czechoslovakia under licence. The manufacture was undertaken by the Avia enterprise at its factory in Čakovice, to which the necessary tooling and rigging were transferred from Voronezh, where the production of Il-10s was discontinued in favour of new jet aircraft.

Preparations for production were not free from problems; the manufacture of the armour shell forming the front fuselage initially presented some difficulties. They were tackled, however, and the first Czechoslovak-built Il-10 took to the air on 26 December 1951, powered by an imported AM-42 engine. It was regarded as a prototype; the first pre-series machine powered by the licence-built M-42 engine was flown on 13 May 1952. The licence-built aircraft differed from the first Soviet version in being armed with a quartet of 23mm NS-23KM (NS-23RM, according to another source) cannon instead of two

Above: **An Avia B-33, the Czech licence-built version of the Il-10.** RART

A new and shiny B-33. This view shows the S-shape of the colour division line near the tail which was characteristic of the Czech-built Il-10s. RART

VYa cannon and two ShKAS machine-guns. The aircraft featured a rear gunner station of the VU-9M type fitted with a 20mm BNT-20E (B-20) cannon instead of the VU-9 turret of the Soviet-produced version. The Czechoslovak-built aircraft received the local designation B-33 (B stands for *Bitevný* – attack); the trainer version was accordingly designated CB-33 (C stands for *Cvičný* – trainer). They featured a number of detail differences from the Soviet-produced aircraft. In particular, the B-33s were adapted for the carriage of Czechoslovak-designed and produced rocket projectiles. They were fitted with four 2RU324 racks for the carriage of four N-150 rockets; other types of projectile included LR-130 non-guided missiles carried in two JRRO launch tubes under the wings. The CB-33 had a locally

Top: **This B-33 has a gun camera in the turret but no machine-gun. Note the dual wing cannon characteristic of the B-33.** RART

Right: **In 1957 the Czechoslovak Air Force introduced a new serial system based on the c/n which replaced the old alphanumeric system. This B-33 is serialled 5514.** RART

Below: **A pre-1957 formation of B-33s serialled MW-34, MW-35, MW-37 and MW-38. The nearest aircraft carries unguided rockets of Czech origin and is equipped with a rear gun camera.** RART

Another air-to-air of B-33s serialled MW-34 and MW-39. RART

V-10, a CB-33 trainer. The CB-33 had a different canopy design from the Soviet-built UII-10. RART

This CB-33 serialled '6 White' is equipped with extraordinarily long missile launch rails under the wings and was probably a weapons testbed. RART

developed rear cockpit canopy design markedly differing from that of the Il-10U. The CB-33s were produced with an armament of four or two NS-32KM cannon, or, in some cases, without armament. The antenna mast on the B-33s and CB-33s was usually slightly canted forward, as distinct from the vertical mast on Soviet-produced machines. Production of the Il-10 in Czechoslovakia lasted for about four years and was discontinued in 1955, a total of about 1,200 B-33s and CB-33s having been built. The machines delivered to the Czechoslovak Air Force were put on the strength of an Attack Air Division formed in 1952. However, the service career of the Il-10s in Czechoslovakia was fairly brief: in 1958 the division was disbanded and the attack element of the Air Force came to be rearmed with attack versions of the locally-produced, licence versions of the Soviet MiG-15 fighter.

The Il-10s were used in Czechoslovakia not only in their primary role. When the Attack Air Division was disbanded some regiments continued to operate the Il-10s as reconnaissance, observation and artillery-spotting aircraft. The B-33s were also used in experiments such as towing a 1:2 scale model of a locally developed target, and as flying test beds for assessing items of equipment and armament.

Roughly 50 per cent of the total output of the Il-10s manufactured in Czechoslovakia were intended for export, the recipient countries including Poland, Hungary, Romania, Bulgaria and even Yemen.

Poland

The Polish Air Force started receiving Il-10 attack aircraft as early as February 1949. By 31 August 1949 there were forty in the Polish Air Force. Early batches coming from the Soviet Union featured the initial armament fit consisting of VYa-23 cannon. In addition to the basic combat version, several Il-10U trainers were received from the Soviet Union. The number of Soviet-produced Il-10s in Poland totalled 120 and they remained in service up to 1959. However, at the beginning of the 1950s Czechoslovakia replaced the USSR as the source of deliveries to Poland. In December 1956 the B-33s and CB-33s in the inventory of the Polish Air Force totalled 281. They went into service not only with the attack

Right: Polish Air Force pilots have a last-minute conversation before taking off in their Il-10s. The nearest aircraft is a Czech-built Avia B-33, as indicated by the S-shaped colour division line near the tail. Note the rocket launch rails and the red/white spinners. Wojskowa Agencja Fotograficzna

Below: Maintenance work on a Polish Air Force Il-10. Note how the technician uses a portion of the engine cowling as a work platform. Wojskowa Agencja Fotograficzna

This Polish Air Force Il-10 (Avia B-33) is pictured in the static park at an air show, as revealed by the data placard in front. Note the red fin cap. Yefim Gordon archive

Right: A Polish Air Force UIl-10 – or possibly Avia CB-33; the direction from which the photograph was taken does not show clearly the rear part of the canopy. Yefim Gordon archive

Below: A Polish CB-33 heads a line of regular Il-10s which are ground-running their engines. The man in the front cockpit of the trainer is obviously a technician (no flying helmet). The Poles referred to the Czech-built trainers as Il-10U. Yefim Gordon archive

An air-to-air shot of a Polish Air Force Il-10U (CB-33) serialled 'U-7'. Yefim Gordon archive

element of the Air Force but also with artillery-spotting units and Naval Aviation units. Some examples went to the OSL-4 Flying School in Dęblin. Some Polish Il-10s and B-33s underwent local modification. Noteworthy was one intended to increase their range. They were fitted with two additional fuel tanks of 400ltr (88gal) each, suspended on bomb racks under the wings, with appropriate changes in the fuel system (the tanks were identical to those used on the LiM-5 jet fighters). The Il-10/B-33 was finally phased out of service in Poland in 1961. After that several machines were used for auxiliary purposes, and two Il-10s were turned over to the Aviation Institute in Warsaw to be used in experiments.

Hungary

The first batch of fifty Il-10s, supplemented by two Il-10U machines, reached Hungary in September 1949. These aircraft were not factory-new, they were transferred from Soviet Air Force units, and some had even served for some time with the North Korean Air Force. The combat machines, which were known in Hungary under the name of *Párduc* (Panther), received tactical numbers in the range Z-101 to Z-150, while the two trainers were allocated the numbers G-901 and G-902. In fact, the two trainers had simplified G-1 and G-2 numbers painted

on the fuselage in white, while many combat machines sported one- or two-digit numbers (for instance, 3 or 16) on the fuselage. The conversion of Hungarian pilots to the new machines began in October 1949. More trainers were needed, and plans were in hand to convert eleven combat machines into trainers. Eventually only three were actually converted (from Z-140, Z-119 and Z-130) because in September 1950 a batch of ten Il-10Us arrived from the USSR. In October 1950 Hungary had in its Air Force inventory sixty-seven Il-10s and fourteen Il-10Us, which were distributed to the sole Attack Air Regiment, the Officer Flying School and the Flight Research Institute. In 1952 a further 100 Il-10s were delivered from the Soviet Union to form an Attack Air Division. Its three regiments were stationed at Tapolca, Börgönd and Székesfehérvár-Tác. In all, 159 Il-10s were supplied to Hungary. They remained in service till the second half of 1956 when the units operating them were disbanded and as many as 120 Il-10s were scrapped.

The operational service of the Il-10s in Hungary was not confined to their primary role as attack aircraft. The type was involved in experiments with the towing of targets. In March 1950 Z-126 was transferred to the Aviation Institute for conversion to the new role. The rear seat was dismantled and a winch installed in its place, enabling the aircraft to extend the towing cable to the required length.

The device was electrically controlled by the pilot, but the experiments were generally unsatisfactory. Another unorthodox application took place in the spring of 1956 when a dangerous situation arose on the Danube due to ice congestion. The Il-10s bombed the ice that blocked the flow of the river.

Bulgaria

Little is known about the use of the Il-10s in the Bulgarian Air Force where they supplanted Il-2s. First deliveries were made from the Soviet Union; later some machines were received from Czechoslovakia (some sources mention thirty-seven Il-10s and three Il-10Us of Czechoslovak manufacture equipping an Assault Air Regiment in Plovdiv).

Romania

The Il-10 and Il-10U aircraft were late in reaching the Romanian Air Force, the first deliveries taking place in March 1953. The first batch consisted of thirty old machines of Soviet manufacture and were used for conversion training undertaken in the 63rd Attack Air Group. In June of that year Romania received 150 (140 in other sources) factory-new B-33s from Czechoslovakia; most of them went to three newly formed regiments, while

Maintenance day at a Hungarian Air Force Il-10 unit, with an armourer cleaning a VYa cannon removed from the nearest aircraft. Yefim Gordon archive

These bombed-up Hungarian Il-10s sport red lightning-bolt unit markings on the tail. The lead aircraft serialled '02 Yellow' has a DF loop aerial while the wingman ('10 Yellow') has none. Yefim Gordon archive

This Hungarian Air Force Il-10 serialled '817 White' was withdrawn from use by the time these pictures were taken (note the lack of armament). It eventually ended in a Romanian museum. Yefim Gordon archive

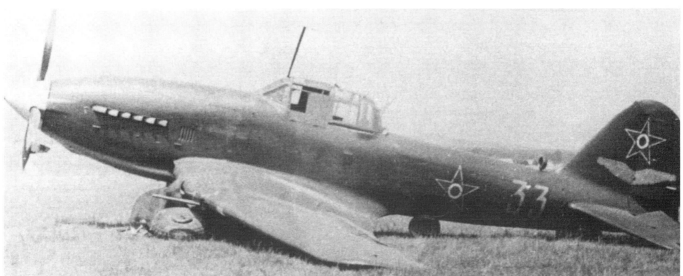

Hungarian Air Force Il-10 '33 Yellow' came to grief during landing, collapsing the port main-gear strut. Yefim Gordon archive

five machines were assigned to the Aviation School in Bobocu. The machines served for several years and were finally phased out in 1960.

North Korea (People's Democratic Republic of Korea)

The Korean People's Army Air Force took delivery of a number of Il-10 attack aircraft immediately before the outbreak of the Korean War. Some sources quote a figure of a mere fifty machines assigned to two regiments; according to other sources, the North Korean Air Force had sixty-two Il-10 aircraft on strength on 25 June 1950. Yet another source states that at one time the 1st Attack Air Regiment of the North Korean Air Force had ninety-three aircraft of this type on strength. These aircraft, together with the Il-10s piloted by Chinese airmen, were committed against the troops of South Korea and the UN. The Il-10s took part in air raids against the capital Seoul and the Kimpo and Suwon airfields. An American report stated that, on one of such missions against the Suwon airfield, a flight of three North Korean Il-10s managed to slip through the opposing fighter cover and destroy a C-54 on the ground.

The Il-10s were used not only in their primary role of attack aircraft, but also as reconnaissance and artillery-spotting aircraft. The North Korean Il-10s were

US Army soldiers examine the charred wreckage of a North Korean Air Force Il-10 wearing the tactical code '39 White' which was shot down by USAF fighters during the Korean War. Yefim Gordon archive

The stripped-out hulk of North Korean Air Force Il-10 '54 White' lies at the scene of a forced landing. The exposed engine is still intact. Yefim Gordon archive

Dismantled Il-10 '55 Yellow' as it was captured in a wrecked hangar at a North Korean airbase overrun by US troops. Yefim Gordon archive

opposed by US fighters which claimed several victories in these encounters. A few Il-10s were captured by US troops. According to some sources, the use of the North Korean Il-10s was restricted to the early period of the war because they allegedly were all destroyed, mostly at their bases, during the counter-offensive launched by the USA. Another source states, however, that the last Il-10s of the North Korean Air Force were withdrawn from service in 1956.

China

According to some sources, the Chinese People's Liberation Army received a total of 175 Il-10s immediately before the Korean War. The aircraft delivered to China had the initial armament version comprising two VYa cannon and two ShKAS machine-guns. Chinese pilots belonging to the 829th Mixed Air Regiment began conversion training on the UIl-10 in Hsuichow on 11 August 1950; a few days later, three pilots of the

Chinese Liberation Army Air Force made their first flights in the Il-10s without instructors. That was the beginning of the type's operation by the Chinese. Unfortunately, few details of their service careers are available. In addition to this participation in the Korean War, Il-10s were also involved in occasional outbreaks of hostilities between the forces of Communist China and the Nationalists in Taiwan. On 9 January 1955 three Chinese Il-10s carried out an air raid on Dachen and sank a warship of the

Captured North Korean Air Force Il-10s '44 Yellow' and '55 Yellow' await shipment to the USA where they would be evaluated. RART

Still in its original North Korean markings, Il-10 '44 Yellow' is seen here at Wright Patterson AFB (Dayton, Ohio) following reassembly. RART

Il-10 '44 Yellow' with the tail jacked up for boresighting the cannons. RART

Nationalist Navy. The Il-10s continued in the People's Liberation Army Air Force long after the type had been phased out by the Soviet Air Force in 1956.

Yemen

In 1957 twenty-four brand-new Czechoslovak-built B-33s and CB-33s were sent to the Kingdom of Yemen where they were assembled by accompanying Czechoslovak personnel. According to some sources, the aircraft were delivered without armament. Obviously, later they were fitted with some sort of armament, which eventually came to be fired in anger. In September 1962 the feudal monarchy was overthrown and the Yemen Arab Republic was proclaimed in its place. This was followed by a Royalist

insurgency, supported by Saudi Arabia and Jordan; the ensuing civil war lasted for several years. In October 1962 the Republican government used its Air Force (presumably the Il-10 attack aircraft) against the insurgents and invading Saudi troops on the northern border; a press report to this effect (*Izvestiya*, 12 October 1962) was accompanied by a picture showing a line-up of the Yemeni Il-10s.

USA

In the course of the Korean War three North Korean Il-10s fell intact into the hands of US forces. Two of them, with tactical numbers 44 and 55, were shipped to the USA and delivered to the Wright Air Development Center at Wright Patterson AFB, Dayton, Ohio, where they

were subjected to comprehensive testing in the summer of 1951. At first they retained North Korean markings, but subsequently the yellow 44 was repainted and provided with USAF markings on the rear fuselage; it carried the ADC registration T2-3000 on the tail.

Indonesia

In 1957 the Republic of Indonesia received, under terms of great secrecy, several B-33s from Poland. They were intended for long-range missions and provided with two supplementary fuel tanks of 400ltr (88gal) capacity each, suspended under the wings. Indonesians, however, were not pleased with the aircraft and they were returned to Poland where they were scrapped.

Left: '44 Yellow', one of the captured North Korean Il-10s, seen at Wright Patterson AFB wearing USAF stars and bars insignia and the additional serial T2-3000. The T stands for test; such serials were allocated to enemy aircraft undergoing evaluation. USAF

Below: An air-to-air view of Il-10 T2-3000; note the large USAF titles under the port wing. USAF

CHAPTER ELEVEN

The Il-8 – a Heavyweight Spin-Off

The Il-2, a single-engined aircraft powered with an engine of moderate output by the standards of the day, can be classed among medium-size, medium-weight attack aircraft. It occupies a place somewhere between the lightweight attack aircraft produced by converting a single-engined fighter for ground-attack duties and a heavy, twin-engined attack aircraft. As related in the first chapter, the latter category was an object of some attention on the part of both political leaders and aircraft designers in the Soviet Union on the eve of war, but after the German invasion this design effort direction slipped into the background. Yet, even at a time when this might well have been considered a luxury, some thought was given to designing heavyweight attack aircraft, which, if successfully developed and put into production, might have become a valuable element in the arsenal of the Red Army.

First Thoughts

Several months before the outbreak of war the Ilyushin design bureau began work on a heavy, armoured attack aircraft with a greater bomb load and longer range than the Il-2. Designated TsKB-60, the original project envisaged an all-metal, low-wing, twin-tailed monoplane powered by two AM-38s. It was planned to produce it in two versions, a single-seater and a two-seater with defensive armament. The aircraft was to have powerful offensive armament. One of the proposed armament fits comprised a 37mm nose cannon, two 23mm cannon and four 12.7mm or 7.62mm machine-guns. The aircraft would be able to carry internally a normal bomb load of 600kg (1,322lb), its maximum load reaching 1,000kg (2,204lb).

The preliminary design was approved on the eve of war, by which time the aircraft had been redesignated Il-6. A mock-up was completed in the spring of 1941. When the war broke out, however, the

OKB and the aircraft factories were too busy increasing output and eliminating defects in the production Il-2, and the project was shelved (the Il-6 designation was later reused for a twin-engined, diesel-powered bomber). It is not quite clear whether Ilyushin was referring to the Il-6 (TsKB-60) or to some new, but similar project in his report dated 16 February 1943 on the activities of his OKB (Plant No.240) in 1942, in which he stated that in the second quarter of the year the OKB had started (or, in fact, resumed?) work on a single-seater, armoured attack aircraft powered by two AM-38 engines. This work, he wrote, had lasted from 20 April until 16 September:

At the stage when the degree of technical completion had reached 75 per cent for the design work, 80 per cent for the mock-up construction and 100 per cent for wind-tunnel model construction, the work was discontinued because the design work was switched over to a new subject – a single-engined attack aircraft powered by the AM-42 engine.

In fact, among Ilyushin's progeny there were several designs answering to that description, and some were precisely in the heavy attack aircraft category. However, Ilyushin's first attempt at creating a single-engined, heavy attack aircraft was connected with the use of a different engine – the M-71 air-cooled radial delivering 2,000hp. In August 1942 Ilyushin submitted a proposal to create a heavy, armoured attack aircraft powered by this engine; it was initially designated BSh M-71. It was a two-seater with the forward-firing armament comprising two 37mm NS-37 cannon and two ShKAS machine-guns; project work on it was completed by July. Its design performance included a maximum speed of 430km/h (267mph) at sea level, which was a considerable improvement on the AM-38-powered Il-2. In September 1942 Commander-in-Chief of the Air Force Novikov suggested to Shakhurin, People's Commissar of the Aircraft Industry, that the BSh M-71 be included in the plan for prototype construction for 1942, the

The Mikulin AM-42 engine. Yefim Gordon archive

The first prototype Il-AM-42 (alias Il-8) attack aircraft seen during manufacturer's flight tests; it was similar in appearance to the standard Il-2. Note the fully enclosed cockpit.
Yefim Gordon archive

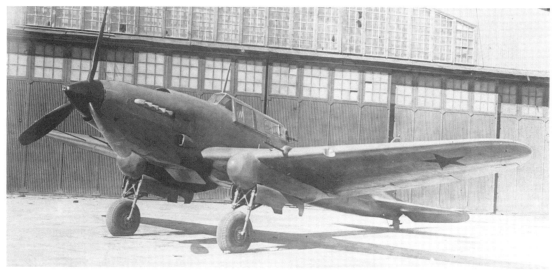

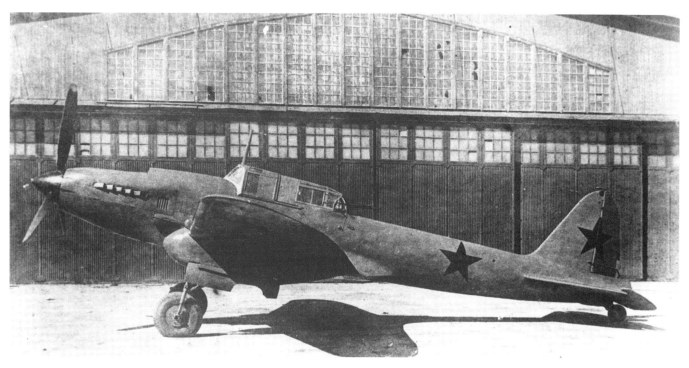

target date for State acceptance trials being 1 March 1943. However, it was not before August that Ilyushin was in a position to present an advanced development project of the aircraft, which by that time was termed Il-8 M-71 (first use of the Il-8 designation).

Unlike the Il-2 M-82, the radial engine on this aircraft was to be completely enclosed by a cowling made of suitably shaped armour plating; it formed part of a shell extending further aft to protect both the pilot and the gunner. The protection afforded to the gunner was especially noteworthy: in addition to the side, rear and ventral armour plating of his cockpit, he was enclosed by a dome-shaped, metal turret made mostly of armour steel and partly of armour glass to provide the necessary view. The design of the aircraft was considered promising by specialists who were also impressed by the degree of protection from the rear. Yet the project was not given the go-ahead. This may have been due, at least in part, to difficulties encountered in the development of the M-71 engine with its numerous teething troubles.

That brings us back to the AM-42-powered derivatives of the Il-2. The new Mikulin AM-42 was an updated AM-38F rated at 2,000hp (1,492kW) for take-off and providing 1,770hp (1,320kW) at 1,600m (5,250ft). The AM-38F delivered 1,700hp (1,268kW) at take-off and 1,500hp (1,119kW) at 760m (2,500ft). In September 1942 Ilyushin's OKB and Plant No.18 were tasked with the design and manufacture of two updated versions of the Il-2 based on the use of the AM-42, which at that time was still at prototype stage. These two machines, sometimes

referred to collectively as Il-2 AM-42, differed in a number of respects. The first was known as the Il-2 AM-42 with refined aerodynamics, or S-42. It featured increased sweep-back on the outer wing panel leading edges, increased aerodynamic balance of the elevator, improved external finishing, retractable tailwheel, extended armour shell protecting both the pilot and the gunner, restressed wing and some other refinements. This machine was under construction, but work on it was not completed due to difficulties with the AM-42 engine.

The second prototype was designated Il-2M AM-42; this was a variant reflecting the concept of a heavy attack aircraft. It had somewhat bigger dimensions compared with the Il-2 AM-38F, and its normal bomb load was increased to 500kg

(1,100lb). The Il-2M incorporated many of the refinements introduced on the S-42; a special feature of the Il-2M was the armour-plated, dome-shaped turret of the same type as on the Il-8 M-71. Testing of this aircraft began in August 1943 at Plant No.240 in Moscow, to which Ilyushin's OKB was transferred from the manufacturer, Plant No.18. In the course of testing, the armour-plated turret revealed its shortcoming – a restricted field of view for the gunner – and was replaced first by a normal glazed turret and then by a flexible mount of the type used on the Il-2 AM-38F. The Il-2M's performance was significantly better than that of the Il-2 AM-38F, which was in no small measure due to the new propeller measuring 4m (13ft 1 1/2 in) in diameter; however, it caused engine vibration and

The second Il-8 (Il-AM-42) at NII VVS during State acceptance trials. The revised canopy design and the new-style insignia are cleary visible. Yefim Gordon archive

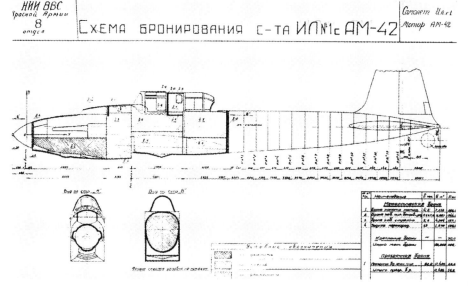

This drawing prepared by NII VVS illustrates the armour protection and fuselage design of the Il-AM-42. Yefim Gordon archive

had to be replaced by a propeller of 3.6m (11ft 10in) diameter with which the aircraft's performance dropped almost to the level of the AM-38F-powered aircraft. The Il-2M AM-42 remained a prototype and was used chiefly for flight-testing the new AM-42 engine.

Fresh Beginning

The concept of a heavy attack aircraft was implemented by Ilyushin on another AM-42-powered machine. In the summer of 1942 he received a request for a proposal for a heavy attack aircraft with a bomb load of up to 1,000kg (2,204lb). It was prompted by the need to attack motorized infantry on the offensive from the air. Building on combat experience with the Il-2, Ilyushin chose a single-engined configuration. The projected aircraft was essentially an oversized Il-2 with better armour protection, longer range and the same armament. While retaining a broad similarity of general layout, basic contours and many design features to those of the Il-2, the new machine was structurally a completely new aircraft of bigger dimensions. Originally known as Il-AM-42, it was allocated the factory designation Il-8. Some refinements were introduced into the aerodynamics of the aircraft. The oil radiator was accommodated side-by-side with the coolant radiator in the duct

similar to that of the Il-2, with the characteristic, big air scoop on the top of the engine cowling. The scoop was enlarged and moved slightly to aft, closer to the cockpit. The Il-8 featured enhanced armour protection. As distinct from the Il-2, the gunner's cockpit on the new aircraft was accommodated within the armour shell. The latter had bigger dimensions and featured thicker plates in the most vulnerable areas. Accordingly, the weight of the plating rose by 150kg (330lb). The rear fuselage was lengthened by 1.25m (4ft 1in) to enhance the effectiveness of the empennage. To allow for the greater diameter of the propeller, the main undercarriage legs were lengthened and the underwing undercarriage fairings were modified accordingly. The gunner's station was provided with the 12.7mm UBK machine-gun. The forward-firing armament of the Il-8 comprised two VYa-23 cannon with a total of 300 rounds and two ShKAS machine-guns with 1,500 rounds. As an option, two NS-37 cannon could be installed in the wing instead of the VYa cannon (the first version of the Il-8 was built in two examples, one of which was armed with the VYa cannon while the other one was fitted with the NS-37 cannon). In addition, a static test airframe was built after some delay. Two versions of the aircraft were under design concurrently. Alongside the baseline attack/bomber version, design work was started on a reconnais-

sance and artillery-spotter aircraft with a slightly shorter range, but with more efficient radio equipment.

The Il-8 prototype took off on 10 May 1943. The project test pilot Vladimir Kokkinaki said that the aircraft was easy to fly and had no surprises. At a weight of 7,250kg (15,983lb), the Il-8 had a top speed of 435km/h (270mph) at sea level and 470km/h (292mph) at 2,240m (7,400ft) – almost 50km/h (31mph) faster than a production Il-2 at low altitudes. The climb rate increased by 15 per cent and range was almost doubled. Thanks to the powerful engine the take-off run was only 318m (1,043ft), while landing speed was 132km/h (82mph). On the down side, the tests were delayed by engine problems; the AM-42 proved unreliable, smoky and plagued by vibration. Nevertheless, the Il-8 powered by the AM-42 with an AV-5L-18B propeller underwent State acceptance trials that lasted from 26 February until 30 March 1944. The first prototype performed forty-four flights, logging 19h 30min; it was tested in two versions: an attack aircraft/bomber and a reconnaissance/spotter aircraft. The results were considered generally satisfactory and the aircraft was recommended for production in both versions, provided that all the outstanding problems were solved.

Ilyushin states in his report to NKAP on the OKB activities in 1944 that 'the Il-8-2 AM-42 [presumably the second example of the original Il-8] was flyable as of 1 January 1944; it passed factory testing during the first quarter of 1944 and was submitted for State acceptance trials on 29 March 1944 instead of 1 April, that is, three days earlier than stipulated.' Trials of the second example were completed on 27 May. (It should be remarked here that the designation Il-8-2 was, rather confusingly, used in documents and literature to denote both the second example of the original Il-8 and the later, reworked version of the Il-8.) The first and the second example of the Il-8 differed in having different rear fuselages: the first had a rear fuselage of wooden construction, while the second had a metal fuselage. The first example was armed with two VYa-23 cannon, two ShKAS machine-guns and one movable UBK machine-gun on the VU-8 turret; the second had two 37mm 11-P37 cannon instead of the VYa.

The second reworked version powered by the AM-42 engine was likewise designated Il-8. The first of two prototypes is seen here at NII VVS during State acceptance trials. These views illustrate the four-bladed propeller, the Il-10 style main landing gear and canopy design; the vertical tail, however, is still similar to that of the Il-2, lacking a rudder horn balance. Yefim Gordon archive

Two more views of the first example of the reworked Il-8 attack aircraft. Yefim Gordon archive

Doubts and a New Start

The document summarizing the results of the State acceptance trials of the Il-8 was endorsed on 12 April. On 5 May Chief Engineer of the Red Army Air Force Repin sent a letter addressed to G. Malenkov and A. Shakhurin in which he asked them to consider the question of immediately putting this aircraft into series production at Plants No.1, 18 and 30; he suggested that thirty aircraft be manufactured in the attack version and ten in the artillery-spotter version by 15 July. Another document shows that at one time Shakhurin envisaged the prospect of the Il-8 supplanting the Il-2 completely on the production lines. On 18 May Shakhurin sent to Malenkov a draft resolution of the State Defence Committee ordering the Il-8 to be launched into production at Plant No.18. However, these plans never materialized. This was presumably because of some

shortcomings which made its service introduction questionable. Indeed, while the speed and the range of the Il-8 were marked improvements on that of the Il-2 AM-38F, its manoeuvrability in the horizontal and the vertical plane proved to be inferior to those of the Il-2 and fell short of current battlefield requirements.

By the end of the test programme the OKB had achieved good progress with the Il-1 (Il-10) (*see* Chapter 7). Hence Ilyushin proposed to redesign the Il-8's engine cooling and lubrication system, armour shell, wings, undercarriage and empennage to match those of the Il-1. This proposal was made in a letter to Shakhurin dated 1 July. An NKAP order to this effect was issued on the same day. All the experience gained by the OKB was used to improve the aircraft. Thus, despite having the original Il-8 designation, the resulting aircraft emerged as a completely new machine. Externally it much resembled the Il-10 from which it differed in

having a longer fuselage and a four-blade propeller. A feature shared by the Il-10 and the new Il-8 variant was the sleek shape of the engine cowling which dispensed with the air scoop on the top; instead, two ducts placed on either side at the junction of the wing and the fuselage were used as air intakes for the coolant and the oil radiator.

The Il-8 in its new guise featured a somewhat different armament fit. The VYa cannon were replaced by those of the NS-23 type. The machine-gun in the rear cockpit was replaced by the more potent UB-20 cannon on the VU-9 flexible mounting. Rear defence was further enhanced by a cassette with AG-2 aerial grenades in the rear fuselage. Modified bomb-bays enabled the aircraft to carry internally a bomb load of up to 1,000kg (2,200lb) as against the 600kg (1,320lb) of the first Il-8 version. Alternatively, two 500kg (1,100lb) bombs could be carried externally on bomb racks.

The reworked Il-8 trestled for landing-gear retraction tests. Yefim Gordon archive

Three more shots of the first example of the reworked Il-8 during trials. Yefim Gordon archive

Changes were introduced into the armour plating as compared to the first version of the Il-8. In particular, the pilot and the gunner were protected from the rear by an armour bulkhead comprising two spaced layers, each of 8mm thickness.

The redesign was complete in July and the prototype conversion was completed in August and September. The revamped Il-8 (sometimes referred to as Il-8-2) made its first flight on 13 October – again with Kokkinaki at the controls. Once again the test programme lagged behind schedule through powerplant problems – testing was suspended on 18 December because of the poor condition of the engine. The new AV-9L-22B four-bladed propeller also was a culprit this time, causing severe vibration during early test flights. However, this problem was solved just before the acceptance trials began shortly after the end of the war, on 27 May 1945; they were completed on 7 July. Several different types of propeller had to be consecutively tested before normal operation was finally achieved with the four-bladed AV-5L-22B.

The reports of the test pilots were generally favourable. They gave due credit to the new aircraft's good stability and ease of handling, high load-carrying capacity and potent armament and good serviceability. Performance figures also showed some improvement as compared with the previous type. The new arrangement of the water radiator and the oil cooler, the more streamlined shape of the armoured fuselage (reminiscent of the Il-10) and other improvements increased the speed to 461km/h (286mph) at sea level and 509km/h (316mph) at 2,800m (9,200ft) at an AUW of 7,610kg (16,766lb). Still, the performance of the modified Il-8 was inferior to that of the Il-10, which had already entered service. In addition, some shortcomings revealed during the tests had to be rectified. However, this proved inexpedient.

When NII VVS project test pilot Col A. Dolgov and engineer S. Frolov submitted the Il-8's State acceptance trials report, the Soviet Air Force First Deputy C-in-C Vorozheikin wrote (on 14 August 1945): 'Further development of the Il-8 is inexpedient because the Il-10, which outperforms it, is in production and the Il-16 is forthcoming.' (The latter is described below; as will be seen, the Il-16 did not justify the hopes pinned on it, unlike the Il-10, which became the mainstay of the attack air units of the Soviet Air Force.) Ilyushin agreed with this decision; yet, for some time he cherished the idea of prolonging the life of the Il-8 by re-engining it with the more powerful AM-43 – a

The gunner's station of the first reworked Il-8, equipped with a Berezin UB-20 cannon. Yefim Gordon archive

further development of the AM-42 featuring direct fuel injection. The plan for prototype aircraft construction for 1945 envisaged the construction of an Il-8 derivative powered by the AM-43 delivering 2,300hp at take-off and 2,000hp at the rated altitude of 2,300m (7,550ft).

There is no evidence as to whether this aircraft was actually built; in all probability this project was abandoned because of difficulties experienced with the AM-43 development (the same fate befell the projected AM-43-powered version of the Il-10). Nevertheless, this was not

Ilyushin's last piston-engined aircraft. Two years later his bureau brought out the Il-20 heavy armoured bomber and attack aircraft which incorporated the designers' accumulated experience. This aircraft, however, is outside the scope of this book.

The second Il-8 featured a slightly different turret design and a Shpital'nyi Sh-20 cannon for self-defence. Yefim Gordon archive

This drawing prepared by NII VVS illustrates the armour protection and fuselage design of the Il-8. The figures indicate the thickness of the armour panels. Yefim Gordon archive

The first prototype of the Il-16 attack aircraft. Yefim Gordon archive

Specification of Ilyushin's Heavy Attack Aircraft		
Aircraft	Il-8-1	Il-8-2
Year	1943	1944
Crew	2	2
Engine	AM-42	AM-42
All-up weight, kg (lb)	7,250 (15,986)	7,610 (16,780)
Total load, kg (lb)	2,005 (4,421)	2,500 (5,512)
Max speed, km/h (mph)		
at sea level	435 (270)	461 (287)
at rated altitude	470 (292)	509 (316)
Time to 1,000m (3,380ft), min	1.97	2.6
Range, km (miles)	1,180 (733)	1,140 (709)
Take-off run, m (ft)	318 (1,043)	520 (1,706)
Landing run	n.a.	595 (1,952)
Bomb load, kg (lb)		
normal	600 (1,323)	1,000 (2,205)
maximum	1,000 (2,205)	–
Cannon and machine-guns	2 VYa + 2 ShKAS 2	NS-23 + 2 ShKAS

Il-16: Final Offspring of the Il-2/Il-10/Il-8 Line

The high performance of the Il-10 and its ability to engage in active air-to-air combat prompted the development of a lightweight attack aircraft with still greater speed and manoeuvrability. Design work

began in 1944 and the aircraft was designated Il-16. (Being a lightweight aircraft, it belongs more naturally in the chapter with the Il-10, but is included here as chronologically the conclusion of the series of Ilyushin's single-seat attack aircraft stemming from the Il-2 and sharing the same basic layout.)

The Il-16 was to be powered by the new Mikulin M-43NV (AM-43NV) liquid-cooled engine with direct injection, delivering 2,300hp (1,691kW) at take-off. Aerodynamically and structurally, the Il-16 was virtually identical to the Il-10 but had slightly smaller dimensions and weight. Coupled with the more powerful engine, this was expected to give it a top speed of 625km/h (388mph) at 3,400m (11,150ft) and 560km/h (348mph) at sea level. Other design performance figures included a ceiling of 9,000m (29,530ft) and a range of 800km (497 miles). These figures and those quoted in brackets below were mentioned in the NKAP order No.43ss, dated 6 February 1945.

The Il-16's armour protection was similar to that of the Il-10, but the armour plate thickness of the engine cowling sidewalls and the cockpit section sidewalls was reduced and the upper front part of the fuselage had larger, soft-skinned areas. The aircraft's forward-firing offensive guns comprised two NS-23 cannon with 280 [300] rounds and two ShKAS machine guns with 1,400 rounds [1,000] installed in the detachable outer wings. Originally the Il-16 was

The second prototype Il-16 differed in having an extended rear fuselage and a taller fin. Yefim Gordon archive

to have a 200kg (440lb) normal and a 400kg (880lb) maximum bomb load, the bombs being carried internally (in two bays in the inner wings) and externally on underwing racks. Later, however, it was decided to increase the normal load to 400kg and the maximum load to 500kg (1,100lb). The rear was protected by a turret-mounted UB-20 cannon with 150 rounds and by ten AG-2 aviation grenades.

Thus, according to the project, the Il-16 was virtually equal in firepower to the Il-10 while having markedly superior speed and manoeuvrability. The front-line units needed such an aircraft, and preparations for series production began even before the Il-16 prototype entered its flight test. The first prototype was completed by Plant No.18 in early 1945, while Plant No.240 – Ilyushin's OKB – had performed the project work on the aircraft. Three prototypes were built, according to some sources. There is a document stating that Plant No.39 (30?) was tasked with building an Il-16 proto-type with the AM-43 engine; the aircraft

was to be submitted for factory tests on 15 June. That was stipulated by order No.43ss. The order contained design performance figures, with revised figures for the bomb load – 400/500kg. It is not clear whether this was an order for yet another example of the Il-16 nor whether it was actually built.

The Il-16 was test flown – as the reader may have guessed – by V.K. Kokkinaki. It was immediately apparent that the torque of the very powerful engine, combined with a short rear fuse-lage, resulted in unsatisfactory longitudi-nal stability characteristics. To improve these the detachable aft fuselage was lengthened by 500mm (1ft 7.7in), the vertical tail area was increased and the rudder was provided with a trim tab. With these modifications the aircraft became more stable and controllable in flight. Nevertheless, the flight testing of the Il-16 was protracted because of the M-43NV engine's deficiencies. All attempts to rectify them failed and in the summer of 1946 the development of the Il-16 was terminated.

Specification of the Il-16	
Year of manufacture	1945
Crew	2
Engine type	AM-34NV
Engine power at take-off (hp)	2,300
Empty weight, kg (lb)	4,135 (9,118)
All-up weight, kg (lb)	
normal	5,780 (12,745)
overload	5,980 (13,186)
Total load, kg (lb)	1,465 (3,230)
Maximum speed, km/h (mph)	
at sea level	529 (329)*
at rated altitude	576 (358)*
Range, km (miles)	800 (497)
Take-off run, m (ft)	400 (1,310)
Offensive armament:	
machine-guns	2 ShKAS 7.62mm
cannon	2 VYa 23mm
Bomb load, kg (lb)	
normal	400 (880)
maximum	500 (1,100)
Defensive armament	
cannon	1 × 20mm
AG-2 aircraft grenades	10

*These figures were obtained with a derated engine possessing lower altitude performance.

The Il-2 and the Il-10 in Museums and Collections

Being a truly famous aircraft, the Il-2 is a coveted item for any aviation museum. Genuine Il-2s surviving today are not overly numerous, and those museums in whose possession they now are can justifiably be proud. Fortunately, there are several in a number of countries which can boast having an Il-2 among their exhibits. The Il-10, likewise, has been preserved in a number of collections. The holdings are reviewed here.

Russia

The Il-2

It is a surprising and grievous fact that not a single example of the Il-2 was preserved for posterity in the Soviet Union after it had been finally phased out of service. It shared the fate of many Soviet aircraft of the Second World War that were thoughtlessly sent wholesale to the scrap heap as soon as they were retired. That was an irretrievable loss to the nation's cultural heritage. Later, when aviation enthusiasts stimulated the general interest of the public for historic aircraft, much effort was devoted to making good this loss by resurrecting the Il-2 and other wartime aircraft from wrecks found in lakes and marshes, notably in Karelia. In the course of the last three decades several examples of the Il-2 have thus been restored. Here are, in short, the stories of some of these aircraft.

The first Il-2 resurrected as a memorial appeared in Kuibyshev (at present Samara) in 1974. Young workers of the Kuibyshev aircraft plant restored an Il-2 which had been manufactured by their factory (Plant No.18) and had taken part in combat actions over Karelia and was there shot down and made a forced landing near the lake of Orijarvi. More than thirty years later the wreckage was discovered by a group of enthusiasts

from Kuibyshev conducting a search for veteran warplanes. Careful research revealed that this particular aircraft had belonged to the 828th Attack Air Regiment. It had been flown by pilot K.M. Kotliarevskiy who survived after his aircraft had been shot down. Less fortunate was his gunner Mukhin whose remains were found in the wreckage. After restoration, the aircraft was placed on a pedestal at the factory gate. Later, on 9 May 1975, it was moved and was mounted on a pedestal at the side of one of the city's thoroughfares, the Moscow highway, at a point where it enters the city.

Another Il-2 wreck was discovered in 1974, on the bottom of the bay of Novorossiysk on the Black Sea by student scuba divers. It was later established that the aircraft had been flown by V. Kuznetsov and A. Reshetinskiy of the 8th GvShAP; they were killed in action on 19 April 1943 when their aircraft was shot down. The wreckage was raised and over the next two years made part of an exhibition of war relics. Then a decision was taken to restore it to a static-display standard. This work was carried out by young workers of the Novorossiysk ship repair yard, enjoying the assistance and support from veteran airmen and specialists from the factory that had manufactured the aircraft. Finally, in 1980 the resurrected aircraft was placed on a pedestal and became an important part of the memorial devoted to the defenders of Novorossiysk, the scene of fierce battles during the war. In this case the restoration was performed to museum standard involving the use of original materials (wood and fabric) where necessary. For this reason it was actually suitable only for indoor preservation. There were plans to erect a glazed pavilion around the aircraft, but they were not put into effect, as far as is known (nothing is known about the present state of the exhibit).

In 1977 two examples of the Il-2 were discovered simultaneously in a marsh in the vicinity of Novgorod. They were recovered and transported to Moscow to the premises of the Ilyushin OKB; the transportation involved an Mi-10K crane helicopter flown by V. Koloshenko, a well-known test pilot. General Designer G. Novozhilov, who was heading the OKB at that time, immediately set up a special restoration team which brought one of the aircraft to a standard suitable for outdoor demonstration as a memorial. Accordingly, only metal was used in all parts of the airframe, an appropriate structural strengthening was undertaken and adequate protection against corrosion was ensured. This memorial was inaugurated at the premises of the OKB on 9 May 1978. This particular aircraft, c/n 301064, had been manufactured by Plant No.30 in Moscow in October 1942 and had been on the strength of the 33rd GvShAP of the 6th Air Army.

The other example of the Il-2 from the Novgorod area, c/n 301060, was also restored, in this case specially for the Air Force Museum in Monino. In accordance with the Museum's wishes, it was restored to a condition permitting it to taxi on the airfield under its own power and imitate take-off runs, although it could not get airborne. The aircraft's engine had been preserved sufficiently well to permit its restoration to a working condition. The aircraft, which thus received a new lease of life, appeared in two films dealing with the wartime period; on 15 August 1980 it was turned over to the Monino Museum and became its permanent exhibit. The most moving moment at the inauguration of the new exhibit was a meeting between a former attack aircraft pilot, retired Lt Col M.A. Fedotov and his former wartime mount. Fedotov had flown this aircraft as a pilot of the 71st Attack Air Regiment of the

A restored two-seater Il-2 preserved on a plinth in Novorossiysk, southern Russia. TASS News Agency

3rd Guards Air Division; on one of his sorties his aircraft was damaged by a German fighter, and he made a forced landing in a swamp, managed to get back to his unit and resumed flying on another Il-2.

The year 1978 saw the recovery of yet another Il-2, which eventually went to a square in Voronezh. The aircraft was discovered by scuba divers in a lake in the vicinity of Rakitnoye village, Belgorod district (famous in the Battle of Kursk). It was an Il-2 with the tactical number '21', manufactured in April 1943. It belonged to the 50th Independent Reconnaissance Air Regiment. The aircraft, which had been shot down on 1 September 1943, was salvaged and the remains of its crew given a worthy funeral. The wreckage was sent for restoration to the Voronezh aircraft factory. The restoration was undertaken with a view to preserving the aircraft as

an open-air monument and included measures intended to protect the aircraft from the elements. The aircraft was raised on a pedestal in the Aircraft Constructors Square in Voronezh and inaugurated on 9 May 1979.

Leningrad, now St Petersburg, also came into possession of its own restored Il-2 aircraft. Wreckage was recovered from Beloye lake in the Leningrad district in 1979. Subsequent research showed it to be an aircraft of the 232nd Attack Air Division, 14th Air Army, which was lost on a combat mission on 18 September 1943. The aircraft was restored by specialists of the Leningrad Military District and inaugurated as a memorial on the premises of a local aviation college (presumably, it is this aircraft that is preserved, according to some sources, in the St Petersburg Military Aviation College Memorial Museum).

Another institution which has acquired a restored Il-2 is the Museum of the Northern Fleet Air Force at Safonovo Air Force base in Severomorsk (Kola Peninsula). The wreckage was found in the Arctic tundra and restored to static-display standard by technical personnel of the local Air Force units.

Another restored Il-2 is among several aircraft preserved as memorials at the museum of the Komsomolsk-on-Amur aircraft factory (the present KnAPO). And yet another Il-2 is preserved at the Museum of the Great Patriotic War in Volgograd (the former Stalingrad); it made its appearance there in 1982, when full-scale mock-ups of three wartime aircraft (the Yak-3 fighter, the Su-2 bomber and the Il-2) were placed on public view near the building of the Panorama of the Battle of Stalingrad. According to some sources, the Il-2 mock-up was assembled

This Il-2 was a gate guard at aircraft factory No.18 in Kuibyshev (now Samara) which built it (now the Aviacor Jont-Stock Co.). TASS News Agency

This Il-2 is mounted on a plinth at the main entrance to the premises of the Ilyushin Design Bureau in Moscow. Although restored as a two-seater, this particular example was originally built as a single-seater. TASS News Agency

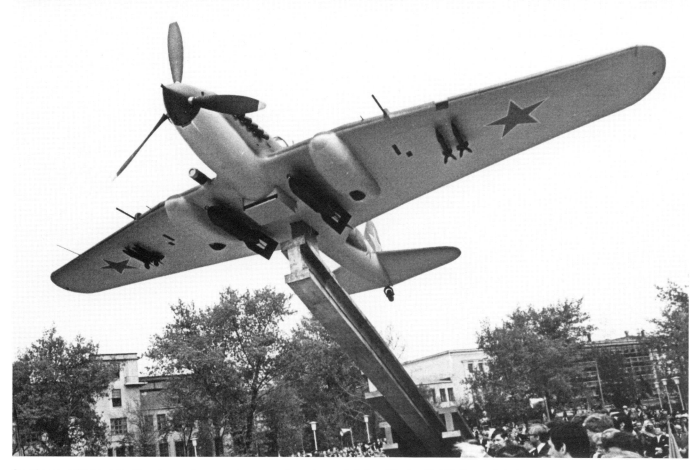

Seen here in 1982, this Il-2 with an impressive array of weaponry is a gate guard at aircraft factory No.64 in Voronezh. TASS News Agency

from original parts of an aircraft which had been preserved at an air unit of the Air Force of the Hungarian People's Republic. High-ranking officials of the Soviet Air Force obtained the consent of the Hungarians to turn these relics over to Soviet representatives who delivered them to Volgograd to be used in restoration. All the aircraft described so far are two-seater versions of the Il-2. The Victory Museum in Moscow has acquired its own example of the Il-2 – this time of the single-seater. It appears to be a mock-up, not a restoration job.

This list is almost certainly incomplete; many more wrecks suitable for restoration were recovered from woods and marshes. Some of them found their way to collectors abroad.

The Il-10

The Air Force Museum in Monino has among its exhibits an example of the Il-10M which was delivered to the Museum

on 17 June 1959. The aircraft was originally painted dark green on upper surfaces and light grey-blue underneath and sported a red star centrally placed on the white propeller spinner. Now it wears camouflage consisting of two shades of green, and the spinner has been repainted all-red. It carries no tactical number.

Belorussia

The Il-10

An example of the initial production version of the Il-10 was placed on a pedestal and preserved as a monument in a Soviet Army garrison in Lida, on the territory of the then Soviet Belorussia, in 1965 to commemorate the twentieth anniversary of wartime victory. After the dissolution of the Soviet Union it was 'inherited' by the newly independent Belorussia. The aircraft had belonged to the 226th Attack Air Division, which was transformed into

the 1st Guards Stalingrad Attack Air Division in March 1943. In the course of the war this air unit was decorated five times with prestigious orders: the Red Banner Order (twice), the Orders of Suvorov and Kutuzov (famous Field Marshals in Russian military history), and the Order of Lenin. Eighty-one pilots of that division were awarded the title of Hero of the Soviet Union. The aircraft was put on display in Lida in response to a request from the veterans of this Division. Painted on its fuselage are the Orders that had been conferred on the Division.

Bulgaria

The Il-2

An example of an Il-2 was preserved in one of the museums in Sofia; from there it was transferred to Plovdiv where it forms part of the collection of the Army Museum at present.

This single-seater Il-2 ('15 White') preserved in the open-air display at the Great Patriotic War Museum in Moscow is a mock-up. It is seen here in July 1997 shortly after its arrival at the Museum. Sergey Komissarov

Above: **By June 2002 the Il-2 mock-up at the Great Patriotic War Museum received a fresh coat of paint and a new tactical number, '21 White'. The star insignia are disproportionately small.** Dmitriy Komissarov

This crude mock-up of an Il-2 is erected on a plinth at a Russian Army garrison. Yefim Gordon archive

If the previous mock-up was crude, this one is ridiculous; aircraft restoration enthusiasts must be rotating in their graves. This excuse for a mock-up was built by Russian Army conscripts who were completing their two-year service term, and was preserved at a Russian Air Force base in (former East) Germany; note the UTI MiG-15 and Yak-27R in the background. Yefim Gordon archive

China

The Il-10

Several examples of the Il-10 are preserved in two museums in the Chinese capital. An Il-10 with a tactical number 6 and c/n 7100-25 is among the exhibits at the Beijing Aviation Museum. As many as five Il-10s are listed as belonging to the collection of the China Aviation Museum at Datang Shan in Beijing. They carry the tactical numbers 33, 80, 83, 96 and 1219.

Czech Republic

The Il-2

Two surviving examples of the Il-2 (both of the two-seater combat version, the so-called Il-2m3) are listed among the exhibits of the Aviation Museum (Letecke Museum) in Prague (Kbely airfield). One of them, c/n 12438, carries a tactical number 38.

The Il-10

Single examples of the B-33 and the CB-33 have been preserved in the same museum. These are: the B-33, c/n B33-5502, tactical number 5502, and the CB-33, c/n CB33-5271, tactical number 5271.

United Kingdom

The Il-2

Some examples of the Il-2 have found their way to the United Kingdom in the shape of wreckage discovered during recent years and deemed suitable for restoration. In 1998 three Il-2s, comprising two single- and one two-seater with a rear gunner station were imported by Jim Pearce. A fourth example was added later. Their subsequent fate is unknown.

Norway

The Il-2

Understandably, Norway was not among the countries that operated the Il-2s nor the Il-10s. However, some years ago it came into possession of an Il-2 now preserved as a museum piece. The story behind the exhibit is as follows: in 1983 a wreckage of an Il-2 was discovered in northern Norway in Sennagressvannet lake, south-east of Kirkenes (the scene of combat when Soviet troops liberated the area in November 1944). The Il-2 was shot down on 22 October 1944; the pilot survived but the tail gunner perished. In 1984 the wreck was raised by a local group and the engine was restored in the area. A

request to the Russian authorities for spares resulted in an offer to rebuild the airframe. In June 1988, in a cooperative act, the wreckage was sent to a factory in the small Soviet town of Revda, near Murmansk where a group of eight enthusiasts spent a year restoring it to static-display standard.

In October 1989 it was ferried back to Norway and placed in a special hangar in Kirkenes (photographs show it in the process of assembly, with the wing panels still not attached). Official inauguration of the exhibit took place in December 1989. The Armed Forces Museum (*Forsvarsmuseet*) in Oslo was designated as the official owner of the exhibit. This is a two-seater, sporting c/n 303560 (indicating that it was manufactured by Plant No.30) and a tactical number 2-white on its rudder and the head of a reindeer on the fuselage sides. Later the aircraft went to a new Borderland Museum (Grenseland Museum) in Kirkenes, in the district (*fylke*) of Sør-Varanger, where it is on permanent view, being officially on loan from the Armed Forces Museum.

Poland

The Il-2

A rare, genuine, original Il-2 (as distinct from restored examples) has been

This Il-10M joined the collection of the Soviet Air Force Museum (now the Central Russian Air Force Museum) in Monino. It is seen here in the late 1960s, still in its original uniform green camouflage with light blue undersides and a white spinner with a red star. Yefim Gordon archive

Below: The Il-10M made a brief excursion from Monino to Moscow-Domodedovo for the 9 July 1967 air show. Yefim Gordon archive

The Il-10M made a brief excursion from Monino to Moscow-Domodedovo for the 9 July 1967 air show. Yefim Gordon archive

Unfortunately, some aviation museums have a habit of repainting their exhibits without bothering about accuracy, and Monino is one of them. In the early 1990s the Il-10 at Monino received this mottled camouflage scheme and an all-red spinner. Yefim Gordon archive

preserved in the Warsaw Museum of the Polish Armed Forces (*Museum Wojska Polskiego*). Carrying a tactical number 23, it is a late-series, two-seater version (known in the West as Il-2m3).

The Il-10

Three examples of the Il-10 have been preserved. One of them forms part of the collection of the Polish Armed Forces Museum and is a Soviet-produced model, c/n 5523, with two VYa-23 cannon and two ShKAS machine-guns, sporting tactical number 011 (a false one). A second is a B-33 of Czechoslovak origin (tactical number 4, c/n B33-3061), armed with four NS-23 cannon and is in the Polish Aviation Museum (*Museum Lotnictwa Polskiego*) in Krakow. The third model, c/n B33-5339, tactical number 11, belongs to the Lubuskie Military Museum (*Lubuskie Museum Wojskowe*) in the town of Letnica, south-west of Zielona Gora.

Romania

The Il-10

An example of the B-33 (Czechoslovak-built Il-10) sporting, surprisingly, Hungarian markings and a tactical number of 81-white (817, according to some sources) is preserved at a museum in Bucarest-Baneasa.

The USA

The Il-2

The USA came into possession of an example of an Il-2 recovered from a lake in the former Soviet Union. The wreckage, in fairly good condition, was delivered to California in 2000 and was put on sale for the benefit of those willing to undertake its restoration. Possibly it is this aircraft that later came to be listed among the exhibits of the National Air and Space Museum, Washington. According to some sources, the Smithsonian Institution, in Washington, is in possession of an Il-2 which had been restored in St Petersburg.

The Il-10

As related in Chapter 10, two captured North Korean Il-10s were shipped to the USA and tested at the Wright-Patterson AFB, Dayton, OH. Their subsequent fate is unknown.

Yugoslavia (Serbia and Montenegro)

The Il-2

A two-seat Il-2, c/n 308331, tactical number 4154, has been preserved at the Yugoslav Aviation Museum (*Muzej Yugoslovenskog Vazduhplovstva*) in Beograd.

The wreckage of this Moscow-built Il-2 (c/n 303561) was discovered in 1983 in Lake Sennagressvannet in northern Norway, south-east of Kirkenes. After recovery in 1984, the aircraft was painstakingly restored in 1988–89 by Russian enthusiasts. Here it is seen in Kirkenes in October 1989 during reassembly. The aircraft is now on display at the local Grensemuseum (Borderland Museum). Sergey Komissarov

Another view of II-2 '2 White' (c/n 303561) in Kirkenes; note the stag's head artwork. Sergey Komissarov

The c/n on the II-2 restored for the Norwegian museum has been applied in error as 3035561. Sergey Komissarov

Left: This well-preserved two-seater Il-2 resides at the *Muzeum Wojska Polskiego* (Polish Armed Forces Museum) in Warsaw in company with other Soviet types. The gunner's station has been closed off with sheet metal to stop rain from getting in. Yefim Gordon

Below: The Il-2 at the *Muzeum Wojska Polskiego* has an equally well-kept Il-10 (c/n 5542) to keep it company. Yefim Gordon

Il-2 Versions

As we have seen, this aircraft was produced in numerous versions and variations – understandably so bearing in mind the huge production run of more than 36,000. It would be an exceedingly difficult task to compile a complete a list of these versions, given the scarcity of detailed information available in many cases and the confusion arising from discrepancies between sources. Attempts to do so have been undertaken by some researchers, notably by I. Rodionov, and by V.I. Perov and O.V. Rastrenin. The authors here have attempted to produce their own list, based largely on the work of these researchers and combining some features of both approaches.

Only a few Il-2 versions, as stated earlier, had their specific designations such as Il-2U, Il-2bis, Il-2I and Il-2KR. These were usually allocated to versions intended for other mission types rather than the basic attack mission. The aircraft featured several engines in the course of its development and career, and this, in accordance with the practice of that period, was reflected in the designations which included the mention of the engine type (such as Il-2 AM-38, Il-2 AM-38F and Il-2 M-82). Single-seater and two-seater versions were not distinguished by special designations and, in case of need, were just described as single- or two-seaters. Other changes that were made in the course of Il-2 production may be generally be classed in one of the following categories:

Airframe Modifications

Changes involving aerodynamic improvements included the increasing of the leading edge sweep-back (undertaken twice in the course of the aircraft's development), increasing the stabilizer area, introducing the fixed flap setting at take-off. Structural changes introduced progressively on the production line were often dictated by the availability or not of materials and included the substitution of wooden rear fuselage and wooden outer wing panels for metal ones early in the aircraft's career, reverting to metal airframe components when the situation allowed; local strengthening of the airframe

(notably, the wooden aft fuselages); redistribution of the thickness of armour plating in different areas of the armour shell; and extending the armour shell aft to include the gunner's cockpit.

Modifications to Aircraft Systems and Equipment

These included items such as the control system, hydraulic system, propellers, instruments, navigation and radio equipment.

Modifications to the Armament

These included the introduction of defensive armament; the use of different types of wing-mounted cannon and rear-firing machine-gun; introduction of different types of gunsight and bombsight; changes in the bomb complement (the introduction of new types of bomb and methods of their external or internal stowage); alterations to guide rails for rocket projectiles to suit the several types; experiments with some unorthodox types of armament (such as mortars and flame throwers).

While not being exhaustive, these give an idea of the number of variables that went into making up the many versions. To characterize each of them fully, it would be desirable to be able to state in each case all the basic variable features: single- or two-seater; all-metal airframe or wooden aft fuselage/wing panels; engine subtype; cannon and machine-gun complement; and special features. It is also useful to know which plant manufactured a particular version (although required to stick strictly to the same standard, the plants inevitably introduced some elements of their own). Unfortunately, in many cases such completeness of information is unattainable. With these reservations, there follows a list of the identifiable versions of the Il-2, including development aircraft, production versions, experimental one-off aircraft and, in some cases, projects which did not reach the hardware stage. The versions are listed, as far as possible, in chronological order.

LT AM-34FRNV (BSh AM-34FRN): this was the original designation of the attack aircraft project as submitted by Ilyushin in January 1938, the LT being the Russian acronym for 'flying tank'. This figurative description soon gave place to the sober BSh (armoured attack aircraft) and the project was known for some time as the BSh AM-34FRN. In the course of the project work, Ilyushin had to relinquish the AM-34FRN engine and opted for the AM-35 with an appropriate change in the designation.

TsKB-55 (BSh AM-35) (BSh-2 AM-35): the TsKB-55 was the Design Bureau designation, while the BSh AM-35 was the service designation. The digit 2 appeared, according to some sources, in the course of testing the prototypes, but is used by most authors irrespective of that, while the designation BSh AM-35 is generally ignored. This was the original two-seater version with an aft-firing machine-gun for defence in addition to its quartet of forward-firing ShKAS machine-guns. Two prototypes were built and subsequently modified repeatedly in the process of testing and development. These were:

TsKB-55 No.1 (BSh AM-35 No.1) (BSh-2 AM-35 No.1): this first prototype of the future Il-2 was completed in July 1939 and made its first flight on 2 October. In the course of testing it underwent various modifications (initially it lacked the radio, mass balances on the ailerons and armour-glass windscreen) and the cooling system (coolant and oil radiators) was subjected to experimentation before the designers arrived at the final arrangement. Later it was modified into the single-seater TsKB-57 (*see* below).

TsKB-55 No.2 (BSh-2 AM-35 No.2): this second prototype of the future Il-2 took to the air for the first time on 30 December 1939 and passed State acceptance trials in the period between 1 and 19 April 1940. In parallel with the first prototype, it was used for experimenting with different arrangements of the cooling system. Later it was modified into the TsKB-55P (*see* below).

TsKB-57 (BSh-2 No.1 AM-38): this became the designation of the first TsKB-55 prototype after it had been converted into a single-seater and re-engined with the AM-38. So modified, the aircraft passed its manufacturer's testing in October 1940. Deletion of the gunner's station made it possible to install an additional fuel tank and thus increase the range. Other changes included shifting the engine forward by 50mm, increasing the leading-edge sweep-back of the wing panels by 5 degrees and increasing the stabilizer area. The fixed armament remained unchanged. According to Perov, in April 1941 the TsKB-57 was modified back to a two-seater configuration, this time as a dual-control aircraft, thus becoming the forerunner of the later Il-2U trainer.

TsKB-55P (BSh-2 No.2 AM-38): this was the second TsKB-55 prototype modified, like the first prototype, to a single-seater configuration and powered, likewise, by the new AM-38 engine. In addition to changes which it shared with the TsKB-57, the TsKB-55 featured several other modifications. Its engine was lowered and the pilot's cockpit raised, which provided the pilot with better visibility; the elongated fairing aft of the cockpit characteristic of the TsKB-57 was replaced by a shorter, glazed fairing. The armament fit was modified to include two wing mounted MP-6 23mm cannon supplemented by two ShKAS machine-guns. Difficulties with the MP-6 canon led to their replacement by ShVAK 20mm cannon. The TsKB-55P acquired the contours similar to those of the future series-produced machine and became virtually the true prototype of the initial production single-seater Il-2 (this new name was allocated to the BSh-2 in December 1940 in accordance with the new Soviet system of aircraft designations).

IL-2 AM-38: early production, single-seater with two Taubin MP-6 cannon and two ShKAS machine-guns. Modified belt-fed MP-6 cannon were installed on one of the first production examples of the Il-2, and a fly-off was arranged between this version and a production example fitted with the 23mm VYa (Volkov-Yartsev) cannon (*see* below). The latter emerged as a winner and the MP-6 was discarded.

Il-2 AM-38: single-seater with the VYa-2 cannon, and two ShKAS machine-guns, early production. Two cannon of this type were installed on one of the first production examples of the Il-2 and were given preference, as noted above, over the MP-6 cannon in the course of comparative testing. Service introduction of this weapon on the Il-2 was initially delayed by production difficulties, but eventually they were surmounted and the VYa-23 became, together with ShVAK, one of the two main types of cannon used on the Il-2 throughout the war.

Il-2 AM-38: single-seater with two ShVAK cannon and two ShKAS machine-guns, early production. The ShVAK 20mm cannon installed on one of the first production examples of the Il-2 were immediately adopted for large-scale production and for some time all Il-2s were manufactured with this weapon before deliveries of the VYa cannon got under way.

Il-2 AM-38: single-seater with the SG-23 (TsKB-14 NKV) 23mm cannon. This weapon was installed in the wings of a single example of an early production Il-2 in addition to the usual pair of the ShKAS machine-guns; the results were considered unsatisfactory and the weapon was discarded.

Il-2 AM-38: single-seater early production with boiler-plate front fuselages instead of armour plating. There is evidence that early difficulties with the delivery of armoured shells by subcontractors to production plants prompted one of them to suggest turning out a small batch of Il-2s with boiler plating as a substitute for the special armour steel. How many were produced (if any) is not known.

Il-2 AM-38: single-seater production version with ShVAK cannon placed inboard of the ShKAS machine-guns. This arrangement was used on some but by no means all aircraft of this type, although it was considered preferable to the opposite arrangement (*see* below) from the point of view of the accuracy of cannon fire.

Il-2 AM-38: single-seater production version with ShVAK cannon outboard of the ShKAS machine-guns. Criticized by some experts now, this arrangement, nevertheless, was used on many ShVAK-armed Il-2s.

Il-2 AM-38: single-seater, mass-produced version with VYa cannon placed outboard of the machine-guns. This arrangement of the weapons was characteristic for the Vya-armed Il-2s when its manufacture got into full swing.

Il-2 AM-38: single-seater with two B-20 cannon. Documentary evidence concerning attempts to install the 20mm Berezin B-20 cannon in the wings of the Il-2 is rather vague, no accounts of actual tests being available.

Il-2 AM-38 (and AM-38F?): single-seater with reinforced wooden rear fuselage (field modification). The low strength of the wooden rear fuselages of the Il-2s prompted frontline units to resort to strengthening this part of the airframe with aluminium extrusions riveted in two pairs externally to the upper and the lower side of the aft fuselage.

Il-2 AM-38: c/n 1878916 with reinforced wooden fuselage and TsAGI filter on the carburettor air intake. This example is interesting as introducing the dust filter, which was absent on the single-seater machines and found widespread use on Il-2s only after the single-seater was supplanted in production by the two-seater machine.

Il-2 AM-38: single-seater production model with factory-built, reinforced, wooden fuselage. As distinct from the field modifications or those made during repairs, the strengthening of the aft fuselages of the Il-2s on the production line was effected internally. Six additional stringers were installed and the skinning thickness was increased by adding a few layers of *shpon* (veneer).

Il-2 AM-38: single-seater production model with wooden undercarriage fairings, wooden cockpit canopy aft fairing and wooden outer wing panels. The 'extra large' amount of wooden elements of the airframe on this particular production version is noteworthy.

Il-2 AM-38: single-seater production model with fixed skis. Joint State Acceptance trials of a machine manufactured by Plant No.381 (c/n 381403), initiated in December 1941 and completed on 21 January, were conducted on fixed skis. The aircraft was identical to the machines of the four initial production batches of Plant No.18. Armament: two ShKAS machine-guns, two ShVAK cannon.

Il-2 AM-38: single-seater production model with retractable skis. Joint State Acceptance tests of a machine manufactured by Plant No.18 (c/n 181904) on retractable skis were completed on 2 February 1942. Armament: two ShKAS machine-guns, two ShVAK cannon.

Il-2 AM-38: single-seater with foamed rubber wheels. Intended to eliminate the danger of landing accidents caused by tyre bursts (due to enemy bullets), this version was under development but failed to find widespread use.

Il-2 AM-38: single-seater with Chechubalin-designed, caterpillar undercarriage (he was an aviation engineer who experimented with this undercarriage on several types of aircraft). Application of this idea to the Il-2 was studied but does not seem to have emerged as a practical solution.

Il-2 AM-38: single-seater with two fixed ShKAS machine-guns for rear defence (prototype). This version was developed by the Ilyushin OKB in mid 1942 as a stopgap measure to provide rear defence for the Il-2 lacking the aft-firing flexible weapon. Two aft-firing ShKAS machine-guns were mounted on a production single-seater, a measure of sighting being effected with the help of mirrors. Tests showed this version of defensive armament to be insufficiently effective and it was not adopted for large-scale production. This was true of another version of fixed defensive armament (*see* below), developed concurrently.

Il-2 AM-38: single-seater with one fixed Berezin UBT machine-gun for rear defence (prototype). Developed to the same requirement as the version described above, it possessed the same shortcomings and, in consequence, shared its fate. Both this and the preceding version had the basic armament fit comprising two ShKAS machine-guns and two ShVAK cannon.

Il-2 AM-38: single-seater with four drop tanks. No details are available on this version (mentioned by Perov and Rastrenin in their study on the Il-2).

Il-2 AM-38: single-seater with fourteen RO-132 launching rails for rocket projectiles. Again, nothing is known about this version apart from its being fitted with the usual complement of ShKAS and ShVAK weapons.

Il-2 AM-38: single-seater with eight RO-82 and eight RO-132 launching rails for unguided rockets (the RS-82 and RS-132, respectively), supplementing the basic armament fit as above. The unusually large number of rockets was presumably carried at the expense of the bomb load.

Il-2 AM-38: single-seater with two 37mm ShFK-37 (Sh-37) cannon and the usual pair of ShKAS machine-guns. A prototype of this version underwent State acceptance trials between 23 September and 12 October 1941. Of the planned production batch of twenty machines, only nine were built, apart from the prototype; they saw action in the Stalingrad area at the end of December 1942 and in January 1943. Insufficient accuracy and reliability of these 37mm cannon prevented this version from being adopted for large-scale production.

Il-2 AM-38: single-seater with the AOG flame-thrower. Testing of this device on the Il-2 was conducted in August 1941 and October 1942. The AOG consisted of the UKhAP-250 universal chemical container with inbuilt ignition system. Tests revealed that the intensity of fire when it reached the ground was too low to produce a worthwhile effect. The device was deemed unsuitable for combat use.

Il-2 M-82: two-seater, first prototype. Powered by the M-82 radial engine, this version was developed primarily with a view to providing the Il-2 with an alternative to the AM-38 engine. Simultaneously the aircraft was made a two-seater with a gunner for rear defence. The armament comprised two ShKAS machine-guns, two ShVAK cannon and one aft-firing UBT-12.7 machine-gun. Converted from a production single-seater manufactured by Plant No.18, the prototype made its first flight on 8 September 1941. The gunner's cockpit was armour-protected and had a blister mounting for the aft-firing machine-gun. Initially the prototype lacked the blister mounting which appeared on 20 February 1942,

according to Perov. State acceptance trials lasted from 4 February to 22 March 1942.

Il-2 M-82IR: two-seater, second prototype, manufactured by Plant No.39. Armament: two ShKAS, two ShVAK, one aft-firing UBT-12.7. State acceptance trials were conducted between 20 February and 25 April 1942. Plans for series production were cancelled when difficulties with the AM-38 engine were overcome and the M-82 engine was deemed more urgently required for Lavochkin fighters.

Il-2 M-82IR: single-seater, manufactured by Plant No.381 before plans for series production were cancelled. Armament: two ShKAS machine-guns, two ShVAK cannon. The reason for reverting to a single-seater configuration is unknown. The engine had some armour plating on the underside of the cowling (the two prototypes had no armour protection on the engines).

Il-2 AM-38: two-seater, frontline conversions. A number of single-seater Il-2s were converted by technical personnel of frontline air units into two-seaters with a gunner station. There were numerous variations as to the type of the aft-firing machine-gun and its mounting; the weapon could be the 7.62mm DA or ShKAS or the 12.7mm UBT machine-gun; turret rings from the Pe-2 or the R-5 were sometimes used.

Il-2 AM-38: two-seater prototype with an aft-firing UBT machine-gun. Converted at Plant No.30 from a production single-seater Il-2, c/n 30887. Forward-firing armament comprised two ShKAS and two ShVAK. The gunner's cockpit was accommodated outside the armour shell. He was protected in the rear by an armour plate, but lacked armour protection at the sides and beneath. This version was developed in parallel with a similar prototype fitted with a ShKAS for rear protection (*see* below) and chosen for mass production after comparative tests. The sub-type was launched into production at three plants in October 1942.

Il-2 AM-38: two-seater prototype with an aft-firing ShKAS machine-gun, produced by Plant No.30 by converting a production single-seater machine, c/n 30897. Forward-firing armament comprised two

ShKAS and two ShVAK. Manufacturer's and State acceptance tests were conducted in parallel with the similar version armed with the UBT machine-gun (*see* above), to which it lost. However, the prototype with the aft-firing ShKAS formed the basis for numerous field conversions.

Il-2 AM-38: two-seater, armament fit: two ShKAS, two ShVAK, one aft-firing UBT on the VUB-3 mounting. Mass-produced from October 1942.

Il-2 AM-38: two-seater, armament fit: two ShKAS, two VYa-23, one aft-firing UBT on the VUB-3 mounting. Mass-produced from October 1942.

Il-2 AM-38: a two-seater version developed by Plant No.1. Independently of the Ilyushin OKB, Plant No.1 designed and built its own version of a two-seater Il-2 with a flexible aft-firing machine-gun. This was done in response to requests from officers of service air units. However, when the Ilyushin OKB designed and tested the prototype of a two-seater version, it was adopted for production by Plant No.1, and the Plant's own design was shelved.

Il-2 AM-38: two-seater, with two ShKAS machine-guns, two ShVAK cannon and one aft-firing ShKAS, converted in the field by factory repair teams from single-seater machines. Development completed in October 1942.

Il-2bis (Il-2 AM-38 two-seater with the BLUB defensive installation): A prototype of this version was built at Plant No.1. Its armament comprised two ShKAS machine-guns, two ShVAK cannon and one aft-firing UBT in a blister installation dubbed BLUB (translated as Berezin's blister installation). The gunner's cockpit was fully armour-protected and occupied the place of the rear fuel tank, instead of which two smaller tanks of the same total volume were installed in the wing centre section bomb-bays. The fuel tanks were armour-protected. The blister installation incorporated armour-glass protecting the gunner. The aircraft passed State acceptance tests in October 1942 and was sent to the front where it was well liked, especially by the gunners. However, the aircraft was not launched into series manufacture mainly due to the problems it could create on the production line.

Il-2M AM-42: this experimental version of the Il-2 was powered by the AM-42 engine of considerably greater output (2,000hp) compared with the AM-38. It was a heavy attack aircraft with an increased bomb load (500kg [1,100lb] instead of 400kg). Its special feature was a turret for rear defence, a steel dome providing excellent protection for the gunner at the expense of vision, which was severely restricted. Eventually this turret was dismantled and replaced first by a normal glazed turret and then by a machine-gun mount of the standard type used on production two-seaters. The aircraft fitted with a propeller of 4m diameter (13ft) showed an improvement in performance in comparison with the standard Il-2; however, the propeller caused severe vibrations and had to be discarded; with a smaller one the Il-2M AM-42 possessed only marginal advantages in performance. It did not progress beyond the prototype stage.

Il-2 AM-42 (S-42): another AM-42-powered, two-seater prototype with improved aerodynamics, the work on which was conducted in Ilyushin's OKB. The work was not completed.

Il-2 AM-38F: two-seater, two ShKAS, two VYa-23, one aft-firing UBT on VUB-3 mounting, in series production from January 1943.

Il-2 AM-38F?: two-seater, a prototype with the VYa cannon modified to accept 14.5mm armour-piercing ammunition. Development work was conducted by Plant No.240 in December 1942; no information on testing is available.

Il-2 AM-38F: single-seater, two ShKAS, two VYa-23, in series production from January 1943.

Il-2 AM-38F: single-seater, two ShKAS, two ShVAK, in series production from January 1943 (this version, as well as the VYa-armed single-seater, were produced for some time with the AM-38F engines concurrently with the two-seater AM-38F-powered model).

Il-2 AM-38F: two-seater with water injection for boosting the engine output. An 80ltr water tank was mounted in the rear cockpit instead of the gunner. Not adopted for series manufacture.

Il-2 AM-38: dual-control, two-seater, boiler-plate front fuselage instead of armour shell, prototypes (requirement issued to the OKB on 16 July 1941). The dual-control version came later to be known as the Il-2U or UIl-2 (*see* below).

Il-2 AM-38: dual-control, two-seater, initial series production (presumably not making use of armour steel).

Il-2U (UIl-2) AM-38F: dual-control two-seater with normal production type armour shell. In series production from April 1943 (variations from batch to batch in rear cockpit glazing and equipment).

Il-2U (UIl-2) AM-38F, c/n 18841133: manufactured by Plant No.18 in April 1945. This aircraft, tested in the NII VVS between 31 May and 8 June 1945, featured improvements in the gunner's cockpit and modifications to the glazing of the front cockpit (armour-glass windscreen, transparent panels in the sides of the sliding canopy instead of the metal ones).

Il-2U (UIl-2): field conversions; some examples of the dual-control version of the Il-2 were produced by technical personnel of field repair shops by converting combat machines.

Il-2U (UIl-2): as target tug; the Il-2U could be fitted with special equipment in the aft fuselage for the purpose of target towing.

Il-2KR AM-38F: two-seater, artillery-spotting and reconnaissance aircraft, series-produced from April 1943 on the basis of both the ShVAK-armed and the VYa-armed versions of the basic Il-2. Apart from being fitted with the AFA-I or AFA-IM aerial camera, it differed from the basic Il-2 in equipment, fuel system and distribution of armour plating. The aircraft was provided with a more powerful RSB-3bis radio instead of the standard RSI-4. The Il-2KR was externally recognizable by the location of its antenna mast, which was moved to the windshield.

Il-2KR AM-38F: field modification with additional cameras in the undercarriage fairings.

Il-2KR AM-38F: field modifications with

additional cameras in the fuselage or on top of the rear fuselage.

Il-2 AM-38F: two-seater with the MV-3 turret. The fully enclosed turret fitted with the UBT machine-gun afforded considerable improvement in the field of fire. Development of the prototype was completed in May 1943. Higher drag created by the bulky turret led to some deterioration of performance; this prevented the installation from gaining wide acceptance.

Il-2 AM-38F: two-seater with fibre fuel tanks featuring protective coating. Both the ShVAK- and the VYa-armed aircraft were manufactured in this configuration.

Il-2 AM-38F: two-seater with two ShKAS and two NS-37 cannon, series manufacture from May 1943. Production was terminated in late 1943 because service testing revealed the poor accuracy of the NS-37 caused by heavy recoil in combination with imperfect synchronization of the cannon.

Il-2 AM-38F: two-seater with two ShKAS and two NS-45 (45mm) cannon. A prototype was built in the autumn of 1943. Tested, but not adopted for series production due to problems caused by heavy recoil.

Il-2 AM-38F: two-seater with two ShKAS and two Sh-45 (45mm) cannon. Prototype was completed in October 1943, but there is no evidence of any testing. The project was abandoned.

Il-2I AM-38F: a single-seater fighter version, intended for attacking enemy bombers. The Il-2I was converted into the new configuration from a production two-seater machine, with wooden outer wing panels, c/n 7581, manufactured by Plant No.1. The armament was restricted to two VYa cannon and two 250kg bombs carried externally. ShKAS machine-guns, rocket launch rails and internal bomb shackles were dismantled, bomb-bays were faired over. Tests conducted in 1943 revealed limited usefulness of the Il-2I in the intended role and the aircraft was not ordered into production.

Il-2 AM-38F: two-seater (ShVAK-armed version) with eight unguided, rear-firing

rockets for rear defence (development completed in July 1943); prototype only.

Il-2 AM-38F: two-seater (VYa-armed version) with two PLGB 150ltr (33gal) drop tanks. Passed State acceptance tests between 29 September and 10 October 1943. The tanks were adopted for service use.

Il-2 AM-38F: two-seater (VYa-armed version) with two PTB 175ltr (39gal) metal drop tanks. Underwent State acceptance tests between 29 September and 10 October 1943. The tanks were not adopted.

Il-2: with damper and counterbalance in the elevator control system. In July 1943 an example of the Il-2 (presumably an AM-38F-powered, two-seater) featuring this modification was under test in the LII (Flight Research Institute). This innovation increased the aircraft's longitudinal stability and ease of handling during manoeuvres, such as banking turns and diving. It was recommended that the modification be incorporated in production aircraft.

Il-2: with horn balances on the elevator. In July 1943 the LII, in response to a task issued by TsAGI, conducted an evaluation of the influence of 5.1 per cent horn balances of the elevator on longitudinal stability and controllability. It was established that this did not affect in any appreciable way stability and controllability.

Il-2: with the M-250 engine (a project). Ilyushin came up with the idea of fitting the Il-2 experimentally with the M-250 engine which was under development then in the KB-2 MAI design bureau (Dobrynin). This heavy, twenty-four-cylinder engine was expected to deliver 2,270hp at take-off. The aircraft was to feature more potent armament, comprising two wing-mounted VYa-23 cannon, two wing-mounted UBT machine-guns and a UBT for rear defence. The bomb load would be 600kg (1,300lb) and 800kg (1,800lb) in overload configuration. Flight speeds were expected to be boosted to 450km/h (280mph) at ground level and 490km/h (304mph) at an altitude of 2,500m (8,200ft). However, the development of the M-250 engine ran into difficulties, and the project had to be abandoned (presumably before reaching the hardware stage).

Il-2 AM-38F: two-seater (VYa-armed version) with new metal wing outer panels featuring increased sweep-back (15 degrees on the leading edges). This modification was intended to compensate for the rearward shift of the CG after the transition from the single- to the two-seater version of the Il-2. This shift caused the worsening of the aircraft's longitudinal stability. Tests conducted in 1943 in the NII VVS showed that the aircraft with the new wings had its CG at 28.0 per cent of the MAC, while the figure for the production machines was 32.3. Longitudinal stability was considerably improved. It took some time for this modification to be adopted due to some difficulties in getting the manufacture of metal wings under way; aircraft with the modified wings started appearing in quantity in mid 1944.

Il-2 AM-38F: two-seater (VYa-armed version) with the UBSh installation (UBT machine-gun) for rear defence. A prototype, development completed in March 1944. The new installation afforded some increase in the field of fire for the aft-firing machine-gun, but on the whole displayed no decisive advantages over the standard VUB-3 mount. Its introduction into service was deemed inexpedient.

Il-2 AM-38F: two-seater (VYa-armed version) with the armour shell extended aft to include the gunner's cockpit. In series manufacture from mid 1944.

Il-2 AM-38F: two-seater (VYa-armed version) featuring additional strap-on armour plating to protect the gunner's cockpit (field conversion sets). Developed in July 1944.

Il-2U AM-38F: dual-control trainer with the armour shell extended aft to include the rear cockpit. In series manufacture from January 1945.

Il-2KR AM-38F: two-seater (VYa-armed version) reconnaissance and artillery-spotting aircraft with the armour shell extended aft to provide protection for the gunner/observer. An example of this version manufactured by Plant No.30 (c/n 308099) was tested in April 1945. The aircraft also featured late-model, outer wing panels with increased sweep-back; the wooden aft fuselage section was shortened by 135mm (5.3in). Despite a favourable test report, this modification was not phased into production because the war was nearing its end.

Il-2 AM-38F: two-seater, c/n 303316, with wooden wings featuring increased sweep-back on the leading edges. The first-stage testing of this machine manufactured by Plant No.30 was completed on 16 May 1944.

Il-2 AM-38F: two-seater, two ShKAS, two VYa, revised defensive armament (one UB-20 cannon instead of the UBT machine-gun). Successfully tested in August 1944. No series manufacture was undertaken due to the low reliability of the UB-20.

Il-2 AM-38F: two-seater (VYa-armed version) with a combined throttle-and-propeller-pitch lever. Developed to a requirement issued in August 1944. Recommended for service introduction.

Il-2 AM-38F: two-seater (VYa-armed version) with duplicate elevator control linkages. Development completed in July 1944 (similar work had earlier been carried out on other sub-types both by the OKB and by service units).

Il-2 AM-38F: two-seater (VYa-armed version) with the AV-9A-158 four-bladed propeller. Tests conducted in 1943 showed that this experimental propeller could not be recommended for production.

Il-2 AM-38F: two-seater, all-metal construction (metal wings and aft fuselages instead of wooden ones). Armament fit – presumably the standard version with the VYa cannon. So configured Il-2s were produced by Plant No.18 from mid January 1945.

Abbreviations

AFA: (*aviatsionnyi fotoapparat*) aerial camera

AG: (*aviatsionnaya granata*) aircraft grenade

AM: engines designed by Alexandr Mikulin

ANT: (*Andrey Nikolayevich Tupolev*) design bureau designations of Tupolev aircraft up to 1937

ASh: engines designed by Arkadwy Shvetsov

AUW: All-Up Weight

AV: (*aviatsionnyi vint*) aircraft propeller (in designations)

AVMF: (*Aviatsiya Voyenno-Morskogo Flota*) Naval Air Arm

B: (*bombardirovshchik*) bomber aircraft

B: (*bronirovannyi*) armoured

B-20: 20mm aircraft gun designed by M. Berezin

BB: (*blizhniy bombardirovshchik*) short-range bomber

BMSh: (*bolshaya modifikatsiya shturmovika*) major attack aircraft modification

BSh: (*bombardirovshchik-shturmovik*) bomber and attack aircraft (BSh-1, licence-built Vultee V-11GB)

BSh: (*bronirovannyi shturmovik*) armoured attack aircraft

CG: Centre of Gravity

DAG: (*derzhatel aviatsionnykh granat*) aircraft grenade container

DB: (*dalnii bombardirovshchik*) long-range bomber

DDBSh: (*dalniy dvukhmestnyi bronirovannyi shturmovik*) long-range, two-seater, close air support aircraft

DI: (*dvukhmestnyi istrebitel*) two-seater fighter

Esbr: (*elektricheskiy sbrasyvatel*) electric bomb release device

F: (*forsirovannyi*) boosted (in engine designations)

FAB: (*fugasnaya aviabomba*) high-explosive bomb

G: (*Grokhovskiy*) prefix in designations of aircraft designed or modified by P.I. Grokhovskiy

Gv: abbreviation of *Gvardeiskiy* (Guards), in combination with, for instance, IAP and ShAP, such as GvShAP

I: (*istrebitel*) fighter aircraft

IAP: (*istrebitelnyi aviatsionnyi polk*) fighter air regiment

IL: (*istrebitel [s drigatelem] Liberty*) fighter aircraft powered by a Liberty engine

ITP: (*istrebitel tiazhoyi pushechnyi*) heavy, cannon-armed fighter

KhAI: Kharkov Aviation Institute

LII: (*Lyotno-issledovatelskiy institut*) Flight Research Institute, Zhukovskiy, near Moscow

LR: (*lyogkiy razvedchik*) light reconnaissance aircraft

LSh: (*lyogkiy shturmovik*) light attack aircraft

LT: (*letayushchiy tank*) 'flying tank' (armoured attack aircraft)

M: (*motor*) engine; prefix in Soviet engine designations

M: (*modifitsirovannyi*) modified, suffix in aircraft designations

MAI: Moscow Aviation Institute

MMSh: (*Malaya Modifikatsiya Shturmovika*) minor attack aircraft modification

MP: (*motor-pushka*) 23mm cannon of Taubin design (MP-6), intended for installation between cylinder banks of liquid-cooled V-engine (also suitable for wing installation)

MV: (*Mozharovskiy-Venevidov*) gun turret designed by Georgiy Mozharovskiy and Ivan Venevidov; aircraft of their design

NII VVS: (*nauchno-issledovatel'skiy institut VVS*) Scientific Research Institute of Air Force

NIP AV: (*Nauchno-issledovatel'skiy poligon aviatsionnykh vooruzheniy*) scientific research test range for aircraft armaments

NKAP: (*narodnyi komissariat aviatsionnoy promyshlennosti*) People's Commissariat [ministry] of Aircraft Industry

NKO: (*narodnyi komissariat oborony*) People's Commissariat [ministry] of Defence

NKOP: (*narodnyi komissariat oboronnoy promyshlennosti*) People's Commissariat [ministry] of Defence Industry

NR: (*Nudelman-Rikhter*) aircraft guns designed by A. Nudelman and A. Rikhter

NS: (*Nudelman-Sooranov*) aircraft guns designed by A. Nudelman and A. Suranov

NV: (*neposredstvennyi vprysk*) direct injection (in engine designations)

OBSh: (*odnomestnyi bronirovannyi shturmovik*) single-seater, armoured attack aircraft

OKB: (*opytno-konstruktorskoye biuro*) experimental/prototype design bureau

OKO: (*opytno-konstruktorskiy otdel*) experimental/prototype design section (headed by V.K. Tairov; used as a prefix in designations of his aircraft)

OPB: (*odnomestnyi pikiruyushchiy bombardirovshchik*) single-seater dive bomber

OSh: (*odnomestnyi shturmovik*) single-seater attack aircraft

P: (*pushechnyi*) cannon-armed

PAU: (*pulemyot aviatsionnyi ychebnyi*) gun camera

PBSh: (*pikiruyushchiy bombardirovshchik-shturmovik*) dive bomber/attack aircraft

PIT: (*pushechnyi istrebitel tankov*) cannon-armed tank destroyer (attack aircraft)

PTAB: (*protivotankovaya aviatsionnaya bomba*) air-delivered anti-tank bomb

PTB: (*podvesnoi toplivnyi bak*) external fuel tank

PV: (*pulemyot vozdushnyi*) 7.62mm aircraft machine-gun (based on 'Maxim' design) by A. Nadashkevich and F. Tokarev

R: (*razvedchik*) reconnaissance aircraft

R: (*redukrornyi*) fitted with a reduction gear (in engine designations)

RBS: (*reaktivnyi broneboinyi snariad*) armour-piercing rocket projectile (RBS-82, RBS-132)

RO: (*raketnoye orudie*) launching rail for unguided rockets (RO-82, RO-132, the figures denote the calibre of the rockets in mm)

ROFS: (*reaktivnyi oskolochno-fugasnyi snariad*) high-explosive fragmentation rocket projectile (ROFS-132)

RS: (*reaktivnyi snariad*) rocket projectile (RS-82, RS-132, figures denote the calibre)

RSI: (*radio stantsiya istrebitelnaya*) fighter aircraft radio station

SAM: (*Samolyot Aleksandra Moskalyova*) designation of aircraft designed by A. Moskalyov

SG: (*Salishchev-Galkin*) 23mm gun designed by Salischev and Galkin

Sh: (*shturmovik*) attack aircraft

ShAD: (*shturmovaya aviatsionnaya divisiya*) attack air division

ShAP: (*shturmovoi aviatsionnyi polk*) attack air regiment

ShB: (*shturmovik bronirovannyi*) armoured close-support aircraft

ShFK: (*Shpital'nyi fiuzeliazhno-krylyevaya*) 37mm fuselage- and wing-mounted cannon (ShFK-37) of Shpital'nyi design

ShKAS: (*Shpital'nyi-Komarnitskiy aviatsionnyi skorostrelnyi*) 7.62mm rapid-firing (1,800 rpm) machine-gun of Shpital'nyi and Komarnitskiy design

ShR: (*shturmovik-razvedchik*) attack and reconnaissance aircraft

ShVAK: (*Shpital'nyi Vladimirov aviatsionnaya kr'nyi* and Vladimirov design

SPB: (*skorostnoi pikiruyushchiy bombardirovshchik*) high-speed dive bomber

ss: (*sovershenno sekretno*) top secret (as suffix to the numbers of official documents)

TB: (*tiazholyi bombardirovshchik*) heavy bomber

TIS: (*tiazholyi istrebitel soprovozhdeniya*) heavy escort fighter

TK: (*turbokompressor*) turbosupercharger

TsAGI: (*tsentralnyi aerogidrodinamicheskiy institut*) Central Aerodynamics and Hydrodynamics Institute

TSh: (*tiazholyi shturmovik*) heavy attack aircraft

TsIAM: (*tsentralnyi institut aviatsionnogo motorostroyeniya*) Central Institute of Aviation Motors

TsKB: (*tsentral'noye konstruktorskoye biuro*) Central Design Bureau

U: (*uchebnyi*) trainer (used as suffix or prefix in aircraft designations)

UB: (*universalnaya Berezina*) 20mm gun of Berezin design (UB-20), suitable for all types of installation

UBT: (*univeralnyi Berezina turelnyi*) 12.7mm turret machine-gun of Berezin design

UKhAP: (*universalnyi khimicheskii aviatsionnyi pribor*) versatile chemical aircraft device (UKhAP-250)

UT: (*uchebno-trenirovochnyi*) trainer aircraft

VA: (*Vozdushnaya Armiya*) air army

VIAM: (*vsesoyuznyi institut aviatsionnykh materialov*) All-Union Institute of Aviation Materials

VISh: (*vint izmeniayemogo shaga*) variable-pitch propeller

VIT: (*vozdushnyi istrebitel tankov*) aerial tank destroyer

VMSh: (*vremennoi mekhanism shturmovika*) literally 'time-setting device for attack aircraft', a sighting device for bombing, automatically releasing the bombs after a preset time interval

VVS: (*voyenno-vozdushnyye sily*) [Soviet] Air Force

VYa: (*Volkov Yartsev*) 23mm gun of Volkov and Yartsev design

Bibliography

Russian-Language Publications (Titles in English)

Books

Air Power of the Motherland (Moscow, 1988)

Beregovoi, G.T., Angle of Attack [memoirs] (Moscow, 1971)

Chernikov, Yevgeniy, The Il-2 Armoured Attack Aircraft (Armada series, Moscow, 1997)

The Il-2 and Il-10. The History of Their Creation and Their Operation, Part 2 (War in the Air series No.8, Moscow, 2000)

Kozlov, P.Ya., Attack Aircraft (Moscow, 1987)

Kozlov, P.Ya., Great Unity. A Documentary Story (Moscow, 1982)

Krasovskiy, Air Marshal S.A., A Lifetime in Aviation [memoirs] (3rd edn, Minsk, 1973)

The Naval Air Force in the Great Patriotic War (Moscow, 1983)

Novozhilov, G. et al., From the History of Soviet Aviation. Aircraft of the Ilyushin OKB (Moscow, 1990)

Perov, V.I. and O.V. Rastrenin, Attack Aircraft of the Red Army 1941–1945, Vol.1. The Aircraft Take Shape (Aviko Press, Moscow, 2003)

Pstygo, I.I., Toilers of the Sky [memoirs] (Ufa, 1995)

Stefanovskiy, P.M., Three Hundred Unknown Quantities [memoirs of a test pilot] (Moscow, 1973)

Shavrov, V.B., History of Aircraft Design in the USSR 1938–1950 (3rd edn, Moscow, 1994)

Yegorov, Yu.A., Aircraft of the Ilyushin OKB (RUSAVIA, Moscow, 2003)

Periodicals

Alinin, Yuriy, 'Sentinels of history are conducting their search', Tekhnika molodyozhi, No.5 (1980)

Bakurskiy, Viktor, 'The Il-2 – our pride or a strategic mistake?', Krylya Rodiny, No.1 (1992), p.7

Chernikov, Yevgeniy, 'Ilyushin's flying tanks', M-Hobby, No.1 (1996), pp.23–6, 33

Chernikov, Yevgeniy, 'The Il-2 – the pride of our country's aviation', Krylya Rodiny, No.5 (2002), pp.1–8

Kolesnikov, Pavel, '"Flying tanks" are attacking', Modelist-konstruktor, No.5 (1982), pp.12–16

Kozlov, P.A., 'Shturmovik from the Black Sea', Krylya Rodiny, No.1 (1981), p.26

Kozlov, P., 'The "Ils" were born in the spring', Aviatsiya i Kosmonavtika, No.2 (1981), pp.20–1

Leontyeva, T., 'A memorial to the warrior aircraft', Krylya Rodiny, No.7 (1979), pp.26–7

Martynov, A., 'The legendary Ilyushin aircraft', Krylya Rodiny, No.4 (1989), p.7

Medved', Alexander, 'Polish air units in the USSR in the years of the Great Patriotic War', Istoriya Aviatsii, No.4 (2001), pp.26–9

Orlov, Vadim, 'Sentinels of history continue their search', Tekhnika molodyozhi, No.11 (1982), pp.10–14

Orlov, Vadim, 'Sentinels of history have their say', Tekhnika molodyozhi, No.2 (1981), pp.22–5; No.3 (1981), pp.22–6

Perov, V.I. and O.V. Rastrenin, 'The Il-2 attack aircraft', Aviatsiya i Kosmonavtika, No.5–6 [special issue] (2001)

Perov, V.I. and O.V. Rastrenin, 'The Il-2 attack aircraft', Mir Aviatsii, No.2–4 (1999) [three articles]

Perov, V.I. and O.V. Rastrenin, 'Battlefield aircraft', Aviatsiya i Kosmonavtika, No.3–6, 8–12 (2001); No.8–11 (2002)

Rodionov, Ivan, 'The Il-2 attack aircraft', Krylya Rodiny, No.6 (1984), p.28; No.7 (1984), pp.27–29

Shikov, Alexandr, 'A class of its own' [history of the development of the Il-2] Krylya Rodiny, No.12 (1991), pp.7–12

Sivkov, Grigory, 'The attack aircraft that remained in history', Nezavisimaya Gazeta (19 April 2002)

Spasibo, Vladimir, 'The Il-2: the truth versus the legend', Nezavisimoye Voennoye Obozrenie [Independent Military Review], No.4 (2002), p.5

Valin, German, 'The unforgettable Il-2', Krylya Rodiny, No.5 (1995), pp.10–12

Yakubovich, Nikolai, 'Attack aircraft/fighter. On the Il-10 aircraft', Krylya Rodiny, No.5 (1997), pp.1–8

Yegorov, Yuriy, 'How the "flying tank" was created', Krylya Rodiny, No.6 (1983), pp.18–20

'How the "flying tank" was resurrected', Aviatsiya i Kosmonavtika, No. (1978), pp.38–39

Publications in Other Languages

Books

Herbert, Leonard, Les Chtourmovik. Docavia (Editions Lariviere, 1999)

Krzemiński, Czeslav, Lotnictwo polskie w pierwszich latach powojennych (Warsaw, 1981)

Liss, Witold, The Ilyushin Il-2 (Profile Publications, No.88, Profile Publications, 1966)

Morgala, Andrzei, Polskie samoloty woiskowe 1939–1945 (Wydawnictwo MON, Warsaw, 1976)

Morgala, Andrzei, Polskie samoloty woiskowe 1945–1980 (Wydawnictwo MON, Warsaw, 1981)

Stapfer, Hans-Heiri, Il-2 Stormovik in Action (Aircraft No.155, Squadron/Signal Publications, 1995)

Periodicals

Punka, Georg, 'Die fliegenden Panzer', Jet & Prop, 3/1999 s, pp.60–4

Several articles in Skrzydlata Polska (Poland) and Letectvi a Kosmonautika (Czech Republic)

Documentary Sources

Documentary chronicle on the history of Soviet aircraft design and construction compiled by Ivan Rodionov and made available for Internet users: www 2.warwick.ac.uk/fac/soc/economics/staff/faculty/harrison/aviaprom

Index

References to illustrations are shown in *italics*